Nineteenth-Century
Rhetoric
in
North America

Nan Johnson

Southern Illinois University Press
Carbondale and Edwardsville

Printed in the United States of America
Edited by Dan Gunter
Designed by Jason Schellenberg
Production supervised by Natalia Nadraga
94 93 92 91 4 3 2 1

Library of Congress Cataloging-in-Publication Data

Johnson, Nan, 1951–
     Nineteenth-century rhetoric in North America / Nan Johnson.
         p.   cm.
     Includes bibliographical references and index.
     1. English language—Rhetoric—Study and teaching—United States—
History—19th century.   2. English language—Rhetoric—Study and
teaching—Canada—History—19th century.   3. Rhetoric—United
States—History—19th century.   4. Rhetoric—Canada—History—19th
century.   I. Title.
PE1068.U5J64   1991
808'.042'07073—dc20   90-20983
ISBN 0-8093-1654-4   CIP
ISBN 0-8093-1655-2 (pbk. : alk. paper)

The paper used in this publication meets the minimum requirements of
American National Standard for Information Sciences—Permanence
of Paper for Printed Library Materials, ANSI Z39.48-1984. ∞

Contents

Acknowledgments

In the course of researching and writing this book, I have sounded out my ideas and plans on several colleagues and friends. Their support has been invaluable. I offer special thanks to Deanne Bogden, Gregory Clark, Robert J. Connors, Sharon Crowley, William A. Covino, Lisa S. Ede, Richard Leo Enos, Winifred Bryan Horner, Andrea A. Lunsford, James J. Murphy, C. Jan Swearingen, Kathleen E. Welch, and Marjorie Curry Woods. I am also indebted to the University of British Columbia, Canada Council, and the National Endowment for the Humanities for funding this project. A final word of thanks to Abigail Jones, without whose support I would never have attempted this project. To her I am endlessly grateful.

Nineteenth-Century Rhetoric

in

North America

This is a work of history in fictional form—that is, in personal perspective, which is the only kind of history that exists.

Joyce Carol Oates, *Them*

The truth is, I have never written a story in my life that didn't have a very firm foundation in actual human experience—somebody else's experience quite often, but an experience that became my own by hearing the story, by witnessing the thing, by hearing just a word perhaps.

Katherine Ann Porter

It is like what we imagine knowledge to be:
dark, salt, clear, moving, utterly free,
drawn from the cold hard mouth
of the world, derived from the rocky breast
forever, flowing and drawn, and since
our knowledge is historical, flowing, and flown.

Elizabeth Bishop, *"At the Fishhouses"*

1

Introduction: A Profile of Nineteenth-Century Rhetoric

The purpose of this commentary is to define the characteristics of the nineteenth-century rhetorical tradition in North America and to argue that the nineteenth century was the last era during which the discipline of rhetoric exerted an acknowledged authority over the philosophical investigation of discourse and formal instruction in oral and written communication. The term *discipline* refers here to the historic role of rhetoric as a branch of liberal philosophy and education self-consciously concerned with discourse and the arts of expression. This history will focus on the theoretical and pedagogical priorities that the nineteenth-century discipline promoted, exploring how rhetoricians in this period defined their own enterprise. What philosophical assumptions were considered authoritative by rhetorical theorists in this period? How did these assumptions influence definitions of rhetorical principles and rules for practice? What rhetorical arts were defined as significant? What civic and cultural function was assigned to rhetorical education? These questions presuppose that an understanding of the nineteenth-century tradition depends on an investigation of the discipline's particular theoretical and cultural contexts. This methodological stance is predisposed by a larger assumption regarding the history of rhetoric: to understand the historic function of rhetorical traditions as

3

Nineteenth-Century Rhetoric

generic, cultural phenomena, we must concede the intrinsically adaptive dynamics of rhetorical theory and practice and the tendency of rhetorical pedagogy to model dominant philosophical and social values.

The most conspicuous characteristic in the history of rhetoric has been its responsiveness to the ever-changing nature of certain intellectual and cultural imperatives: (1) governing epistemological assumptions regarding the relationships between thought, language, and communication; (2) dominant philosophical views of human nature and the nature of affective response to discourse; (3) conventional and institutional perceptions of appropriate modes of formal communication; and (4) the perceived role of the study and practice of rhetoric in the maintenance of social and political order.[1] The disposition of theory, the evolution of rhetorical genres, and the function of rhetoric in the promotion of standards of literacy in any period in history are influenced directly by the shifting substance of these imperatives. Such factors have shaped what rhetoric has been deemed the art *of*. For example, Plato insists in the *Phaedrus* that the "function of speech is to influence souls" and that a "man who is going to be a speaker must know how many types of souls there are" (63). Underlying Plato's definition of the aim of rhetoric is the ethical bias that the arts should facilitate humankind's struggle to overcome the passions through reason and thus gain access to the knowledge of the Ideal. Plato's definition of rhetoric's edifying function also relies on the notion that eternal truth is knowable only through the processes of higher rationality.[2] By contrast, Aristotle stresses the truth-value of consensus over the authority of "immutable" truths; consequently, the *Rhetoric* assigns a more strategic function to rhetoric, viewing it as an agency by which practical wisdom or *doxa* is related to decision making concerning the good or health of the state.[3]

A more contemporary illustration of how ethical, epistemological, and ontological developments influence rhetorical theory can be observed in George Campbell's *Philosophy of Rhetoric* (1776). Campbell claims that the ends of speaking are reducible to four; "every speech being intended to enlighten the understanding, to please the imagination, to move the passions, or to influence the will" (10). Campbell's definition of rhetoric

4

was influenced by those views that had preoccupied eighteenth-century philosophy and liberal thought. As students of eighteenth-century rhetoric are quite aware, Campbell's concept of the human mind as comprising discrete faculties of the will, the imagination, the understanding, and the passions is attributable to the epistemological speculations of popular eighteenth-century philosophers such as David Hume and Thomas Reid, who pursued the assumptions of the Baconian-Lockian perspective that language links empirical knowledge with the mental faculties.[4]

These examples do not exhaust the philosophical issues that influenced classical theory and subsequent traditions; however, they do point to the overt influence that changing philosophical imperatives have had on theories of rhetoric and definitions of its scope and aim. Just as rhetorical theory has been affected by shifting philosophical views, so too has rhetorical practice been affected by social changes that have encouraged the development of new genres of rhetoric and/or transformations within the canonical guidelines. Pragmatic theories of rhetoric have tended to retain the classical system of treating rules for practice in terms of analyses of the divisions and canons of rhetoric; however, the theoretical substance of these rhetorical elements has been in a constant state of transformation. Shifting social and political conditions have promoted the development of "new" modes of formal communication and have supported alterations in the theoretical base of canonical precepts. Features of medieval and eighteenth-century rhetoric illustrate the effects of such forces on pragmatic rhetoric. The attention of medieval rhetoric to *ars dictaminis, ars praedicandi,* and *ars poetica* reflects a diversification of practice prompted by at least two contextual factors: the discourse activities encouraged and instigated by church bureaucracies and the cultures that supported them and the diversifying requirements of rapidly expanding political and economic states.[5] Similarly, contextual circumstances compelled the expansion of the rhetorical divisions in the late eighteenth century and early nineteenth century. One of the major ambitions of the New Rhetoric was to provide a theoretical and pragmatic account of the type of rhetoric suited to scientific and philosophical communication. Both Campbell and Richard Whately (*Ele-*

ments of Rhetoric, 1828) treated the rhetorical process of conviction (the rhetoric of information) as a major constituent of theory and identified various forms of expository prose as distinct rhetorical categories. The development of the divisions of rhetoric beyond the traditional genres of deliberative, forensic, and epideictic in this period as well as others is attributable to cultural and social changes that exerted demands on the discipline of rhetoric to articulate new guidelines for proliferating rhetorical discourses.

The evolution of the rhetorical canons of invention, arrangement, style, memory, and delivery reflects a similar process of responsive transformation. As changing philosophical attitudes have shifted, reorganized, and reshaped conventional standards about what modes of discourse are most effective and relevant, so too have these same dynamics influenced how the canons have been revised and reassessed. Even a brief recapitulation of the fortunes of style illustrates that canons have been transformed in response to changes in the dominant philosophical climate and shifts in attitudes toward rhetorical decorum. Nearly synonymous with *de copia* in Renaissance rhetoric, style underwent a radical redefinition at the hands of eighteenth-century rhetoricians and grammarians, who were strongly influenced by the powerful post-Renaissance linguistic ideals of perspicuity and brevity as well as the popular rationalist assumption that the "plain style" mirrored the processes of higher intellection. [6] Another dramatic transformation of a canonical element is exemplified by the eighteenth-century expansion in the English tradition of delivery into a rhetorical art in and of itself. This expansion, the result of work by theorists such as Thomas Sheridan (*Lectures on Elocution and the English Language,* 1759) and John Walker (*The Melody of Speaking,* 1787), would not have evolved in this fashion had seventeenth-century developments in epistemological philosophy and aesthetics not forged theoretical links between the workings of the sensory and mental faculties and the agencies of the the voice and the body. [7]

To assume that what rhetoric is perceived to be in any given age depends on the organic interplay between the disposition of the discipline and the intellectual climate and social complexity of the times is to propose that there has always been a discipline of rhetoric, but that it has never been exactly the same one.[8] From a historical point of view, the formal discipline of rhetoric has represented itself consistently as that enterprise which governs the theory and study of formal discourse; however, what various societies in various eras have perceived that enterprise to embody has changed continually. To investigate the configuration of any particular rhetorical tradition necessarily obliges us first to recognize that throughout the history of rhetoric, rhetorical theory and pedagogy have displayed a dynamic tendency toward responsive transformation. An account of the nature of the nineteenth-century rhetorical tradition implies an investigation of the philosophical assumptions, theoretical models, and cultural mandates that shaped nineteenth-century theory and practice.

Many commentators on the history of rhetoric have observed that "we have yet no reliable history or bibliography of the dissemination of rhetoric texts in this period" or an "authoritative history" of developments in rhetoric during the nineteenth century (Vickers 22; Connors, Ede, and Lunsford 2). It is true that existing scholarship has not produced an overview of nineteenth-century rhetorical theory and practice; rather, research has focused on discrete elements of theory or on the status of individual arts. However, valuable information regarding the theoretical foundations and favored practices of the nineteenth-century discipline can be gleaned from this body of research, information that points toward significant generalizations. Research on nineteenth-century rhetoric has come in two waves of interest and from two distinctly different scholarly quarters. The first wave, beginning as early as 1930 and peaking in the 1950s, was initiated by scholars working in the discipline of speech communication; the second, more recent wave of attention has been prompted by a renewal of interest in rhetoric in the last decade among teachers and rhetoricians working in departments of English. Despite differences in focus, coverage, and evaluations offered by these two movements, these investigations have provided a number of complementary insights into nineteenth-century theory and practice.

Appearing in the pages of *Quarterly Journal of Speech* and *Speech Monographs,* in early collections of historical scholarship on the American tradition, and in numerous doctoral dissertations written between 1935 and 1955, the earliest investigations of nineteenth-century American rhetoric provided the first accounts of its theoretical and pedagogical nature. The most conclusive of these pioneering efforts were Warren Guthrie's analysis of eighteenth-century English theoretical influences on the early nineteenth-century academy and the rise of the first indigenous American rhetorics ("The Development of Rhetorical Theory in America, 1635–1850") and several notable articles in *History of Speech Education in America: Background Studies,* edited by Karl R. Wallace. These investigations provided overviews of the development of elocution, oratory, and debate and general descriptions of academic courses offered between 1800 and the turn of the century.[9]

Showing a tendency to view the nineteenth-century tradition in terms of the fortunes of the oral arts, speech communication histories have largely been devoted to tracing theoretical influences and pedagogical trends in the relationship between classical rhetoric and the development of speech education. Typical subjects of early scholarship include the influence of "classical doctrines" and canons in nineteenth-century theory, homiletics, and oratorical practice; the popularity of campus exercises and extracurricular activities featuring declamation, original speeches, and debate; and the stylistic and argumentative techniques of emerging modes of public speaking. More recent work in this vein has explored the nature of Victorian and nineteenth-century American understandings of Ciceronian rhetoric, changing views of the inventional obligations of the platform speaker from 1800 to the late 1880s, and the influence of liberal philosophy on the academic tradition.[10]

This initial scholarship suggested that the nineteenth-century American tradition was slow to free itself from the powerful influence of the eighteenth-century British tradition; however, it began to show theoretical

A Profile

and pedagogical creativity at midcentury. This creativity developed in response to the needs of a democratic society and the aims of an increasingly pragmatic system of education.

> Up to this point [1850] we have seen that American rhetoric was strongly under the control of English doctrine and works. . . . Now American rhetoric is prepared to come of age, for three American works of originality appear within a decade. W. G. T Shedd's commentary on and translation of Francis Theremin's *Eloquence a Virtue,* Henry N. Day's rhetorical writings, and M. B. Hope's *Princeton Textbook on Rhetoric* chart a vigorous course toward an ever more practical philosophy of persuasion. Differing in many respects, the works unite in asserting the functional significance of rhetoric. (Guthrie 16: 107)

In addition to providing this outline of influence and development, Guthrie and others established an important generalization regarding the status of the nineteenth-century rhetorical arts: the majority of early chronicles affirm Guthrie's initial observation that the theory and practice of elocution enjoyed massive popularity throughout the nineteenth century, while the exclusive attention to oratory of the eighteenth-century college curriculum gave way to equal attention to composition and the "critical and belles-lettristic phase of rhetorical training" in the early decades of the nineteenth century (Guthrie15: 67). Although early scholars recognized the expanding curricular concerns of nineteenth-century rhetoric, an expansion that ensured the status of oratory and belles lettres as the most favored arts, they argued that the study of oratory underwent a rebirth in the late nineteenth century through the popularity of forensic debate and the development of speech communication as a discrete academic specialization. In one of the earliest surveys of speech education in American colleges, Hochmuth and Murphy define significant features of "the main line of development of rhetorical training" in the last quarter of the nineteenth century in terms of the prominent position of oratory, widespread instruction in elocution, the rising popularity of forensics courses, and a general

Nineteenth-Century Rhetoric

"enthusiasm for debate" (169). The general attitude toward nineteenth-century rhetoric that emerges in this initial body of documentation is one of admiration for the successful development of an indigenous American tradition and for the durable popularity of various oral arts.

Authored primarily by a group of English studies scholars intent on asserting the relevance of rhetorical theory to composing theory, the second wave of scholarship has focused on the historical relationship between nineteenth-century rhetoric and the evolution of rhetorics of composition. Although the most ambitious investigation of this connection has been provided by James A. Berlin in *Writing Instruction in Nineteenth-Century American Colleges* (1984), numerous articles in recent issues of *Rhetoric Society Quarterly, College English,* and *College Composition and Communication,* and in collections such as *The Rhetorical Tradition and Modern Writing* (Murphy, 1982) and *Essays on Classical Rhetoric and Modern Discourse* (Connors Ede, and Lunsford, 1984) have evaluated a wide range of previously unexamined topics bearing on the evolution of rhetorics of composition: theories of invention in nineteenth-century rhetoric texts; the influence of nineteenth-century notions of style and grammar on standards for composition; the development of the genres of written discourse; and the influence of nineteenth-century rhetoricians on twentieth-century pedagogical traditions in composition theory.

This more recent body of scholarship reiterates rather than expands earlier conclusions regarding the influence of eighteenth-century rhetorics and tends, like early histories of nineteenth-century rhetoric, toward a "specialization" focus in its nearly exclusive attention to the history of the art of composition. However, scholarship of the last decade significantly extends previous accounts by drawing attention to the powerful theoretical and curricular status of rhetorics of composition in the nineteenth-century academy and by identifying and analyzing the treatises of those rhetoricians who shaped academic instruction in composition in the little examined period after 1850 (Scotsman Alexander Bain and widely read American rhetoricians A. S. Hill, John Franklin Genung, and Barrett Wendell). Berlin offers the most extensive analysis of nineteenth-century composing theory

A Profile

to date in his exploration of the influence of "classical," "psychological-epistemological," and "romantic" theories of rhetoric on nineteenth-century instruction in composition (*Writing Instruction*).

In addition to establishing additional documentation of major theoretical influences and practices, what is distinctive about recent scholarship on nineteenth-century rhetoric is its overall assessment of this era as that period most responsible for the theoretical impoverishment of the rhetoric of composition and the academic marginalization of rhetoric studies in modern English studies.

> The period 1850–1900 in American certainly cannot be called one of the great eras of rhetoric, even though there was a brief flash of more vital activity in the closing years of the century. The subject was too heavily academic during most of this period to allow it much vigor. In no part of rhetorical doctrine can this be seen so clearly as in the matter of audience awareness—that is, the recognition of rhetoric as the art of communication.[11] (Kitzhaber 223–24)

The extensive influence in the nineteenth-century of belletristic rhetorics modeled on Hugh Blair's popular eighteenth-century treatise *Lectures on Rhetoric and Belles Lettres* has been identified by Kitzhaber and a host of composition studies scholars as a negative theoretical and curricular force that accelerated the erosion of rhetoric's historic function in society and in the academy, a process completed by the early twentieth century. Research of the last decade has characterized nineteenth-century rhetoric as a "fragmented" discipline that lost the stability of a traditional classical system as a consequence of the domination of belletristic views that encouraged superficial pedagogical aspirations for rhetoric.[12]

Frequently citing classical rhetoric as the most comprehensive view of the discipline ever devised, negative assessments of nineteenth-century rhetoric have relied on explicit or implicit contrasts between elements of classical and nineteenth-century rhetoric to assert the now nearly universal criticism that the classical tradition was further fragmented and corrupted

11

during this period. While such claims are provocative, they must be assessed with caution if the circumstances of nineteenth-century rhetoric are to be understood. Pejorative critiques of the nineteenth-century tradition draw their force from the assumption that rhetorical traditions that deviate from classical philosophies of rhetoric (Aristotelian or Ciceronian) are unstable or inherently compromised.[13] This classicist stance in nineteenth-century scholarship follows a noticeable tendency in historiography within rhetoric studies: the adoption of the stance that the "classical tradition" represents the original, most comprehensive, and only "true" configuration of rhetorical theory and praxis and that subsequent traditions should be measured against the features of this superordinate tradition.

The classicist stance has predisposed various characterizations of the state of rhetoric in earlier periods, including the view of the Middle Ages as a period of theoretical dispersal; the general regard for the Renaissance as a period of "recovery" for classical rhetoric; and the popular view of the eighteenth century as a period when the integrity of the classical system was corrupted within the English tradition by the rising popularity of belletristic poetics and "scientific" philosophies of rhetoric. The problematic consequence of adopting such a stance in accounts of the nineteenth-century tradition, or any other tradition for that matter, is that such a posture focuses attention on a fixed notion of what rhetoric ought to be rather than on what an individual tradition actually entails. Comparing the theoretical priorities and pedagogical practices of subsequent traditions to a classical model obscures the fact that every discipline of rhetoric is the creature of historical circumstances.[14]

Modern scholarship displays yet another partisan tendency in methodology that runs contrary to the ambition to examine the characteristic elements of the nineteenth-century tradition—a specialization or praxis bias. Although the "specialization" focus of early and recent scholarship in many instances is simply a consequence of the selective interests of the distinct scholarly venues in which rhetoric is presently studied, significant numbers of nineteenth-century commentaries present evaluative accounts of the fortunes of individual rhetorical arts. These accounts foster the

A Profile

impression that the disciplinary range of nineteenth-century rhetoric can be or should be identified with one art. The bulk of scholarship on nineteenth-century composition instruction associates one of the pedagogical commitments of rhetoric in this period with the scope of the entire discipline in a synecdochic construct.[15] A praxis bias can be identified in a host of early investigations that define the nineteenth-century tradition strictly in terms of the status of argumentation, public address, or the study of oratory. The praxis bias is so pervasive in historical scholarship on nineteenth-century rhetoric that it could easily be assumed that to trace the history of oratory or composition and to account for the history of the discipline are one and the same gesture. Not restricted to nineteenth-century scholarship, the praxis bias can be identified in a number of ways in which the narrative of the rhetorical tradition has been told. For example, Thomas Wilson's *Art of Rhetoric* is discussed mainly as a work that recovers the classical canons and reinscribes public speaking as a major division of rhetoric; however, Wilson's frequent references to the invention and style of prose make it clear that he regards the canons as applicable to both oratory and prose composition. Consider as well the pejorative notice (or neglect) of the arts of elocution and criticism in accounts of the eighteenth-century and nineteenth-century traditions despite their prestige during those periods.

Like the classicist stance that indicts rather than explores the unique theoretical, philosophical, and cultural influences on various postclassical traditions, the praxis bias does not account for the degree to which rhetorical practice evolves in response to changing needs of societies and cultures, accommodating not only an ever-changing theoretical disposition but also an ever-rearranging coalition of "traditional" and innovative arts. The assumptions explicitly or implicitly posed by classicist and praxis-oriented scholarship have perpetuated an approach to the study of nineteenth-century rhetoric that focuses evaluatively or selectively on certain features of the tradition. A commentary that seeks to profile nineteenth-century rhetoric against the backdrop of its indigenous circumstances must resist the assumptions of such partisan critiques in favor of an analytical reading of nineteenth-century scholarship as a body of work from which general conclu-

sions regarding the nature and function of rhetorical theory can be elicited,
conclusions that clarify how the nineteenth-century tradition responded to
the intellectual and social will of its age. When existing scholarship is
reviewed from this perspective, significant presumptions regarding the
character of nineteenth-century theory, the range of the nineteenth-century
rhetorical arts, and the cultural function of rhetorical education can be
derived.

Nineteenth-century rhetoric has been described consistently as a
composite: "early nineteenth-century American school rhetoric [was] an
amalgam of classical and eighteenth-century discourse theory" (Crowley,
"Evolution" 146). Both initial and recent research into the theoretical
foundations of nineteenth-century rhetoric points to three overt influences:
"firm classical foundations," belletristic interests in "criticism and literary
taste," and epistemological approaches to rhetoric as a "science" closely
related to the study of the "mental faculties." All existing evidence indicates
that nineteenth-century theory depended on a combination of the same
classical, epistemological, and belletristic assumptions that marked the
theoretical foundations of the New Rhetoric. Although various scholars
have described this characteristic "amalgam" as "confusing," such evaluations do not mitigate against the working assumption that nineteenth-century
theory was synthetic. This synthetic character can be traced to the durable
influence of eighteenth-century models such as Campbell's *Philosophy of
Rhetoric* and Hugh Blair's *Lectures on Rhetoric and Belles Lettres* as well
as Richard Whately's early nineteenth-century work, *Elements of Rhetoric*.
Nineteenth-century rhetoricians followed their immediate predecessors in
combining classical treatments of the canons of invention, style, and arrangement with epistemological discussions of the laws of the mind and
belletristic treatments of the principles of taste, style, and the literary
genres.

One of the central ambitions of this commentary is to explore the
premise that nineteenth-century theory was essentially synthetic, being
derived from the integration of classical elements with eighteenth-century

bellestristic and epistemological approaches to theory and practice. The significant consequence of this synthesis is that the nineteenth-century tradition extended the theoretical and pedagogical claims of the New Rhetoric (chapters 1 and 2). Early nineteenth-century treatises such as Samuel Newman's *Practical System of Rhetoric* (1827) and Alexander Jamieson's *Grammar of Rhetoric and Polite Literature* (1844) imitated the organization of Campbell and Blair's treatises and incorporated the philosophical and pragmatic principles popularized by the New Rhetoric. Reiterating the classical elements incorporated in the theoretical and pedagogical substance of the New Rhetoric, nineteenth-century treatises outlined epistemological and critical standards for rhetorical principles and practices. This theoretical configuration was typical of nineteenth-century treatises in general—even those such as Henry N. Day's *Elements of the Art of Rhetoric* (1850) and A. S. Hill's *Principles of Rhetoric* (1878), which imitate the treatises of Campbell, Blair, and Whately less directly. By the 1880s, classical, belletristic, and epistemological precepts had become absorbed into an unprecedented theoretical hybrid. Texts such as John Franklin Genung's *Working Principles of Rhetoric* (1900) extended the influence of this theoretical synthesis into the early decades of the twentieth century.[16]

In addition to the repeated observation that nineteenth-century theory relies on a combination of classical, belletristic, and epistemological assumptions, scholars investigating the nineteenth century have pointed to a gradual but distinct shift from a dominant pedagogical interest in oratory early in the century toward a more inclusive pragmatic interest in public speaking, elocution, belles lettres, and composition by 1880. This diversity has been lamented by those who perceive it as problematic for the status of argumentation, oratory, and the study of classical principles. Nonetheless, even the most persistent critics of the "dispersed" state of nineteenth-century rhetoric practice conclude that nineteenth-century rhetoric extended traditional praxis beyond oratory and public speaking to include the arts of prose composition and critical analysis. This extended theory of practice will be explored in chapters 3 and 4, in which the claim will be made that the nineteenth-century discipline displayed far more allegiance to the multifaceted eighteenth-century vision of rhetorical practice than it did to a classical tradition oriented solely to the study of public speaking. Nineteenth-century theorists defined an extensive, inclusive range for the rhetorical arts by conflating epistemological and aesthetic rationales for public speaking, the composition of written discourse, and critical analysis. As the century progressed, theoretical attention to a widening range of rhetorical arts moved the pedagogical interests of rhetorical education ever closer to the pedagogical ideal of the eighteenth-century belletristic tradition, an ideal that assigned equal importance to the arts of oratory, composition, and criticism.

A number of scholars have argued that the status of rhetoric in the academy declined in the nineteenth century; in fact, though, the pedagogical, philosophical, and theoretical interests of the discipline were supported vigorously by the liberal arts curriculum which consistently affirmed the cultural function of rhetorical education (see chapters 5 and 6). Rhetorical education played a crucial role in bolstering the idealism of nineteenth-century liberal education, an enterprise that was committed to the development of an intellectually progressive and culturally enlightened society. From the perspective of nineteenth-century educators in the United States and Canada, only an education in the rhetorical arts could foster those virtues that every intelligent and civilized individual must possess: "the cultivation of . . . taste . . . the exercise of the imagination . . . the development of . . . intellectual traits and feelings . . . and clearness and power of expression."[17]

One of the most distinctive characteristics of the nineteenth-century tradition was its unquestioned authority over institutional standards of literacy and the general public's notion of why the educated individual should learn to speak and write eloquently. Rhetoricians in the period perceived themselves as responsible for accounting for the nature of discourse, the techniques of rhetoric, and the development of the intellectual and moral virtues that enabled the speaker or writer to communicate in an effective and beneficent fashion. Extremely idealistic in their view of the consequences of rhetorical study, nineteenth-century rhetoricians promoted

A Profile

the notion within the academy and in the public mind that the acquisition of rhetorical expertise is commensurate with the cultivation of a liberal mind and admirable, enlightening emotions. At no point during the century did prominent rhetoricians define the nature and aims of rhetoric in isolation of this ideological point of view. To observe the means by which the nineteenth-century tradition exerted this belief is to become better acquainted with the significant cultural role that rhetoric played in this era and to recognize the success with which the discipline promoted a theoretical and pedagogical program uniquely suited to its historical circumstances.

There is no art whatever that hath so close a connexion with all the faculties and powers of the mind, as eloquence, or the art of speaking, in the extensive sense in that I employ the term . . . if the logical art, and the ethical be useful, eloquence is useful, as it instructs us how these arts must be applied for the conviction and the persuasion of others. It is indeed the grand art of communication, not of ideas only, but of sentiments, passions, dispositions, and purposes.

George Campbell, *The Philosophy of Rhetoric*

Belles Lettres and criticism chiefly consider him [man] as a Being endowed with those powers of taste and imagination, that were intended to embellish his mind, and to supply him with rational and useful entertainment. They open a field of investigation peculiar to themselves. . . . They bring to light various springs of action that without their aid might have passed unobserved; and that, though of a delicate nature, frequently exert a powerful influence on several departments of human life . . . they strew flowers in the path of science.

Hugh Blair, *Lectures on Rhetoric and Belles Lettres*

The finding of suitable ARGUMENTS to prove a given point, and the skilful arrangement of them, may be considered as the immediate and proper province of Rhetoric, and of that alone.

Richard Whately, *Elements of Rhetoric*

2

Foundations of Nineteenth-Century Theory: The New Rhetoric

The theoretical substance of nineteenth-century rhetoric was founded on a composite of classical assumptions and epistemological and belletristic premises initially popularized in the late eighteenth-century English tradition known as the "New Rhetoric." The New Rhetoric evolved from the efforts of theorists such as George Campbell (*The Philosophy of Rhetoric*) and Hugh Blair (*Lectures on Rhetoric and Belles Lettres*) to reconcile the principles and practices of rhetoric with theories of the mind, logic, and language that had emerged from the Baconian-Lockian tradition.[1] Nineteenth-century rhetoric relied substantially on Campbell and Blair's innovations and on the subsequent extension of their revisions by Richard Whately in *Elements of Rhetoric*. In theoretical terms, the nineteenth-century tradition can be understood as executing a refined synthesis of those theoretical commitments that promoters of the New Rhetoric were the first to combine: a philosophical approach to rhetoric that examined the nature and aims of rhetoric in terms of the processes of the "mental faculties"; the view that the study of rhetoric applies to all major forms of communication, oral and written; an aesthetic/ethical commitment to the critical study of rhetorical theory and the development of taste; and a neoclassical approach to rhetoric as the art of adapting discourse to purpose, audience, and occasion.[2]

George Campbell and the Epistemological Rationale for Rhetoric

The philosophical redefinition of the aims of rhetoric within the New Rhetoric constituted a reexamination of the processes and forms of rhetoric in terms of contemporary theories of the mind and communication. Campbell, the most influential eighteenth-century proponent of this epistemological approach, defines rhetoric as "eloquence," or "that art or talent by that the discourse is adapted to its end"—a definition conditioned by the stipulation that the nature of rhetorical adaptation is constrained by "those principles of our nature" that affect "modes of arguing, or forms of speech" (1). Campbell's major effort is to outline the epistemological realities embodied in the obligations of rhetoric "to enlighten the understanding, to please the imagination, to move the passions or to influence the will." Campbell's redesign of the aims and procedures of rhetoric proved to be one of the most powerful accomplishments of the New Rhetoric, an accomplishment that shaped the philosophical context in which rhetoric would be defined throughout the nineteenth century. Nineteenth-century theory would be indebted not only to Campbell's general restructuring of the philosophical foundations of rhetoric but also to the reexamination and reiteration of standard elements and principles of theory that *The Philosophy of Rhetoric* provides. Nineteenth-century treatises modeled on the theoretical architecture of *The Philosophy of Rhetoric* also embodied those neoclassical commitments that were distinct features of Campbell's treatise: an attention to the materials of argument, the divisions of rhetoric, the canon of style, and the working presumption that the art of rhetoric lies in adaptation to aim, audience, and occasion. Campbell's advocacy of the study of rhetoric as an inquiry providing scientific insight into human nature and the organic principles that governed communication inspired a legion of supporters among nineteenth-century rhetoricians in North America who regarded *The Philosophy of Rhetoric* as an authoritative commentary on the philosophy and practice of rhetoric.

Campbell clearly regards his treatise as a philosophical work; he seeks to "exhibit . . . a tolerable sketch of the human mind" and to "disclose its secret movements, tracing its principal channels of perceptions and action, as near as possible to their source" as a means of coming to a more scientific and critical understanding of "the radical principles of that art, whose object it is, by the use of language, to operate on the soul of the hearer, in the way of informing, convincing, pleasing, moving, or persuading" (xliii).[3] One of the characteristic assumptions underlying Campbell's method is the notion that the principles of rhetoric are a consequence of the nature of mental activities and that to study one is to come to know the other. Campbell understands the essential relationship between the rhetorical process and the mind in these terms: particular faculties activate discrete intellectual and emotional responses; particular rhetorical forms and techniques facilitate these functions. Campbell explains that if a speaker wishes to instruct an audience or to "explain some doctrine unknown, or not distinctly comprehended by them, or by proving some position disbelieved or doubted by them," an appeal must be made to the understanding, through perspicuity or argument; when a speaker wishes to affect the imagination, it must first be engaged by "exhibiting to it a lively and beautiful representation of a suitable object . . . the principle scope for this class being in narration and description" (2–3); if the speaker seeks to influence the conduct of his hearers (persuasion), the will must be addressed, an appeal that requires "an artful mixture of that which proposes to convince the judgement, and that which interests the passions, its distinguished excellency results from these two, the argumentative and the pathetic incorporated together" (4). The rhetorician must understand not only the unique characteristics of the faculties but also how the mental processes are linked together in an intimate, dynamic chain:

> In general it may be asserted, that each preceding species . . . is
> preparatory to the subsequent; that each subsequent species is
> founded on the preceding; and that thus they ascend in a regular
> progression. Knowledge, the object of the intellect, furnisheth ma-
> terials for the fancy; the fancy culls, compounds, and by her
> mimic art, disposes these materials so as to affect the passions; the
> passions are the natural spurs to volition or action, and so need
> only to be right directed. (2)

The challenge facing the rhetorician in responding adequately to such complex mental activities is learning how to adapt rhetorical materials in such a way that this chain of mental activities is engaged in the proper sequence with the desired result. In Campbell's philosophy of rhetoric, the aims of enlightening the understanding, pleasing the imagination, moving the passions, and influencing the will constrain the nature of rhetorical proof, shape the substance of types of discourse, and constrain the stylistic processes of rhetoric.

Within the general provisions of examining rhetorical practice in terms of faculty psychology, Campbell's theory of rhetoric is predisposed by certain other assumptions regarding the principles of human nature, including the assumption that those ideas that develop in the mind do so as a consequence of the essentially "associative" nature of mental activities (resemblance, contiguity, and causality); the view that the mind relies on empirical experience as a source of knowledge and as a guide to the logic of associative relations; and the notion that *vivacity* or liveliness of ideas is the quality primarily responsible for attention and belief.[4] Campbell's perception of the impact of vivacity on the logical workings of the mind is closely related to his acceptance of the epistemological assumption that the mind draws inferences and deductions through the logical dynamics of associative links. The veracity of any rhetorical utterance comes about as a result of the rhetorician's ability to replicate the laws of association in the structure of discourse and to infuse language with those qualities most likely to bring tangible referents and experiences to mind. Campbell redefines the rhetorician's burden as one directly responsible for shaping discourse in such a way that the empirical truth of an explanation or argument is indisputable. Consequently, Campbell views rhetorical evidence and style in terms of an obligation to scientific principles of probability and verisimilitude.

Campbell views rhetoric as a process that presupposes rather than generates "truth," arguing that "logic forges the arms that eloquence teacheth us to wield" (34). It is the function of rhetoric to present logical substance, substance that is simply information in isolation of an apprehending mind that recognizes factual truth only when empirical veracity has been established by the force of rhetorical content and form. By taking into consideration the circumstances of the subject and the hearers, the rhetorician "manages" logical substance in such a manner that the ends of discourse are achieved and "doubts, disbelief, and mistake" overcome (33). Campbell's idea of truth is synonymous with empirical credibility, or that which appears to be consistent with, or can be inferred from, experience; the managerial obligation that rhetoric has to logic consists of presenting only that substance that conforms to normative conceptions of "the nature of things" and doing so in forms that reify the experiential circumstances associated with the subject or idea. This view of rhetoric as a process of selecting content and managing form implies a distinctly different function for invention from that outlined in classical theory. From Campbell's philosophical point of view, notions of experience and the probable are based not on consensus, public opinion, or a "mean" determined by the common good or utility but on what most closely approximates self-conscious empirical and rational experience: "to eighteenth-century British writers on rhetoric, the syllogistic structure was not the natural form of thought, and although some arguments would appropriately fall into that form, and could be analyzed and discussed in terms of their major premise, their minor premise, and their conclusion, the basic pattern of rhetorical argument for the new age was that which would lead the audience to recognize intuitively the truth of the author's statement or would lead him to establish its truth from related facts or truths" (Howell 443–44).

Although not actually addressing invention per se, Campbell outlines those principles of natural logic and categories of rhetorical evidence that he contends constrain the processes of moral reasoning on which rhetorical conviction and persuasion depend. Deeming syllogistic or dialectical reasoning as contrary to the natural dynamics of inquiry, Campbell attends instead to analytic methods of reasoning from experience, consciousness, and common sense, methods that he defines as the only means by which we can acquire natural knowledge regarding "actual existences" (62). Ascribing rhetorical proof to the realm of "moral evidence," Campbell explains that unlike logic, which sets out abstract principles, rhetoric deals with the "actual connections" between abstract or scientific truth and the realities of human intellection and responses. As a consequence, the rhetorical process of proof is essentially a matter of identifying those modes of presentation that appeal to the common sense or the consciousness of the hearers, the former being the intellectual ability to intuit or deduce reasonable certainties and probabilities from the knowledge accrued from experience and the latter being the natural state of self-awareness of empirical and sensory existence that compels each person to validate personal perception and feelings as valid sources of true knowledge. The inventional obligation of rhetoric is to develop subject matter in conjunction with those types of evidence that appeal most directly to natural intellection: evidence from direct experience; evidence from analogy (which Campbell defines as reasoning from "indirect experience or "more remote similitude"); and evidence from testimony, the presentation of individual observation and experience (40–70).[5] In an attempt to reconcile the obligations of rhetoric with the more sophisticated cognitive and psychological insights of eighteenth-century philosophy, Campbell does not contest the traditional notion of invention as discovery so much as he redefines the nature of what the rhetorician is to discover; Campbell shifts theoretical emphasis from the formulaic character of enthymemic proof to a concern with the identification and presentation of argumentative or explanatory evidence or materials. One way to understand what Campbell does with the notion of rhetorical evidence is to see his efforts to categorize rhetorical evidence in terms of epistemological appropriateness as the designing of a new set of common topoi consisting of the categories of natural logic: experience, analogy, and testimony.

In addition to providing a rationale for a substantive redefinition of the principle of rhetorical proof, a philosophical regard for the empirical and rational foundations of mental response also governs Campbell's analysis of other rhetorical principles. In his discussion of pathetic and ethical appeal, the divisions of rhetoric, and the canon of style, Campbell conflates discrete features of traditional theory with modern pronouncements on the epistemological dynamics that constrain usage and audience response. Campbell's debt to the rhetorical tradition indicates the degree to which the New Rhetoric was based on a revision of traditional elements of theory. Campbell tends to co-opt features of classical rhetoric when discussing how rhetorical forms appeal to the understanding, the imagination, the passions, and the will; nevertheless, his attention to traditional elements of theory (argumentation, ethos, pathos, the divisions, the canon of style) would have the long-range effect of reinscribing these elements within rhetorical theory.

Reiterating classical advice that the rhetorician must adjust the "fitness of arguments" to the "different orders of men" addressed, Campbell's observes that the "sense" advanced must fall within the hearer's "sphere" of knowledge or else the faculties of reason will not be engaged. One means of ensuring such an appeal to the hearer's frame of mind is to gratify the imagination through "vivacity, beauty, sublimity and novelty." Such qualities attract the attention of the imagination, which in turn engages the hearer's beliefs. Just as it is necessary to stimulate the imagination to induce belief, the rhetorician must appeal to the passions if action is the intended end of speaking. Within the dynamics of persuasion, the faculties work in particular concert:

> In order to persuade, there are two things which must be carefully studied by the orator. The first is to excite some desire or passion in his hearers; the second is to satisfy their judgment that there is a connexion between the action to which he would persuade them, and the gratification of the desire or passion which he excites. . . .

passion must be awakened by communicating lively ideas of the
object. . . . a passion is strongly excited by sensation. (210)

Accordingly, the rhetorician must attempt to shape rhetorical content in
terms of the circumstances chiefly instrumental in operating on the passions:
probability, plausibility, importance, proximity of time, connection of
place, relation of the principals to the hearers, and interests of the hearers
or speaker in the consequences. Paralleling many features of classical
advice on pathetic appeal, this analysis of "circumstances" functions in
Campbell's theory of rhetoric in much the same way as does Aristotle's
treatment of character and emotions in book 2 of the *Rhetoric,* as a guide
to the nature of pathetic response and the constraints that such affective
disposition places on the shape and content of persuasive discourse (212–
23).[6]

Campbell again recasts traditional classical advice in his discussion
of "the consideration which the Speaker ought to have of Himself," an
impression "obtained reflexively from the opinion entertained of him by
the hearers or the character which he bears with them" (224). Campbell
reiterates the importance of securing goodwill and authority (ethos) but
discusses these issues in terms of a larger burden that falls to the speaker,
that of generating sympathy, an emotional reaction analogous to the com-
pulsion toward resemblance that controls the imagination. Perceiving the
gaining of sympathy as a necessary step in affecting the passions, which in
turn engage the will, Campbell views ethos in terms of its epistemological
function as a natural strategy for securing the attention of the interrelated
mental faculties and not as an optional mode of appeal that may or may not
be suited to subject or occasion: "Whatever . . . weakens that principle of
sympathy must do the speaker prejudice in respect of his power over the
passions of his audience. . . . Now, the speaker's apparent conviction of
the truth of what he advanceth, adds to all his other arguments an evidence,
though not precisely the same, yet near akin to that of his own testimony"
(224).

The New Rhetoric

Campbell credits classical sources such as Quintilian's *Institutio Oratoria* and quotes frequently from Horace's *Art of Poetry* throughout his discussion of how the orator should regard himself and his hearers. Moreover, he is consistently in the debt of a more general classical principle in his discussion of the divisions and the canon of style: the dictate that the rhetorician must design arguments with constant reference to subject, hearer, and occasion. As he supplements traditional advice with attention to the epistemological dynamics governing rhetorical occasions, usage, and style, Campbell extends the theoretical perimeters of these standard topics by associating rhetorical adaptations of form and style with specific dynamics of the faculties and also by drawing attention to those aspects of human nature that are inevitably implicated in compositional practices. Offering a definition of the divisions as forensic rhetoric, political rhetoric, and pulpit oratory, Campbell briefly discusses the requirements of these divisions in very general advice on how the speaker is to adapt arguments to the subject, audience, and occasion. Elaborating in greater detail on the occasional variables that influence consideration of ethos and pathos, Campbell's discussion of the divisions pays more attention to the dynamics between speaker and audience in various rhetorical scenes than it does to the formal and argumentative requirements of "orations delivered at the bar, those pronounced in the senate, and those spoken from the pulpit" (99). Although Campbell rehearses traditional advice regarding the importance of presenting an "admirable character" and of assessing the "age, rank, fortune, education, and prejudices" of the persons addressed, his discussion of the preacher's obligation to arouse the passions in order to change the heart and disposition is indicative of the epistemological rationale that consistently accompanies the neoclassical affirmations offered in *The Philosophy of Rhetoric*. Following the discussion of the ends of preaching is an elaborate philosophical explanation of "the simple passions of which the mind is susceptible" (the pleasant and the painful) in which Campbell accounts for the epistemological chain of events with which the orator or poet is involved. When the strong passions must be excited, there is an attraction of association among the passions, as well as among the ideas of the mind. . . . pain of every kind generally makes a deeper impression on the imagination than pleasure does, and is longer retained by the memory. . . . under the name pity may be included all the emotions excited by tragedy [pity and terror]. . . . pity is not a simple passion, but a group of passions strictly united by association, and as it were blended by centering in the same object. (132)

In his discussion of the modes of discourse, Campbell repeatedly makes the point that in order for discourse to affect the faculties and thereby ensure conviction or persuasion, the ideas presented must appear credible, in the sense that the members of the audience must be able to associate the information or premises with their own empirical experience or be able to intuit or deduce such an association. An insistence on the rhetorician's obligation to the empirical veracity of experience and the associative nature of mental activity predisposes Campbell's revision of rhetorical theory, even when neoclassical assertions are prominent, as in the case of his discussion of grammatical purity and the major qualities of style. Campbell makes the point that rhetoric has as close a kinship with the laws of grammar as it does with the laws of natural logic because the credibility of discourse also depends on grammatical "purity," or the conventional status of words and syntax. Paralleling quite closely traditional guidelines regarding appropriateness in style, Campbell observes that the rhetorician must make use of grammatical materials to present ideas in forms corresponding to the "fixed principles" of "reputable custom," "national use," and "present use" (260–70).[7] What marks Campbell's discussion of the grammatical aspects of style as a feature of the New Rhetoric is the justification he offers for compulsory attention to grammatical convention: Campbell assumes that adherence to grammatical custom contributes to the success with which eloquence conveys sentiments into the minds of others because grammatical laws embody "the relations which subsist among the things signified" (261). While the rhetorician's general effort is a far more encompassing one than that of the grammarian, the orator can only add the "higher qualities of

The New Rhetoric

elocution" to structures that already reflect a prerequisite level of conventionality sufficient to allow the hearer to associate words with their referents. In Campbell's epistemological view of rhetorical dynamics, grammatical deviations (such as barbarisms and solecisms) are problematic because they inhibit the processes of association, whereas "grammatical truth" or "purity" facilitates these connections:

> Language is the sole channel through which we communicate our knowledge and discoveries to others, and through which the knowledge and discoveries of others are communicated to us. By reiterated recourse to this medium, it necessarily happens, that when things are related to each other, the words signifying those things are more commonly brought together in discourse. Hence the word and names themselves, by customary vicinity, contract in the fancy a relation additional to that which they derive purely from being symbols of related things. Further, this tendency is strengthened by the structure of language. . . . The consequence is, that similar relations in things will be expressed similarly; that is by similar inflections, derivations, compositions, arrangement of words, or juxtaposition of particles, according to the genius or grammatical form of the particular tongue.[8] (259)

Although rhetorical style depends on the foundations of grammatical purity, the general aim of rhetorical style in speaking and writing is to provide those "higher qualities" that give grace and energy to discourse. Campbell defines these major qualities of style as *perspicuity* and *vivacity*. Perspicuity (clarity) is essential to any effort to inform the understanding, intelligibility being to "the understanding what light is to the eye" (216). Within the dynamics of faculty psychology, an appeal to the understanding is always necessary whether the speaker or writer's aim is simply to inform (conviction) or whether engaging the understanding is subordinate to "pleasure, emotion or persuasion." Offenses against perspicuity can occur in diction or syntax: the use of obscure words, faulty arrangement of words, contradictory uses of terminology, vague pronoun references, the "injudicious" use of technical words and phrases, long sentences, and any form of ambiguity. More general violations in composition can be caused by any form of what Campbell describes as *the unintelligible,* an offense against reasoning that can result in conveying "no meaning at all." A major cause of the unintelligible is confusion of thought: when the speaker or writer has only "half-formed" thoughts on a subject, these confused and imperfect perceptions are reflected in sentence structures that obscure meaning. Other stylistic problems that render speech unintelligible include "specious verbosity" ("the puerile"), the recapitulation of "learned nonsense," an overly "profound" subject or register, and subject matter that credits the "marvelous" over the dictates of common sense (216–55).

The theory of perspicuity set out by Campbell reasserts classical teachings regarding clarity; in fact, what Campbell treats under perspicuity, classical texts such as the *Ad Herennium* discuss under the heading of "Taste" (purity and perspicuity) and "Artistic Composition" (4.11.16–18).[9] It is the attention to the epistemological realities associated with claims on the understanding that constitutes the innovative aspect of Campbell's treatment of perspicuity as a preferred quality of style. The same type of attention shapes Campbell's discussion of vivacity, that quality of style which has the most influence on the imagination and thereby an influence on the passions and the will. In his treatment of vivacity, Campbell co-opts features of traditional theories of style (diction, tropes, arrangement of sentences) within a larger discussion of which rhetorical styles affect the faculties most successfully. It is a standard feature of classical advice on style to suggest that "proper terms" (Aristotle describes these as "special names") convey greater specificity; what Campbell adds to this precept is an attention to the function such diction serves in creating vivacity, or vivid ideas. "The more general the terms are, the picture is the fainter; the more special they are, it is the brighter . . . it will sometimes have a considerable effect on enlivening the imagery, not only to particularize, but even to individuate the object presented to the mind" (286–90). Focusing on comparatively few tropes and foregoing distinctions between figures of diction and thought, Campbell discusses tropes in terms of their primary functions of creating vivacity (a sense of felt experience) and enhancing intelligibility.[10] Campbell's discussion of tropes is analogous to traditional advice on how the figures of diction and thought confer "distinction" on style; however, the quality of distinctiveness that Campbell considers significant is the figurative effect that renders an image sufficiently lively "to fix the attention" of the imagination on the particular (e.g. antonomasia [*pronominatio*]) or on a more general association (synecdoche [*intellectio*] and metonymy [*denominatio*]).

Hugh Blair and the Belles Lettres Rationale for Rhetoric

The context in which Campbell reviews the nature and function of figurative language indicates the general theoretical commitment of *The Philosophy of Rhetoric*—the intention to explain the dynamics of rhetoric in terms of the principles of human nature. Campbell's ambition to document how these principles are implicated in the rhetorical process also occupied other eighteenth-century commentators. Joseph Priestley's *Course of Lectures on Oratory and Criticism* (1777) relies on the assumption that "two sources of the principles of human nature and pleasures of the imagination . . . explain the efficacy of rhetorical devices . . . the association of simple ideas [and] a moderate exertion of the faculties" (xliv). Although Priestley's treatise did not achieve the same degree of influence as Campbell's text, his interest in an epistemological approach to rhetoric suggests the degree to which this perspective had become the foundation of rhetorical theory by the late eighteenth century, serving as a guiding set of assumptions not only for Campbell's manifesto but also for those works that reconcile modern philosophy with a critical approach to rhetoric. The distinctive characteristic of the belles lettres approach to rhetoric, embodied in the widely circulated works of Lord Kames (*Elements of Criticism,* 1762) and Hugh Blair (*Lectures on Rhetoric and Belles Lettres*), was a theoretical attention to taste as a human faculty and to those qualities of rhetorical style that most effectively move the faculties of reason and the passions to higher thought and emotion, a state synonymous with the exercise of taste. The philosophical drive of the eighteenth-century belles lettres movement can be understood as the desire to "discover . . . a foundation for reasoning upon the taste of an individual" and to design a "science of rational criticism" that could serve as the foundation for a general art of rhetorical composition (Kames 11–12).[11] The articulation of a rational philosophy of taste and its implications for critical standards and rhetorical practice was the aim of Blair's *Lectures,* and this work more than any other was responsible for popularizing the belles lettres approach to rhetorical theory and practice in the nineteenth century.[12]

In *Lectures on Rhetoric and Belles Lettres* Blair offers a synthesis of classical teachings and contemporary theories of aesthetics and rhetoric, a synthesis that reiterates several features common to the theoretical stance of *The Philosophy of Rhetoric* and the New Rhetoric in general: the assumption that the procedures and practices of rhetoric are founded on and responsible to the faculties of reason; the view that the rhetorical process presumes and manages the materials of logic and grammar; the assumption that the art of rhetoric involves the arrangement, style, and presentation of sense but not the invention of truth; an attention to the divisions of formal oratory (eloquence of the bar, eloquence of popular assemblies, and eloquence of the pulpit); and a general debt to classical concerns with intention, audience, and occasion. Blair's corroboration of these theoretical features emphatically confirmed the New Rhetoric as an emerging tradition that was both innovative and recapitulative in its theoretical interests. Distinctive elements of Blair's theory of rhetoric contributed to the substance the orientation of nineteenth-century theory and pedagogy: a definition of rhetoric as encompassing the study and practice of oratory, writing, and criticism; an explanation of the doctrine of taste and an elaboration of those critical standards for rhetorical composition that conform to its dictates; an explicit attention to the importance of *imitatio* in the development of taste and rhetorical skills; and a theoretical approach to the divisions of oratory and the canons of rhetoric that incorporate both neoclassical and belletristic viewpoints.

Campbell explicitly refers to oratory throughout his treatise and implies by his frequent references to writing in his discussion of style that his discussion of the philosophical principles of rhetoric applies to both public speaking and composition; however, among the New Rhetoricians it is Blair who is responsible for popularizing a definition of eloquence as the art of public speaking and composition. By presenting his treatise as a discussion of "the arts of speech and writing" (3), Blair reiterates the same rationale for the study of rhetoric advocated by Adam Smith in his course of lectures on "a system of rhetoric and belles-lettres" given at Edinburgh and the University of Glasgow at midcentury (1745–60): "the best method of explaining and illustrating the various powers of the human mind, the most useful part of metaphysics, arises from an examination of the several ways of communicating our thoughts by speech, and from an attention to the principles of those literary compositions which contribute to persuasion or entertainment."[13] Like Smith, who considered rhetoric to be the study of how the principles of communication can be adapted to the arts of speaking, Blair perceived the study of rhetoric and belles lettres as including the traditional divisions of "Oratory and Public Speaking" (eloquence of popular assemblies, the bar, and the pulpit) and "the most distinguished kinds of Composition both in prose and verse" (historical writing, philosophical writing, dialogue, epistolary writing, fictitious history, and pastoral, lyric, didactic, descriptive, epic, dramatic, and comic poetry). Blair's definition of the range of rhetorical genres makes considerably more explicit the scope of study implied by Campbell's view of eloquence as "the grand art of communication" addressing "ideas, . . . sentiments, passions, dispositions," the dissemination of "valuable knowledge," and the enforcement of "right rules of action upon others" (xlix).

Blair's belletristic orientation prompted yet another innovative revision of the aims of rhetoric and nature of theoretical study. Intending his treatise for the edification of those who "propose, either by speech or writing, to address the Public" and for the instruction of those who wished to "improve their taste with respect to writing and discourse, and to acquire principles which will enable them to judge for themselves in that part of literature called the Belles Lettres," Blair considers the study of rhetoric to comprehend both the study of eloquence and criticism (5). Conflating eloquence and composition in one system, Blair merged the traditional domains of rhetoric and poetics under the auspices of the study of taste and its application to communication and the critical study of literature. Blair's incorporation of such a critical component into rhetorical theory made theory responsible for articulating fundamental principles that govern the impact of all genres and for promoting the pedagogical standard that a complete education in rhetorical theory and practice involves the acquisition of a critical sensibility.

A theoretical commitment to the doctrine of taste and the epistemological views that doctrine assumes is the philosophical ground for Blair's conflation of the study of oratory with the critical and pragmatic study of composition and literature. Whereas Campbell is mostly concerned with identifying the dynamics of the mind that dictate the principles of rhetoric, Blair pursues a more pragmatic interest. He focuses on defining those rhetorical principles that allow writers and speakers to improve their intellectual powers and habits of mind and that enhance their ability to communicate ideas:

> All that regards the study of eloquence and composition, merits the higher attention upon this account, that it is intimately connected with the improvement of our intellectual powers. For I must be allowed to say, that when we are employed, after a proper manner, in the study of composition, we are cultivating reason itself. True rhetoric and found logic are very nearly allied. The study of arranging and expressing our thoughts with propriety, teaches us to think, as well as to speak accurately. By putting our sentiments into words, we always conceive them more distinctly. . . . so close is the connection between thoughts and the words in which they are clothed. (6–7)

Blair awards to the acquisition of taste, or the development of critical judgment, a special function in strengthening the powers of the mind and the arts of expression. "Taste" designates that common faculty of the mind that can be understood as an innate response to beauty, a response that enhances the powers of the imagination and the passions by directing intellectual and emotional attention to the beauties of nature and art. Aiding the understanding by enhancing the powers of the imagination and the intensity of sensory impressions of experience, taste embodies a natural response to harmony, to elegance, and to the sublime (qualities of beauty).[14] The cultivation of taste and the study of critical principles (rhetoric) extends philosophical insight into human nature by foregrounding those "delicate springs of action" that lie outside the scrutiny of science proper:

> The exercise of taste and of found criticism, is in truth one of the most improving employments of the understanding. . . . For such disquisitions are very intimately connected with the knowledge of ourselves. They necessarily lead us to reflect on the operations of the imagination, and the movements of the heart; and increase our acquaintance with some of the most refined feelings which belong to our frame. (10)

Blair's regard for the edifying function of taste goes beyond an argument for its influence on the powers of reason to include an advocacy for its impact on the development of moral character and civil commitment. Ascribing to taste a specific role in educating the mind to a liberal state in which it may respond to elevated sentiments such as "public spirit, the love of glory, contempt of external fortune, and the admiration of what is truly illustrious and great," Blair draws a direct link between the cultivation of taste and the development of intellectual, moral, and civil virtues. Defining rhetoric as a discipline that directs the cultivation of taste, Blair views the study of rhetoric and belles lettres as a process of edification, a means by which the individual can prepare for the discharge of "the higher and more important duties of life" (12–13). The strictly epistemological or "scientific" view of rhetoric within the New Rhetoric (represented by Campbell) made a case for the cognitive foundations of rhetoric that would constrain nineteenth-century theory; Blair's belletristic ideology established an equally influential claim for the role of the rhetoric in the cultivation of liberal and moral culture, a claim that would find wide acceptance in the nineteenth-century tradition in North America.

The general rationale of Blair's *Lectures* is founded on a presumption of the intellectual and moral worth of attending to taste as an "improvable faculty" and on the assumption that the study of rhetoric and belles lettres will inevitably result in the acquisition of taste in its most perfect state. The epistemological/aesthetic rationale on which the belletristic approach to rhetoric relies assumes that the composition of eloquence and written discourse is obligated to taste insofar as the aims of rhetoric entail a necessary obligation "to please" the imagination. Blair argues that the imagination serves reason in a special way because it allows the mind to apprehend aspects of truth (the sublime and the beautiful) that cannot be directly perceived by the understanding. The study of belles lettres is the means of understanding those principles that guide the exercise of taste and appeal most powerfully to the imagination. Blair defines the major principles of taste as: sublimity, grandeur in subject, passion, and/or form that fills the mind with "great ideas"; beauty, an aesthetic quality of style, sentiment, or object created by the collaboration of several qualities (color, regularity, and motion) which inspire "an agreeable serenity" and lasting pleasure; and novelty, a comparatively less intense influence on the imagination but one that produces "a vivid and agreeable emotion" in response to the unusual, the uncommon, or the new (22–96).[15] As natural qualities reflecting the substance of experience, sublimity, beauty, and novelty represent primary qualities of taste and the first principles of criticism. Other pleasures of taste include imitation and description, which please the imagination by recalling the primary beauty or sublimity of the object exhibited and intensifying the connection between perception and experience. Blair points out that eloquence and poetry rely on imitation and description more than does any other art and can represent the world of natural and moral experience in "colors very strong and lively" (93). This particular assumption reveals an essential characteristic of the belletristic approach to rhetoric—a concern for the degree to which particular types of discourse engage the imagination, that faculty with the greatest disposition toward tasteful qualities of sense and form. By identifying the critical principles that best appeal to the faculty of taste and applying these to outline proper practices in rhetorical composition, the study of belles lettres encourages the development of taste to higher levels of excellence.

In the belletristic rationale for rhetoric, it is the critical ability to judge and appreciate the qualities of taste that ultimately confers success on the efforts of those writers and orators who strive to move the passions or the imagination; therefore, the study of the principles of taste is a mandatory aspect of rhetorical training. The cultivation of taste is achieved by the study of critical principles and by practice in deploying these principles in criticism, composition, and oratorical performance. Blair insists that the the study of "the most admired productions of genius" (an exemplary canon) ensures the acquisition of taste because such models reveal qualities of sense, sentiment, and form that have exerted "long-lasting and universal appeal" to human nature. One of the most distinctive aspects of belletristic theory is the assumption that the study of rhetoric necessarily involves the study of "the proper models for imitation": "by them we are enabled to collect, what the sense of mankind is with respect to those beauties, which give them the highest pleasure. . . . In every composition, what interests the imagination and touches the heart, gives pleasure to all ages and nations. There is a certain string, which being properly struck, the human heart is so made, as to accord to it" (17). Belletristic rhetorical theory insists that great works illustrate not only tasteful rhetorical effects but also the admirable ideas and elevated sentiments that the would-be writer or speaker should aspire to express. In this sense, the principle of *imitatio* is as crucial an element of belletristic rhetorical theory as it is of traditional poetics.[16]

The articulation of the doctrine of taste, the formulation of rhetoric as a critical theory, and the designation of rhetoric as a general art of communication are Blair's innovative contributions to the New Rhetoric. However, Blair further contributes by offering reviews of traditional elements of rhetorical theory such as the divisions of oratory and the offices of arrangement, style, and delivery. Like Campbell, Blair relies substantially on neo-Ciceronian premises and definitions in his treatment of such

Nineteenth-Century Rhetoric

issues; however, he supplements standard advice regarding these elements
of theory with attention to the epistemological and aesthetic principles
that affect communication and affective response. This theoretical stance
indicates the degree to which belletristic rhetoric shared in the revisionist
intentions of the New Rhetoric.[17] In his treatment of the divisions of
rhetoric, Blair combines neoclassical assumptions with updated notions of
what types of affective dynamics influence the composition and presentation
of the major modes of public speaking. Blair approaches the "scenes" of
oratory in terms of classical analogues, observing that "Eloquence of Popular Assembles" involves both deliberative and demonstrative elements and
that "Eloquence of the Bar" compares with the classical category of judicial
rhetoric; however, "Eloquence of the Pulpit," a distinctly "modern" form
of oratory, "cannot be properly reduced under any of the heads of the
ancient Rhetoricians" (47). Blair's treatment of each form of oratory in
terms of aim, audience, subject, method (arrangement), style, and delivery
is distinctly neoclassical, yet his discussion also attends to the particular
epistemological realities associated with the form and impact of oratorical
composition. (Blair pays particular attention to the range of affective response involved in preparing the sermon.) Throughout his discussion of the
major divisions, which is far more detailed in its treatment of characteristic
features of oratory than is Campbell's, Blair consistently reiterates Ciceronian admonitions regarding the consideration of aim, audience, and occasion, while also stressing the strategic relevance of "natural" appeals to the
mental faculties:[18]

> In all kinds of Public Speaking, but especially in Popular Assem-
> blies, it is a capital rule to attend to all the decorums of time,
> place, and character. No one should ever rise to speak in public,
> without forming to himself a just and strict ideal of what suits his
> own age, and character; what suits the subject, the hearers, the
> place, the occasion; and adjusting the whole train and manner of his
> speaking on this idea. All the ancients insist much on this. (58)

> The end of all preaching is, to persuade men to become good. All
> persuasion . . . is founded on conviction. The understanding must

38

be applied to in the first place, in order to make a lasting impression on the heart: and he who would work on men's passions, or influence their practice, without first giving them just principles, and enlightening their minds, is no better than a mere declaimer.[19] (105)

Blair's approach to the "conduct of a discourse" (arrangement) exemplifies a similar theoretical tendency to assert principles of classical doctrine in conjunction with the characteristic philosophical rationale of the New Rhetoric, a rationale that explains rhetorical strategies in terms of what best inspires the mind's natural inclinations to process ideas and feelings in terms of experience. In his discussion of arrangement, Blair offers a neoclassical definition of the parts of an oration as "the Exordium or Introduction; secondly, the State, and the Division of the Subject; thirdly, Narration, or Explication; fourthly, the Reasoning or Arguments, fifthly, the Pathetic part; and lastly, the Conclusion" (157). Just as Campbell reasserts classical elements of the canon of style on an epistemological foundation, so too Blair reiterates classical advice on oratorical structure in combination with observations regarding the parity between the aims of arrangement and effective impact on the faculties. To read Blair's discussion of the discrete functions of the parts of an oration is to encounter a host of traditional assumptions regarding arrangement: the function of the introduction is to gain the interest and favor of the audience and to introduce the significance of the subject ; the function of the division (when appropriate) is to outline the method of discussion; the "Argumentative or reasoning Part of a Discourse" should be arranged with a concern for the hierarchical placement of material arguments and the "inconspicuous" placement of weak arguments (157–202).[20]

Although Blair frequently cites "ancient" sources in his treatment of arrangement, he just as frequently supplements time-honored advice with comments directing the speaker's attention to the epistemological influences that must be considered when composing a speech. For example, in his approach to "the pathetic part of a discourse" Blair argues that when the aim of the orator is to persuade or move the will, the passions—"the great springs of human action"—must be moved or the dynamics of the

39

mind that induce action will not be engaged. In addressing exactly how the passions can be affected, Blair observes that the best rhetorical strategy for putting the hearer in a conducive frame of mind is vivid engagement of the emotions: "To every emotion or passion, Nature has adapted a set of corresponding objects; and without setting these before the mind, it is not in the power of the Orator to raise that emotion. . . . The foundation, therefore, of all successful execution in the way of Pathetic Oratory is, to paint the object of that passion which we wish to raise, in the most natural and striking manner; to describe it with such circumstances as are likely to awaken it in the minds of others" (192). In this description of the function of the pathetic part of an oration, Blair assigns a special role to the passions in inducing a sufficient recognition of experiential fact to provoke the will into action. By so doing, Blair underscores his treatment of this traditional element of oratorical structure with a philosophical attention to natural processes of mental activity—in this case an assumption of the essentially empirical basis of intellectual and emotional response.

Blair's theoretical interest in the natural is also revealed in the ways in which he revises standard treatments of style and delivery. Frequently reiterating the traditional principle that a consideration of audience and the constraints of occasion must influence all aspects of composition, Blair treats style primarily in terms of how the "author's manner of thinking" can be conveyed, stressing those qualities that enhance appeal to the mental faculties. Although there are significant parallels between Blair's discussion of the major qualities of style (perspicuity and ornament) and Campbell's treatment of perspicuity and figurative language, Blair reviews these features in terms of the aesthetic impact they create as well as in terms of how style ensures distinct impressions and comprehensible syntax.[21] For example, Blair discusses perspicuity ("purity, propriety, and precision") in diction and sentence structure as a quality of style embodying "a sort of negative virtue, or freedom from defect." Blair regards clarity as an important principle of positive beauty. "We are pleased with an author, we consider him as deserving of praise, who frees us from all the fatigue of searching for his meaning . . . whose style flows always like a limpid stream, where we see to the very bottom" (186).

Blair's conflation of an aesthetic view of rhetorical effects with a cognitive philosophy of language is obvious in his tendency to foreground the activities of the imagination and its sensitivity to the natural and the beautiful. The focus predisposes Blair's discussion of ornament and figurative language (lecture 13), in which he argues that just as hearers and readers are pleased by clarity, so too are they affected by the imagination's response to "Ornament," or the grace and beauty of sentence construction and the figures. Observing that uniformity in sentence length is tiresome, Blair points to the advantages of mixing the "style periodique" and the "style coupe" to derive an elegant style based on "variety and harmony," qualities that increase the attention of the imagination to language and ideas. In his recommendations for the use of these general styles and for the necessary character of sentence structure (204–73), Blair acknowledges the epistemological importance of comprehensibility (pe. spicuity) but stresses the function of sentence arrangements that stimulate the mind's response to beauty: unity (the presence of a connecting principle: one object must reign and be predominant), strength (rendering a lively impression), and harmony (agreeableness to the ear). "The fundamental rule of the construction of Sentences, and into which all others must be resolved, undoubtedly is, to communicate, in the clearest and most natural order, the ideas which we mean to transfer into the minds of others. Every arrangement that does most justice to the sense, and expresses it to most advantage, strikes us as beautiful" (245). Arguing that the imagination "revolts" when sense is expressed in harsh and disagreeable sounds, Blair insists that sentence structure should strive to provide the pleasure of "melody" through words composed of "smooth and liquid sounds" and "musical" arrangement (248, 252). These suggestions do not in any way contradict traditional advice regarding the style of sentences; in fact, Blair's views on sentence construction reiterate the Aristotelian case for the value of periodic style and the importance of "rhythm" in composition (*Rhetoric* 3.8.). What makes Blair's treatment of stylistic issues distinctive is the way in which he interprets traditional tenets from the perspective of both epistemological and belletristic doctrines.

Blair's discussion of figurative language reveals the degree to which the belles lettres rationale characteristically conflates classical features and epistemological and aesthetic perspectives. Classifying figures as either figures of passion or figures of imagination, Blair observes the distinction between figures of words and figures of thought, but he considers this traditional distinction less significant than the principle that "Figurative Language always imports some colouring of the imagination, or some emotion of passion, expressed in our Style" (276). Observing that figures should arise from the subject and be based on "solid thought and natural sentiment," Blair is primarily interested in making the point that figures intensify impressions of experience and thus affect the emotions and the imaginative responses that spur belief and action: "[A figure] sets mirrors before us, where we may behold objects, a second time, in their likeness. It entertains us, as with a succession of the most splendid pictures" (28). Essentially in agreement with Campbell that certain figures (metaphor, allegory, personification, apostrophe, comparison [simile], antithesis) are best suited to stimulate the associative processes of the faculties, Blair's more extensive discussion of these figures defers to classical views of style while focusing on the elevating effects of those tropes that convey ideas through similitude and resemblance. Citing classical sources on several aspects of ornament—including the appropriateness of "simple" figures when expressing dignified ideas, the importance of not mixing "kinds" of metaphor, and the function of "orationis lumina" (figures that add luster and beauty to discourse)—Blair incorporates classical precepts in a larger discussion explicitly concerned with the aesthetic function of the "capital" figures in stimulating the natural processes of the mind, an interest clearly displayed in his treatment of "Comparison":[22]

> The pleasure we take in comparisons is just and natural. We may remark three different sources whence it arises. First, from the pleasure which nature has annexed to that act of the mind by

The New Rhetoric

which we compare any two objects together, trace resemblances
among those that are different, and differences among those that
resemble each other; a pleasure, the final cause of which is, to
prompt us to remark and observe, and thereby to make us advance
in useful knowledge. This operation of the mind is naturally and
universally agreeable. . . . Secondly, the pleasure of Comparison
arises from the illustration which the simile employed gives to the
principal object; from the clearer view of it which it presents; or
the more strong impression of it which it stamps upon the mind:
and thirdly, It arises from the introduction of a new, and commonly a splendid object, associated to the principal one of which
we treat; and from the agreeable picture which that object presents
to the fancy; new scenes being thereby brought into view, which,
without the assistance of this figure, we could not have enjoyed.
(333–44)

Blair's discussion of style illustrates a prominent philosophical assumption of the New Rhetoric: the faculties of the mind are predisposed to
process ideas in terms of resemblance and association. In addition to his
articulation of the doctrine of taste and the unique role of rhetoric in
its cultivation, one of Blair's major contributions to eighteenth-century
rhetorical theory is his reconciliation of aesthetic response in terms of
this basic epistemological assumption and his subsequent definition of
the particular functions that rhetorical strategies—in this case, the use
of figures—have in inciting the mind's natural reaction to pleasurable
experience.

Blair's inclusion of delivery in his discussion of "general heads
relating to Eloquence of Public Speaking" reiterates the theoretical and
pragmatic relevance of this traditional canon to the general study of rhetoric
and represents another instance in which neoclassical principles are reshaped by considerations of the philosophical and aesthetic imperatives of
the natural. Blair's regard for the importance of the canon of delivery is
clear: "it is intimately connected with what is, or ought to be, the end of
all Public Speaking, Persuasion; and therefore deserves the study of the
most grave and serious Speakers, as much as those, whose only aim is to

Nineteenth-Century Rhetoric

please" (204). Blair's definition of delivery as "the management of the voice and gesture" is reminiscent of classical and postclassical definitions of this canon, but his major interest is in recommending practices of delivery that increase the impression ideas and emotions make on others: judgments regarding delivery must be governed by taste as well as by a concern for what is natural and typical (*Ad Herennium* 3.11). Many of Blair's specific recommendations regarding delivery are drawn from Thomas Sheridan's *Lectures on Elocution* (1762) and reflect the interests of eighteenth-century elocutionary theorists who advocated a theory of delivery drawn from the study of the natural disposition of voice, expression, and gesture in ordinary conversation. Blair assumes, as did the leading elocutionists of his time, that this "natural manner" is far more effective in engaging the passions and the imagination than affectations and actions learned by rote and applied indiscriminately to any subject or any occasion: "the capital direction, which ought never to be forgotten, is to copy the proper tones for expressing every sentiment from those which Nature dictates to us, in conversation with others; to speak always with her voice; and not to form to ourselves a fantastic public manner, from an absurd fancy of its being more beautiful than a natural one" (220).[23]

Blair's interest in delivery betrays epistemological and aesthetic values typical of the New Rhetoric's philosophical preoccupation with the realities of human nature; however, his reiteration of the constituents of delivery as management of the voice and of gesture and his acknowledgment of the usefulness of classical advice on this canon align his treatment of delivery with traditional approaches. As with his comments on arrangement, style, and the divisions of rhetoric, Blair's examination of the canon of delivery reiterates the significance of a systemic element of rhetorical theory and proclaims the major theoretical interest of the belles lettres rationale: a concern for how the varied dynamics of natural response to the beautiful affect the forms of language and the presentation of discourse.

The articulation of the doctrine of taste and the function of rhetoric and belles lettres in its cultivation constitute the major innovations in the *Lectures;* however, Blair's contribution to the New Rhetoric must also be evaluated in terms of how the *Lectures* affirm traditional elements of the classical system. Just as Campbell's innovative redesign of the philosophical foundations of rhetoric relies on and makes use of a variety of classical precepts and assumptions, so too does Blair's particular effort to outline a critical theory of rhetoric conflate neoclassical elements and belletristic theoretical assumptions. Blair's *Lectures* extend the New Rhetoric's project of philosophical redress by reconciling rhetorical principles with an aesthetic view of affective response. In the pursuit of this aim, Blair outlines a theory of rhetoric that is both more synthetic and distinctly more systematic than Campbell's philosophical treatise. Blair's belletristic approach to rhetoric reviews and revises more classical elements of theory and outlines a discussion of the modes and processes of rhetoric that imitates the systematic and prescriptive approach of the neoclassical tradition. Nineteenth-century theory proved highly dependent on Blair's more inclusive revision of traditional elements of theory (arrangement, style, delivery, divisions of rhetoric) as well as on his belletristic rationale, which assumed the obligation of rhetoric to the cultivation of taste, the relevance of critical study to the acquisition of a complete rhetorical sensibility, and the extension of the range of rhetorical genres to include oral and written discourse. The nineteenth-century tradition would also be influenced dramatically by the ideological claims of belletristic philosophy. In the *Lectures* Blair popularizes the assumption that there is a cause-and-effect relationship between the cultivation of taste (through the study and practice of rhetoric) and the acquisition of intellectual, moral, and civil virtue. Although this position represents the general stance of the New Rhetoric, Blair is more explicit in his declaration of the implicit virtues conferred by the study of rhetoric because his formal epistemological-aesthetic interests direct more theoretical and pragmatic attention to how the faculties of taste and the imagination affect the development of higher thought and emotions. Subsequently, the case made in the *Lectures* for the liberal influence of the study and practice of rhetoric is more distinct. Nineteenth-century rhetorical theory and education relied not only on the belletristic and neoclassical theoretical elements featured in the scheme of Blair's treatise but also on the belletristic rationale

45

that the *Lectures* advance: that the study of belles lettres and rhetoric supports the development of taste, intellectual ability, and moral virtue by defining how the principles of taste should be applied to the sense and form of conventional discourse.

Fundamental Assumptions of the New Rhetoric

The major treatises of the New Rhetoric award explicit attention to how affective constraints (characteristic functions of the faculties—the understanding, the passions, the imagination, and the will) govern the effects of discourse. While belletristic theory focuses on the aesthetic capacity of rhetoric to evoke tasteful responses, Blair's *Lectures* define the processes, forms, and effects of rhetorical practice in terms of the principles of human nature; thus, Blair's work parallels Campbell's effort to account for the philosophy of rhetoric. As the texts primarily responsible for popularizing the tenets of New Rhetoric, Campbell's *Philosophy of Rhetoric* and Blair's *Lectures* not only established the epistemological point of view as a normative foundation for rhetorical theory but also awarded a priori status to specific assumptions derived from this perspective: (1) The aims of rhetoric in general and of particular modes and techniques of rhetoric are linked necessarily to affective intentions. (2) Due to the philosophical veracity of its procedures and aims, the study of rhetoric can be understood as a science, that is, as an enterprise that reveals basic principles of nature (human nature). (3) Rhetorical discourse stands in a unique relationship with the faculty of taste; therefore, rhetoric must also be understood as an art, or a means of adapting critical principles to composition. (4) Through the study and practice of rhetoric, the faculty of taste can be cultivated, an education essential to the intellectual and moral health of individuals and of society in general.

For both Campbell and Blair, these imperatives served as a basis for the reevaluation of particular traditional assumptions and the reinscription of others. The most significant alteration to the traditional scope of rhetorical theory provoked by the rationales of the New Rhetoric was the extension of the domain of rhetoric to include all forms of belles lettres as well as the modes of public speaking. It is extremely important to an understanding of the integrity of the New Rhetoric to note that this restructuring of rhetorical praxis was prompted first and foremost by the implications of a basic philosophical position: the assumption that rhetorical theory and practice are agencies by which the nuances of reasoning and affective response can be verified. The dynamics of communication are implicit in the principles of human nature and vice versa; therefore, all forms of communication are philosophical endeavors implicated in and by their generic forms and subjects. From this point of view, which already presupposes the scientific and aesthetic importance of rhetoric as a body of revealed and revealing theory, all forms of communication are relevant to the study of the interrelationship between human nature and language. In *The Philosophy of Rhetoric* Campbell posits exactly this rationale for the range of rhetoric and implies by his attention to public speaking and frequent references to poetry and explanatory discourse that his view of the theoretical and pragmatic domain of rhetoric necessarily comprehends "the general rules of composition" in the "same medium, language" (xlix). Blair's *Lectures* outline what the general study of rhetoric involves: the critical and pragmatic study of all forms of discourse including public speaking, historical writing, philosophical writing, epistolary writing, fictitious history, dialogue, poetry, and drama. One way to understand the systematic impact of Blair and Campbell's extension of the range of rhetoric is to view this innovation as a substantial redefinition of the divisions component of rhetorical theory.

In addition to reformulating a working understanding of the types of discourse that the study of rhetoric must address, the New Rhetoricians also redefined the canon of invention. By redefining invention as the management of rhetorical evidence and the selection and arrangement of types of arguments, Campbell and Blair maintain a Ramistic view of rhetoric and logic as closely related but distinct disciplines; however, it is obvious in *The Philosophy of Rhetoric* that eighteenth-century reformulations of the canon of invention were also the consequence of the philosophical context that directed the revisionist efforts of the New Rhetoric in general. The New Rhetoric proceeded on the assumption that conviction and persuasion are promoted only by the dynamic reactions of the faculties. Such reactions are compelled by an inherent predisposition to experience, consciousness of empirical and sensory experience, and "commonsense" intuitions regarding the association between new ideas and experience already accrued. Campbell observes that it is the function of rhetoric to identify the materials of rhetorical discourse and to "manage" the substance of arguments (evidence) in such a way as to convince the hearer that the matter presented is indicative of experience. Blair shares the view that it is not the function of rhetoric to "discover reasons" but rather to "manage those reasons with most advantage" (180). Blair gives no attention to what constitutes the "most advantage"; however, the compatibility of his position on invention with Campbell's can be inferred from the emphasis Blair places on the implicit worth of the orator's own "thorough knowledge of the subject, and profound meditation on it" as a source of arguments (182). Blair prefers the speaker's own experience and "consciousness" as an inventional source over the classical "commonplaces," which he regards as potentially useful but still an "artificial" source. Blair's position reveals another instance of the philosophical reverence for the natural that underlies the treatment of argumentative invention in the New Rhetoric. Rhetoric selects, shapes, and arranges the information that logic derives; the inventional force of the rhetorical process lies in the manner in which information is adapted to the hearer or reader's perception of what constitutes truth, which as Campbell points out, "consisteth in the conformity of our conceptions to their archetypes in the nature of things" (Campbell 35).

Between their two treatments of arguments, Campbell and Blair collectively formulate "the disposition and conduct of Arguments" as an inventional or managerial obligation dealing with the following issues: analytic and synthetic arrangement of arguments; arrangement of arguments according to topic and strength; the selection of argumentative proof or "moral evidence" derived from experience, analogy, and testimony; and circumstances influencing "the passions." Although the New Rhetoricians treated principles comparable to ethos and pathos, these appeals were considered qualities of discourse relevant to style and the selection of materials, not as inventional modes in and of themselves in the Aristotelian sense. Campbell and Blair stipulate that sensitivity to affective disposition and the presentation of an attractive character in the speaker facilitate emotional responses prerequisite to achieving persuasion, a rhetorical effect that depends on the engagement of the passions in the inducement of the will and the establishment of a general "communicative principle" that Campbell defines as sympathy (90–96). By treating "the consideration which the Speaker ought to have of the Hearers" and "the consideration which the Speaker ought to have of Himself" as inevitable considerations in persuasion, "the pathetic part" of discourse, and the effect of stylistic qualities such as vivacity and beauty, Blair and Campbell reiterate traditional wisdom regarding the necessity for an orator to convey sincerity, goodwill, and authority as well as to assess (and appeal to) the particular nature of the hearer's habit of mind.

Other standard features of the classical system such as the canons of style and delivery were subjected to revisions in the New Rhetoric, which redefined constituents of these canons in terms of particular epistemological or aesthetic functions. The New Rhetoricians' treatment of style addressed three major issues: perspicuity, vivacity, and ornament (beauty). Considering these aspects of style in terms of epistemological dynamics such as intelligibility and aesthetic appeal, Campbell and Blair collectively identify constituents of style that contribute most to appeals to the understanding (conviction) and the passions (persuasion): grammatical usage and syntax; clarity in diction, sentence structure, and sentence arrangement; rhetorical qualities of sentence arrangement (unity, strength, harmony); and the use of figures (metaphor, allegory, personification, apostrophe, comparison, simile, and antithesis) to create force and elegance. Blair's account of how delivery renders words fully significant by embodying natural sentiments in tones and gestures is similarly constrained by a pervasive interest in the organic principles of human nature. Typical of the New Rhetoric's recapitulation of traditional principles of theory within a changed philosophical framework, Blair's account of delivery as "the Language of Nature" reasserts its importance to the study of rhetoric while shifting theoretical and pragmatic attention to a consideration of the natural as a superordinate guide to effective practice.

It is important to observe the degree to which the New Rhetoric revised the traditional rhetorical system if we are to understand the extent to which the philosophical imperatives of the eighteenth century imposed on the definitions of rhetorical principles and praxis that emerged in the English tradition after 1750. However, it is equally important to note which classical presumptions and canonical features the New Rhetoric preserved. Several unaltered neo-Ciceronian elements figure prominently in the substance of the New Rhetoric: (1) the theoretical commonplace that effective rhetoric proceeds from a thorough understanding of purpose, subject, audience, and occasion; (2) the assumption that the study of theory, diligent practice, and imitation are a fundamental means of "improving in Eloquence"; (3) an attention to the activities or canonical nature of the rhetorical process (attention to the substance and form of arguments, the arrangement of discourse, style, and delivery); (4) theoretical and pragmatic attention to the nature and conduct of formal species of oratory; and (5) the classical view of rhetoric as crucial to individual development and cultural harmony. Such reinscription of classical precepts demonstrates the characteristic dependence of the New Rhetoric on a synthesis of traditional precepts and principles derived from a general epistemological rationale and/or a belletristic perspective.

Richard Whately and the Promotion of the Epistemological Rationale

In agreement with the general epistemology of Campbell and Blair's treatises, Richard Whately reiterates the governing philosophical rationale

The New Rhetoric

of the New Rhetoric in *Elements of Rhetoric* (1828), the only post-eighteenth-century British treatise equal to Campbell and Blair's works in the nineteenth-century tradition in North America. Whately contributed to the influence of the New Rhetoric by reasserting several of its crucial elements: (1) a concept of rhetoric as the art of writing and speaking; (2) a notion of the inventional function of rhetoric as the management of proofs (selection and arrangement of arguments); (3) the assumption that the rhetorical process follows from the investigative procedures of logic; (4) a theoretical approach to arguments that distinguishes between appeals to the understanding and appeals to the feelings (passions and the will); (5) a treatment of style that examines the major qualities of style—perspicuity, energy (vivacity) and elegance—in terms of appeals to the understanding and the feelings; (6) a treatment of delivery that emphasizes the "natural" method in management of the voice and gesture; and (7) an affirmation of the general relevance of classical theory to the modern study of rhetoric.[24]

In addition to affirming the philosophical and canonical authority of major features of the Campbell-Blair system (features already bearing the mix of neoclassical elements with the distinctive rationales of the New Rhetoric), Whately also made a unique contribution to the development of rhetorical theory by supplementing and extending the implications of key theoretical principles. *Elements of Rhetoric* provides a more formal and detailed treatment of conviction (arguments to the understanding) and the arrangement of arguments and outlines a more systematic treatment of persuasion (influencing the will). These features of Whately's theory of rhetoric were incorporated into nineteenth-century treatises in conjunction with his general theoretical and pedagogical interest in the the rhetoric of composition.[25]

Intended to outline "A System of Rules for Argumentative Composition," Whately's text pretends neither to the philosophical depth of *The Philosophy of Rhetoric* nor to the critical and pragmatic scope of *Lectures on Rhetoric and Belles Lettres*.[26] Concerned primarily with establishing a "regularity of system" in the procedures for the discovery and arrangement of arguments, Whately relies on the fundamental theoretical assumption that rhetorical discourse makes unique demands on the understanding in the process of conviction, and on the imagination, the passions, and the will in the process of persuasion. Upholding Campbell's stipulation that conviction and persuasion have different ends and therefore require different means, Whately provides an extensive treatment of the classes of arguments suited to the aims of conviction: to give satisfaction to a candid mind; to convey instruction to those who are ready to receive it; and to compel the assent or silence the objections of an opponent (108). Whately's discussion of conviction focuses on two classes of arguments: a priori arguments, or arguments from cause to effect that establish fact, and a posterori arguments, or arguments from sign, example, and testimony from which factual cause or condition can be deduced (33–52). Whately's account of the forms of moral evidence (experience, analogy, testimony) is both more systematic and more concerned with pedagogical application than is Campbell's; however, his treatment of conviction is not innovative, as its claims regarding rhetorical proof reiterate Campbell's explanation. Like Campbell, who stresses that the function of rhetorical proof is to establish the validity of an idea in terms of experience and common sense, Whately stresses that arguments must "convince" hearers and readers of the factual nature (verifiable by the senses) or probable nature (verifiable by judgment or common sense) of particular propositions. For Whately, who frequently cites his *Elements of Logic* as a reference in his discussion of conviction, the function of rhetorical proof is to identify and present those proofs or reasons that establish a particular proposition as logically sound.[27] What distinguishes this treatment of conviction is the degree of formalization that Whately confers on the theoretical descriptions of arguments from testimony and example, his unprecedented discussion of presumption and burden of proof as important considerations in the process of conviction, and his attention to the function and form of refutation in the conduct of arguments to the understanding (53–167). These innovations contributed significantly to nineteenth-century treatments of conviction and argumentation.

Campbell mainly concerns himself with identifying those types of evidence that ensure successful engagement of the deductive and associative dynamics of the understanding; Whately is far more explicit regarding the logical formulations of what he defines as "Arguments from Signs" or arguments from testimony and example. Observing that argument from testimony is related mostly to jurisprudence, Whately observes two kinds of "Testimony" that can be used to support the truth of a premise: testimony regarding "matters of fact," in which a witness testifies to matters verified by the senses, and testimony regarding "matters of opinion," in which a witness offers a judgment based on common sense or deduction. As a form of argument from signs, testimony convinces by presenting evidence of an effect from which a cause or condition can be inferred. The hearer's willingness to accept the evidence of testimony as "signs" supporting the asserted proposition can be affected by certain variables: the intellectual character of the witness ("credulity" and "incredulity"), the number of witnesses speaking to the weight of the evidence, the degree to which the testimony appears to be "undesigned" or free from fabrication, adequate evidence on "very minute points" of the argument, uncontradicted negative testimony, and the presentation of "concurrent" testimonies that establish the same conclusion (58–76). Whately presupposes rather than explicitly attends to the epistemological realities governing the process of conviction and the requisite nature of rhetorical proof; nevertheless, his guidelines for the design of appeals to the understanding clearly reflect the philosophical assumptions regarding the workings of the mind so fundamental to the revisionist project of the New Rhetoric. In his treatment of arguments from example (another form of arguments from sign), Whately makes the point that such arguments rely on the power of inference, or the tendency of the understanding to extrapolate a generalization from a "fair example" of a class (86): "The third kind of Arguments to be considered . . . may be treated under the general name of Example; taking that term in its widest acceptation, so as to comprehend the Arguments designated by the various names of Induction, Experience, Analogy, Parity of Reasoning, &c., all of which are essentially the same" (85–86). The argument from example is successful only to the degree that the analogic connections claimed appear reasonable to the common sense of the hearers. Whether attempting to convince using arguments establishing a "parallel case" or simply attempting to explain or make an idea more clearly understood ("illustration"), the rhetorician making use of arguments from example must be able to construct cases that substantiate the point in question by appealing to the hearer's empirical sense of what is "probable in terms of the constraints of experience or resemblance" (85–95).[28]

Under the heading "Of the various use and order of the several kinds of Propositions and of Arguments in different cases," Whately also offers advice regarding the selection and order of arguments in terms of different epistemological aims. He observes that a priori arguments (from cause to effect) are best suited when "instruction" (explanation) is the aim, whereas arguments from sign (testimony and example) are best used when it is necessary to silence the objections of an opponent through refutation. Claiming that arguments from analogy are "unanswerable," Whately points out that arguments from sign provide the most weight in "controversy" and that the use and order of such arguments must be assessed in terms of "presumption and burden of proof" (108–12). Whately's discussion of presumption and burden of proof provides an insight into exactly what factors of experience and common sense influence recognition of the true and the probable. Defining presumption as "a pre-occupation of ground" that stands "till sufficient reason is adduced against it," Whately points out that a proper analysis of which side of an argument holds the presumption and which side has the challenge of "burden of proof" is a determination that can affect the whole character of the discussion. Presumption, by far the strongest argument to make use of in conviction, lies with "every existing institution" and against "anything paradoxical, i.e. contrary to the prevailing opinion." To make use of presumption is to co-opt the "deference" or authority that listeners generally accord to matters carrying presumption; deference is crucial to perception of the truth and will not be be secured in matters of fact or of opinion if the authority of presumption is denied (114–15). Presumption may be rebutted by positing an opposite presumption, shifting the burden of proof to the other side: "the identification of another presumption that rebuts the former one necessarily entails an analysis of prevailing opinion and general conventional notions of fact" (124–25).

Whately explains that refutatory arguments also may be used to assert unpopular or paradoxical truths or to combat "deeply-rooted prejudices." Treating refutation as a standard part of the conduct of an argument, Whately identifies two modes of refutation: proving the contradictory nature of the opposing proposition and overturning the arguments on which the opposing proposition relies. Refutation can be lodged by the "direct method," the denial of the premises or reasons of the opposing proposition, or by the "indirect method," objecting to the conclusiveness of the reasoning (149). Just as in the consideration of the substance of arguments from cause and effect and sign, the logic of refutatory argument draws directly on affective predisposition: "It is generally the wisest course . . . not only to employ such arguments as are directly accessible to the persons addressed, but to confine oneself to these, lest the attention should be drawn off from them" (166).

Whately's discussion of the arrangement of arguments attends only to conviction and offers advice based on conventional philosophical assumptions regarding how the understanding functions. Whately insists that the progressive method of argumentation, "beginning with the more general remarks, and gradually narrowing as it were, the circle, till the particular point in question was reached," is the most effective means of engaging the hearers' attention and positive response as "the interest is the better kept up by advancing successively from the more to the less general" (144). Whately recommends that the strongest arguments, those from cause to effect, take precedence in arrangement because they prepare the way for the receptions of other arguments (arguments from sign) by establishing or refuting factual conditions in terms of the "natural" and the "plausible" (137). The ordering of premises and conclusion (the proposition to be established) also must be based on how the attention of the understanding is best engaged and on presumptive or deferential factors that might influence the hearers. When the conclusion is well established, the opinion or proposition can be stated initially and followed by the proofs or reasons. If the conclusion is not well established, Whately recommends that it is better to state the proofs first, or at least some of them, and then introduce the conclusion, "thus assuming in some degree the character of an investigator":

> When the Conclusion to be established is one likely to hurt the feelings and offend the prejudices of the hearer, it is essential to keep out of sight, as much as possible, the point to which we are tending, till the principles from which it is to be deduced shall have been clearly established; because men listen with prejudice, if at all, to arguments that are avowedly leading to a conclusion which they are indisposed to admit; whereas if we thus, as it were, mask the battery, they will not be able to shelter themselves from the discharge. (142)

Whately's treatment of the arrangement of arguments reiterates Blair's general advice regarding the arrangement of arguments according to strength and the effectiveness of conducting an argument to the understanding by proceeding step by step toward a full statement of the proposition, thus proving it "by instalments" (the "progressive" method).[29] Whately's formal discussion of the order of premises and conclusions in the structure of an argument provides guidance not provided by either Campbell or Blair. Similarly, the attention Whately pays to the placement and nature of refutation in arrangement reintroduces a classical feature of argument not treated previously in the New Rhetoric. While Whately's treatment of arrangement affirms the status of issues such as the merits of the progressive method and the doctrine of caeteris paribus, his discussion of the preferred order of argumentative materials, like his treatment of the nature of arguments, is more comprehensive and more formal than either Campbell's comparatively vague coverage or Blair's extremely brief explanation. The popularity of Whately's theory of arrangement in the nineteenth-century tradition was no doubt partially a consequence of its essential compatibility with Blair's widely imitated approach to this canon but must also be traced to the fact that it is more detailed and more systematic than either Blair's or Campbell's.[30]

The New Rhetoric

Whately's approach to conviction contributed very specific elements to the theoretical substance of the canon of invention reconstructed by Campbell and Blair as the process of managing argumentative materials: a distinction between classes of arguments, the different ends and uses of arguments directed to the understanding, the imperatives of presumption and burden of proof, the nature and function of refutation, and the structure of proposition and premises. Following the example of Campbell and Blair, who treat the conduct of discourse with the arrangement of argumentative materials, thus collapsing the traditional distinction between *inventio* and *dispositio,* Whately treats the matter of the distinctive structural units of argument as a topic related to the arrangement or "order" of the argument. Breaking with Blair, who reiterates the traditional six-part structure for discourse, Whately restricts his discussion of arrangement to an explication of the function of introductions and conclusions in the conduct of argument. Whately presupposes that the type and combination of arguments used imposes order on the argumentative material that falls between the introduction and the conclusion. While Whately's advice regarding conclusions parallels Blair's in its attention to the problems of conclusions that stop suddenly or go on too long, his discussion of introductions offers yet another systematic innovation that would become a standard feature of subsequent nineteenth-century theory.[31] Citing his agreement with Aristotle that formal introductions are not always necessary, Whately argues that it is necessary "to premise something before we enter on the main argument" (168), using formal introductions, "prefaces," "advertisements," or "titles." Whately argues that particular types of introductions are designed for specific purposes in conviction: the *introduction inquisitive* establishes why the subject is significant; the *introduction paradoxical* establishes the validity of a point despite its seeming improbability; the *introduction corrective* clarifies that the subject at issue has been neglected or misunderstood; the *introduction preparatory* explains some peculiarity in the mode of reasoning to be adopted; and the *introduction narrative* provides necessary background description for the reader or hearer (170–71). Whately's designation of this range of introductory forms gives more systematic attention to the structure

Nineteenth-Century Rhetoric

of argument and also extends the range of the canon of arrangement by focusing specific attention on its function in discourses intended to be read. Despite the fact that Whately's approach is less traditional in its attention to Ciceronian structure, his discussion of the introduction in terms of a wider range of formats and varied intentions of arguments proved highly influential on nineteenth-century theory, particularly on rhetorics that treated the forms of conviction (explanation, instruction, the gaining of assent) as major modes of composition.

In addition to his innovative treatment of arrangement, Whately's definition of the major classes of arguments and his outline of how the substance of such arguments should be arranged were widely adopted by nineteenth-century theorists. Whately's "system of rules" for argumentative composition was reiterated by every major nineteenth-century treatise that discussed conviction as a major rhetorical process; these rules were particularly popular with rhetoricians who treated invention. Other components incorporated into nineteenth-century theory included Whately's treatments of persuasion and style. Whately's approach to these standard elements of the New Rhetoric remains compatible with Campbell and Blair's pronouncements but tends, as is the general disposition of his method, to "systematize" these theoretical issues in a pedagogically useful manner. Overall, Whately's discussion of persuasion reinforces the normative status of central assumptions of Campbell and Blair's accounts of how to address the will: (1) Whately treats ethos and pathos as issues bearing directly on address to the feelings, or persuasion, and provides detailed discussion of strategies for "raising a favorable impression" and adjusting eloquence "for whom it is intended" (215–25); and (2) he defines description and comparison in terms of the specific functions that such rhetorical modes have on exciting the feelings. This approach restates Campbell and Blair's shared premise that description ("copious" detail and expansion) facilitates the formation of vivid and distinct ideas, whereas comparison heightens emotion by presenting "a parallel between the case in hand and some other that is calculated to call forth . . . emotions" (197). Whately's treatment

The New Rhetoric

of persuasion as the art of influencing the will reiterates Campbell's discussion of "circumstances influencing the passions"; however, Whately confers a more systematic outline on his discussion of "Address to the Feelings" by defining two major parts of persuasion—conviction and exhortation—and by providing an explicit list of the "Active Principles" of human nature that affect the feelings: "Affections, Desires, Self-love, and the Moral-faculty" (184–88). Whately's assumption that persuasion involves appeals to the understanding and the passions is entirely consistent with the stance of the New Rhetoric; however, his emphatic distinction between the "intellectual faculties" (addressed through conviction) and the emotional faculties, or "Feelings, Propensities, Sentiments" (addressed "indirectly" through rhetorical forms), categorizes epistemological circumstances and rhetorical aims more formally than either Campbell or Blair's discussions of the psychological-rhetorical foundations of conviction and persuasion. This systematic categorization would prove the most popular framework for treatments of "address to the will" (persuasion) in nineteenth-century treatises.

Like his treatment of persuasion, Whately's approach to style reinforces standard features of the New Rhetoric. Whately's treatment of style combines epistemological and belletristic principles in a condensed equivalent of Campbell and Blair's treatments of this canon. Offering nothing unique in his treatment of the features of this canon (choice of words, their number, their arrangement), Whately draws heavily on the New Rhetoric in his definition of perspicuity, energy (his term for vivacity), and elegance as the major qualities of style (274–329). Whately's discussion of style is most conspicuously indebted to Campbell's treatment of vivacity, paying only passing attention to elegance on the assumption that the rules laid down for energy "conduce" as well to beauty. Whately's use of the term *energy* and his more systematic discussion of how to achieve this quality proved more popular in nineteenth-century theory than did Campbell's original treatment of vivacity. Whately's version of the triad perspicuity, energy, and elegance was widely adopted as a framework for the general qualities of style, although nineteenth-century treatises tended to offer a standard Blairian treatment of elegance rather than imitate Whately's nominal treatment of beauty.[32]

Whately's influence on the nineteenth-century tradition becomes noticeable at midcentury, whereas the influence of Campbell and Blair on the structure and content of rhetorical treatises in North America is obvious as early as the 1820s. Blair's *Lectures* and Whately's *Elements* served as the material for numbers of treatises outlining abbreviated versions of these theories; even more frequently, nineteenth-century theories combined systematic elements of Blair and Whately's theories with Campbell's philosophical doctrine, thus depending on the authority of all three works. The combined impact of Campbell, Blair, and Whately set powerful theoretical precedents for the nineteenth-century tradition, precedents that ensured the longevity of the philosophical assumptions of the New Rhetoric. The nineteenth-century tradition in North America relied substantially on the unique epistemological and belletristic rationales of the New Rhetoric and promoted these theoretical rationales as well as the neoclassical and innovative features of the late eighteenth-century British tradition.

Nineteenth-century theory incorporated all of the key assumptions of the epistemological rationale of the New Rhetoric:

1. The procedures and forms of rhetoric are compatible with the principal channels of perception and action in the mind (the faculties), which function as a consequence of associative relations drawn from experience and common sense.

2. Rhetorical proofs, arrangement, and style must embody associative relations (resemblance, contiguity, causality) in order to engage the faculties of the mind in their discrete and interactive functions.

3. Intelligibility, liveliness of ideas, and intensity of emotional impressions are rhetorical effects that engage the attention of the faculties in identifying tangible referents and experiences and deducing links between new information and sensory detail and knowledge already held. Certain rhetorical forms and techniques facilitate these effects in appealing to the understanding and the passions:

The New Rhetoric

—rhetorical proofs drawn on experience, analogy, or testimony
—persuasive appeals to the passions drawn on probability, plausibility, circumstances of time and place, relation of the subject to the hearer, and interest of the hearer in the subject
—the use of description, comparison, and narration
—arrangement of arguments
—grammatical purity
—qualities of perspicuity, vivacity (energy), and elegance (the sublime and the beautiful)
—the use of associative figures such as metaphor, simile, analogy, etc.
—comprehensibility in delivery and the use of "natural" gestures

Indebted primarily to Blair's theory of taste, nineteenth-century rhetoric also incorporated the fundamental principals of the eighteenth-century doctrine of taste:

1. Taste, an innate response to the beautiful, is one of the intellectual powers. It embodies a response to harmony, to elegance, and the sublime that facilitates the function of the understanding and the imagination. The cultivation of taste is synonymous with the development of intellectual virtue and moral character.

2. Taste, an improvable faculty, is directly affected by the study of rhetoric, which provides an education in the nature and effects of those principles of discourse that embody the qualities of taste.

3. The rhetorical process is obligated to taste insofar as the form and substance of rhetoric must please the imagination or move the passions to higher emotion. These epistemological effects aid the understanding and prompt the will. Particular modes of rhetorical discourse and certain styles incorporate principles of taste and facilitate the powers of the imagination:

—rhetorical subject matter or genres attending to the "sublime" (the grand) in natural or moral objects (sentiments)
—descriptive style drawn from simplicity and conciseness
—boldness and variety in style drawn on the use of associative figures and ornament

Nineteenth-Century Rhetoric

—rhetorical subject matter or genres attending to the beautiful in natural and moral objects (sentiments)
—imitation and description in style that attends to color, figure, and motion
—rhetorical subject matter or genres attending to novelty
—perspicuity and ornament in style

The classical rationale of the New Rhetoric affirmed neoclassical definitions and features that were incorporated into the nineteenth-century tradition:

1. The study and practice of rhetoric benefits the individual and society.

2. Rhetoric involves the adaptation of discourse to aim, audience, and occasion.

3. Rhetoric is the counterpart of logic.

4. The study of rhetorical principles, practice, and imitation are the fundamental means of improving in rhetoric.

5. The processes of rhetoric are invention, arrangement, style, and delivery.

The major systematic features of the New Rhetoric became standard features in nineteenth-century theory:

1. A definition of rhetoric as the art by which discourse is adapted to its aim.
2. Definitions of the aims of rhetoric: to enlighten the understanding, please the imagination, move the passions, influence the will.
3. Scope of rhetoric: oral and written discourse.
4. Divisions of rhetoric: oratory (the bar, the pulpit, public speaking) and composition (historical writing, philosophical writing, epistolary writing, fiction, poetry, and drama).
5. Invention: selection and management of proofs
   —Address to the understanding (conviction): types of rhetorical proof (experience, analogy, testimony, cause to effect) which appeal to the understanding; presumption and burden of proof; refutation

The New Rhetoric

—Arrangement of arguments according to progressive strength, induction and deduction, amplification of particulars

—Address to the feelings or exhortation (persuasion): types of appeal to the passions (subsequently the will), probability, plausibility, circumstances of the hearers (pathos), and impression of the speaker (ethos).

6. Conduct of the discourse (arrangement): introduction (inquisitive, paradoxical, corrective, preparatory, narrative), division of subject, narration, reasoning or argument, the pathetic part, conclusion.

7. Style: grammatical qualities (purity in usage and syntax); rhetorical qualities: perspicuity in diction, sentence structure, and sentence arrangement; vivacity (energy) and beauty (with regard to the use of metaphor, allegory, personification, apostrophe, comparison, simile, antithesis).

8. Delivery: management of the voice (volume, articulation, pace, pronunciation, emphasis, pause, and tone); management of gesture and expression.

By the philosophy of rhetoric, I here refer to those principles in the science of the philosophy of mind, and in the philosophy of language, on which are founded those conclusions and directions which are applicable to literary criticism and the formation of style.

Samuel P. Newman, *A Lecture on a Practical Method of Teaching Rhetoric*

Discourse, as the product of a mind working freely, and directly aiming at an effect in another mind similarly constituted, involves and requires the exercise of Taste. Rhetoric, accordingly, presupposes the science of Taste or Aesthetics. It assumes aesthetic principles and applies them to the production of discourse. . . . As the art of communicating thought, rhetoric presupposes Logic, or the science which unfolds the laws of thought. . . . As the art of communicating thought by means of language, rhetoric also presupposes Grammar, or the science of language. . . . Rhetoric is the doctrine of discourse.

Henry N. Day, *Elements of the Art of Rhetoric*

Rhetoric is the art of adapting discourse, in harmony with its subject and occasion, to the requirements of a reader or hearer. . . . The various problems involved in such adaptation constitute the field of the art of rhetoric.

John F. Genung, *The Practical Elements of Rhetoric*

3

Nineteenth-Century
Rhetorical Theory:
Legacy and Synthesis

To understand the nature and development of nineteenth-century theory in North America, we must recognize that the influence of the late eighteenth-century British tradition on subsequent developments in the theory and practice of English rhetoric was profound. For the first half of the nineteenth century, the treatises of Campbell and Blair enjoyed unchallenged dominion over the theoretical orientation of rhetoric and were regarded within the evolving disciplines in the United States and Canada as authoritative sources on the philosophical, critical, and pragmatic principles of rhetorical theory and praxis. By the 1840s Whately's treatise had achieved similar status. At midcentury indigenous treatises began to emerge in the United States, yet these works relied extensively on the philosophical interests and the systematic architecture advocated by Campbell, Blair, and Whately.[1] The influence of the New Rhetoric over the development of rhetorical theory in nineteenth-century North America was deployed, then, in two processes: by direct or primary influence—Campbell, Blair, and Whately's treatises circulated as primary sources—and by secondary influence, as the theories of these three were models for the philosophical orientation, theoretical presuppositions, and systematic features of nineteenth-century theory. These two processes of influence cannot be understood simply as chronological developments; the major treatises of the New Rhetoric circulated in the North American academy as required reading as late as 1890.[2] Their influence is obvious throughout the century in the development and proliferation of "second-generation" New Rhetorical theories, theories that were self-consciously indebted to Campbell, Blair, and Whately's theories or that relied on a combination of the theoretical rationales and systematic schemes popularized by the New Rhetoric movement.[3]

Whether assessed in terms of primary or secondary influence, the claims and commitments of the New Rhetoric were constant factors in the development of the North American tradition. In fact, the doctrinal force of the New Rhetoric was never supplanted in nineteenth-century theory; rather, nineteenth-century rhetorical theory and practice extended the project of the New Rhetoric by ratifying its fundamental philosophy and rationales and by promoting its composite structure of epistemological, belletristic, and neoclassical principles and practices. The epistemological and belletristic rationales underlying the New Rhetoric and the neoclassical commitments that these rationales explicitly and implicitly supported constituted the theoretical foundation of nineteenth-century theory and shaped its pragmatic enterprise. Understanding the nature and extent of this legacy is a key to appreciating the ways in which nineteenth-century theory promoted the New Rhetoric through a unique synthesis and adaptation of its theoretical dimensions and an unprecedented extension of its pedagogical interests.

One of the most reliable generalizations that can be made about the disposition of nineteenth-century theory is that it displayed a marked dependence on the epistemological justification for rhetorical principles and practices that was central to Campbell, Blair, and Whately's theories. Within nineteenth-century theory in North America, "new" definitions of the nature and function of rhetoric continued to be regarded as normative precepts in need of articulation. Embracing the general philosophical rationale of the New Rhetoric without qualification, nineteenth-century theory supported the following assumptions: (1) the aims of rhetoric and the function of particular modes and rhetorical techniques are linked directly to affective intentions (to enlighten the understanding, please the imagination, move the passions, and influence the will); (2) effective procedures and forms of rhetoric are compatible with the the dynamics of the faculties, which function in accordance with associative relations based on experience and common sense; and (3) due to the philosophical verifiability of its procedures and aims, the study of rhetoric can be understood as a science, an enterprise that reveals basic principles of nature.

Nineteenth-century theorists displayed a strong interest in "the philosophy of rhetoric," sharing with their eighteenth-century predecessors the assumption that an understanding of how the rules and principles of rhetoric are related to operations of the mind is a prerequisite to the successful practice of rhetoric. Even theorists who assumed rather than explained principles of "mental science" (in the fashion of Blair and Whately) defined rhetorical principles, modes, and techniques in terms of epistemological functions.[4] The dominant and normative rationale for nineteenth-century theory was the assumption that the art of rhetoric relies on adaptation of fundamental principles along the lines of epistemological constraints. In *Philosophy of Rhetoric* (1866) John Bascom offers a definition of the function of rhetoric that indicates the extent to which this rationale predisposed nineteenth-century conceptions of the communicative force of rhetoric:

> Rhetoric is an art. It strives to render aid to action, to prescribe its methods. What is the action whose rules are furnished by rhetoric? It is the mind's action, we answer, in communicating itself, its thoughts, conceptions, feelings, through language. . . . Expression of thought in language in all its varieties is but one department, governed by the same fundamental principles. . . . We define rhetoric as the art which teaches the rules of composition. By composition we understand the expression in language of thoughts, emotions, for some definite end. . . . The philosophy of rhetoric is the reference of its rules to the principles of mental and moral science on which they are dependent. Mind expresses itself according to its own laws, toward its own ends. When affected from abroad, it is by the influence of mind—of those for whom

the composition is prepared. Whether composition is sought as a
means of expression or of persuasion, its end is reached in mind,
and mind gives the governing principles.[5] (13–15)

Bascom's observation that the rules of rhetoric are derived from the
"laws" of mental and moral science is a direct reiteration of the philosophical
stance of the New Rhetoric—that is, that rhetoric is constrained by "principles of our nature" and that its ends are to be managed in conjunction
with the dynamics of the mental faculties. Such explicit treatments of the
epistemological nature and function of rhetoric were conventional as early
as the 1820s in widely circulated North American treatises and remained a
formal object of theoretical attention in influential works as late as 1900.
Offering a belletristic interpretation of the epistemological rationale in *A
Practical System of Rhetoric* (1827), one of the first widely circulated
nineteenth-century American treatises, Samuel P. Newman reveals how
energetically the early tradition assimilated an epistemological rationale for
the aims and modes of written rhetoric:

Writings are distinguished from each other, as didactic, persuasive, argumentative, descriptive and narrative. These distinctions
have reference to the object, which the writer has primarily and
principally in view. Didactic writing, as the name implies, is used
in conveying instruction. . . . When it is designed to influence the
will, the composition becomes of the persuasive kin. . . . Another
kind of composition, and one which is found united with most
others, is the argumentative. Under this head, are included the
various forms of argument, the statement of proofs, the assigning
of causes, and generally, those writings, which are addressed to
the reasoning faculties of the mind. Narrative and descriptive writings relate past occurrences, and place before the mind, for its
contemplation, various objects and scenes.[6] (28)

In his definition of the divisions of writing in terms of distinctly
different types of appeals to the mental faculties, Newman relies on the

Legacy and Synthesis

most basic tenet of the New Rhetoric—that the aims of rhetoric are to be understood in terms of enlightening the understanding, pleasing the imagination, moving the passions, and influencing the will. This general assumption accounts for the discrete rhetorical obligations of argumentation, narrative, and description. In a somewhat more philosophical treatment of the "characteristics" of rhetoric as founded on "the Sciences," John F. Genung's account of the ways in which rhetoric conforms to the "laws of sound thinking" in *The Working Principles of Rhetoric* (1900) is representative of the firm hold that the epistemological view still retained at the turn of the century:

> The requirements of a reader or hearer are determined not by his
> mental capacities alone, but by his whole nature; which, in one
> way or another, as subject and occasion dictate, is to be acted
> upon by the power of language. The common psychological divi-
> sion of man's spiritual powers will indicate broadly three main
> lines of adaptation. There is first the power of intellect, by which
> a man knows, thinks, reasons. Discourse that addresses itself to
> this power aims merely to impart information or convince of truth;
> and its adaptation consists in giving the reader facilities to see and
> understand. . . . Secondly there is the power of emotion, by
> which a man feels and imagines. Discourse that addresses itself to
> this power aims to make men not only understand a truth but real-
> ize it vividly and have a glow of interest in it; and the adaptation
> is effected by using language that stimulates and thrills. . . .
> Thirdly, there is the power of the will, by which a man ventures
> life and action on what he believes or thinks. Discourse that ad-
> dresses itself to this power must make men both understand
> clearly and realize intensely; it must therefore work with both in-
> tellect and emotion; but through these it must effect some definite
> decision in men's sympathies or conduct. . . . From the consider-
> ation of these human powers and capacities, with the countless
> limitations that culture, occupation, and original character impose
> upon them, it will easily be seen how broad is the field of rhetori-
> cal adaptation, and how comprehensive must be the art that mas-
> ters and applies its resources.[7] (3–4)

Nineteenth-Century Rhetoric

Nineteenth-century theory consistently attended to the general assumption that the principles of rhetoric are founded on a "consideration of human powers and capacities," and it relied on this rationale for stipulations regarding principles and practices in exactly the same way that the New Rhetoricians applied epistemological veracity as a standard for the rules of rhetoric. In *Lectures Read to the Seniors in Harvard College* (1856) Edward T. Channing, the Bolyston Professor of Rhetoric and Oratory at Harvard from 1819 to 1851, addresses the importance of understanding rhetoric as a "helpmate of nature," a body of rules "derived from experience and observation" showing how to make the expression of thoughts effective "in the way that nature universally intends, and which man universally feels" (31–32). Citing Campbell's *Philosophy of Rhetoric,* Channing points to the importance of understanding the "scientific" principles of rhetoric and its basis in "mental philosophy:"

> The teacher . . . will have to speak of the imagination and the passions as giving a tone and a character to human speech. . . .
> The faculty of taste, also must be introduced as the great moderating or tempering power, that wars against excess, against false associations of images and the unbecoming intrusion of startling but disturbing ideas, and which, in these ways and by positive suggestion of true and apposite beauty, keeps down all unnatural vivacity and gives proper brightness to the genuine.[8] (31)

It was the main project of the New Rhetoric to justify both the science and the art of rhetoric in terms of the philosophical constraints that compel rhetorical impact. Assuming this same ambition, nineteenth-century theory not only promoted general assumptions of the epistemological viewpoint but also reiterated assumptions of the New Rhetoric regarding the function and interplay of mental principles and the requisite nature of rhetorical materials and forms. The New Rhetoric defined the divisions of rhetoric in terms of epistemological appeals and also asserted that rhetorical processes depend on the inducement of mental faculties to interrelate in a prerequisite sequence. The theoretical distinction between conviction as a rhetorical aim that appeals primarily to the understanding and persuasion as an appeal primarily addressed to the will (a key element in the New Rhetoric) was also common in nineteenth-century theory, as was the attending assumption that the processes of conviction and persuasion involve an interanimation of the faculties. In *Elements of the Art of Rhetoric* (1866) Henry N. Day's treatment of "Explanation, Conviction, Excitation, and Persuasion" as the "objects of all proper discourse" relies not only on a conventional epistemological view of the function of rhetoric but also on the principle that the mental faculties arc linked together in an intimate, dynamic chain:

> Explanation precedes conviction, as the truth must be understood before it can be believed; explanation and conviction naturally precede excitation, as the object of feeling must be perceived and generally be believed to exist before feeling can be awakened; and persuasion properly follows the other three processes, as in order to a change of will, the feelings are generally to be aroused, the judgement convinced, and the understanding informed.[9] (43)

Nineteenth-century theory was indebted generally to the point of view that Day expresses: the order and combination in which the faculties are engaged completely predispose whether or not the rhetorician (1) can produce a new conception or modify one already existing (conviction) or (2) can influence conceptions and awaken feelings in the service of persuasion. In *The Science of Rhetoric* (1877) David. J. Hill observes that an understanding of such "mental phenomena" is crucial to the rhetorician since the intention to convey new ideas to the mind can be accomplished only by engaging the mental faculties in their proper cognitive relations:

> Men are moved to action by three steps: 1) an idea is presented to the mind for cognition; 2) the idea produces a state of feeling; 3) the feeling excites action. . . . Without cognition there could be neither feeling nor conation; and without feeling there could be no conation. . . . [F]eeling . . . forms the bridge, and contains the motive, by which we are aroused from mere knowledge to appe-

tency, to conation, by reference to which we move ourselves so as to attain the end in view. (44)

In this summary of the "laws of action" of the mind, Hill affirms not only the general scientific foundations of rhetoric but also the more specific assumption that the cognitive impact of rhetoric is the consequence of, and thoroughly dependent on, the interanimation of the faculties in the process of thought. Nineteenth-century theory treated this assumption as a basic principle of the philosophy of rhetoric, following the example of the New Rhetoric by asserting that rhetoric must facilitate communication in keeping with the "laws of thought"—those associative, intuitive, and deductive links that represent the necessary conditions of valid thinking.

Relying on the epistemological assumption that associative links of various types allow the faculties of the mind to process new information, sensory detail, and knowledge in terms of experience and common sense, Campbell, Blair, and Whately stress that rhetorical force is measurable in terms of the intensity of the associative relations (resemblance, contiguity, causality) that rhetorical materials, forms, and techniques can create. Campbell and Whately address the issue of associative relations at the logical level mainly in terms of the materials of rhetorical proof; Blair supports a similar view of the importance of logical intelligibility in successful appeals to taste; and all three argue for the relevance of associative relations in persuasion and in stylistic choices. That nineteenth-century theory depended on the doctrine of association in just as pervasive a manner is exemplified in its stance toward argumentation. This stance relied heavily on Whately's treatment of classes of arguments and thus presupposed the epistemological rationale guiding Whately's attention to the associative and deductive force of proofs such as testimony, induction, and cause and effect.[10] In *The Principles of Rhetoric* (1878) A. S. Hill's discussion of argumentative "evidence" advances a doctrinaire view of the materials of proof. Echoing the New Rhetoric's definition of proof as that which is furnished directly by the senses and consciousness through experience and common sense, or indirectly through the senses or the consciousness of others (testimony, tradition, or documents), Hill affirms the importance of the empirical veracity of argumentative structures. Hill presupposes the empirical foundations and associative force of causality and probability and stresses that a change of mind or appeal to the understanding is best promoted by propositions that demonstrate a literal or probable reality. These crucial principles of the doctrine of association are implicit in his classification of arguments drawn on "antecedent probability, example, and sign":

> A classification . . . convenient for our purposes is that which dis-
> tinguishes arguments according to the sources from which they
> come,—accordingly as they are derived 1) from the relation of
> cause to effect, 2) from resemblance which persons and things
> bear to one another in certain particulars or under certain aspects,
> 3) from the association of ideas. Arguments of the first class are
> called arguments from Antecendent Probability; those of the sec-
> ond class, arguments from Example; those of the third class, argu-
> ments from Sign. (344)

In his discussion of argument from antecedent probability, Hill stresses that this type of argument rests on the logic of inference from experience—inference as a process of asserting what is likely to be from what is or from what has been. Such an argument employs a principle of common sense: certain causes produce certain effects; "the stream of tendency . . . will continue to flow in the direction once taken" (354–55).[11] Hill's willingness to assert "the stream of tendency" as a logical constraint on strategies of argumentation reveals how thoroughly the associative view of thought is integrated into both the general and more detailed examinations of rhetorical strategies and devices in nineteenth-century theory. Nine-teenth-century treatments of figurative language also demonstrate the extent to which theoretical attention to the laws of thought influenced definitions of rhetorical techniques. In imitation of the systematic tendency of the New Rhetoric to treat stylistic structures in terms of epistemological dynamics, Bain's discussion of "the figures of speech" in *English Composition and*

Nineteenth-Century Rhetoric

Rhetoric: A Manual (1866) treats major figures in terms of their function in facilitating epistemological links such as similarity, comparison, and contrast. As he explains that the general predisposition of the "intellectual powers" to various representations of resemblance ensures the effectiveness of the "Figures of Similarity" (simile, metaphor, personification, allegory, and synecdoche), Bain rehearses essential principles of the epistemological rationale:

> The intellectual power named Similarity, or Feeling of Agreement, is the chief inventive power of the mind. By it similitudes are brought up to the view. When we look out upon a scene of nature, we are reminded of other resembling scenes that we have formerly known. . . . The tracing of Resemblance among the objects, and the events of the world, is a constant avocation of the human mind. . . . Every kind of reasoning implies similarity, or the identity of two or more things.[12] (3–4)

Bain's approach to the figures and Hill's treatment of argumentation are representative of the extent to which nineteenth-century theory promoted the general and specific claims of the epistemological rationale and extended the philosophical authority of "scientific" principles over the developing tradition in North America. Nineteenth-century treatises that defined the aims and processes of rhetoric primarily in terms of mental phenomena and the laws of thought conventionally applied the epistemological point of view in the examination of major systematic features:

—Introductory accounts of the philosophy of rhetoric and/or the principal ends of speaking and writing (e.g., Newman, *Practical System* iii; Bain, *English Composition* 1)
—Treatments of invention as a means of identifying materials and forms in terms of discrete appeals to the understanding, the passions, the imagination, and the will (e.g., Newman, *Practical System* 21–28; Day, *Elements* 35)
—Treatments of forms of conviction as particular types of address to the understanding: explanation, narration, description, analy-

sis, exemplification, comparison and contrast, and argument (Newman, *Practical System* 28–29; Genung *Working Principles* 478–650)

—Treatments of arrangement of arguments and disposition of the discourse in terms of the requisites of the state of the mind addressed and the proper order of conclusive reasoning (e.g., Day, *Elements* 116–32; A. S. Hill, *Principles* 177–248)

—Treatments of persuasion as constituted by appeals to understanding through conviction and explanation and appeals to the passions or feelings through excitation (e.g., A. S. Hill, *Principles* 386–400)

—Treatments of style that respect the mind of another through the character and advantage of figures and the rhetorical and grammatical qualities of style (e.g., Day, *Elements* 171–288)

—Treatments of delivery (elocution) as primarily a matter of giving "nature free room for making her spontaneous suggestions" and "by making . . . natural and necessary experiments upon her power" (Channing 54–55)

The epistemological rationale was a founding philosophy not only for those treatises that favored a scientific treatment of rhetorical theory but also for those that relied overtly on a belletristic orientation or on a synthesis of epistemological and belletristic approaches to theory and practice. Just as it is crucial to an understanding of the New Rhetoric to note that the eighteenth-century belletristic tradition (exemplified by Blair's *Lectures*) was in complete philosophical sympathy with Campbell's theoretical revision of rhetorical principles, so too the belletristic approaches to theory in the nineteenth century should be understood as sharing common philosophical ground with distinctly scientific treatments of principles and praxis. Nineteenth-century treatises that adopted Blair's critical rationale as an organizing perspective implicitly incorporated the same interest in the articulation of a rational philosophy of taste that predisposed Blair's investigation of rhetoric as a science of criticism. Following the example of Blair's method, which assumes the epistemological function of rhetoric as primary but directs attention to rhetoric's use of the laws of thought in the service of taste, nineteenth-century belletristic theory defined the processes, forms, and effects of rhetorical practice in terms of the same critical rationale. Nineteenth-century theory relied on a critical rationale that affirmed major principles of eighteenth-century belletristic rhetoric: (1) the assumption that taste is the most intellectual power, one that embodies a response to harmony, elegance, and the sublime through the responses of the understanding, the imagination, and the higher passions; (2) the assumption that the cultivation of taste through the study of rhetoric is synonymous with the development of intellectual virtue and moral character; and (3) the assumption that particular rhetorical forms, materials, and techniques enhance taste by facilitating the powers of the imagination and the passions.

Throughout the nineteenth century, a series of influential treatises advocated a belletristic rationale for rhetoric and imposed critical standards on definitions of rhetorical principles and practices. Formally indebted to Blair in the majority of instances, these "second-generation" New Rhetorics gave special attention to explanations of the doctrine of taste and the unique role of the study of rhetoric in its cultivation. Such promotion of the critical rationale, like the long-lived attention to the scientific rationale within the North American tradition, is observable in the theoretical orientation of treatises appearing throughout the century. In the marked belletristic disposition of works such as Alexander Jamieson's *Grammar of Rhetoric and Polite Literature: Comprehending The Principles of Language and Style, the Elements of Taste and Criticism; With Rules for the Study of Composition and Eloquence* (1820) and G. P. Quackenbos's *Advanced Course of Composition and Rhetoric* (1855), explicit theoretical attention to the doctrine of taste and to a critical rationale for rhetorical theory and practice reflects the theoretical authority that the belletristic approach to rhetoric had achieved by midcentury. Jamieson offers a definition of taste and of the nature and function of criticism that is explicitly faithful to eighteenth-century assumptions:

> Taste is that faculty of power of the human mind which is always appealed to in disquisitions concerning the merit of discourse and writing; it is the power of receiving pleasure from the beauties of

nature and art. The word taste, under this metaphorical meaning, has borrowed its name from the feelings of that external sense by which we receive and distinguish the pleasures of food. This faculty is common, in some degree, to all men; for the relish of beauty, of one kind or another, belongs to human nature generally. . . . True criticism is the application of taste and of good sense to the several fine arts. The object which it proposes is, to distinguish what is beautiful and what is faulty in every performance; from particular instances to ascend to general principles; and so to form rules or conclusions concerning the several kinds of beauty in works of genius.[13] (192, 200)

Implicit in Jamieson's characterization of the faculty of taste is an essential premise of belletristic theory: the cultivation of taste is intrinsically related to the exercise of common sense brought to an explicit level of aesthetic apprehension. At this level of "relish" for the beautiful, one is more able to appreciate (through criticism) those profound truths that art alone, in its role of strewing "flowers in the path of science," can reveal. Quackenbos reiterates this same view of taste as a faculty founded on reason and sensibility: "We are pleased through our natural sensibility by impressions of the beautiful, aided . . . by the imagination; but an exertion of reason is first required to inform us whether the objects successively presented to the eye are beautiful or not" (161). Quackenbos and Jamieson echo Blair's account of the epistemological foundations of taste by defining the imagination and the understanding as its major operations and by presenting taste as a faculty that involves highly evolved emotional and intellectual senses. Newman's similar explanation in *A Practical System of Rhetoric* treats the principles of taste under headings that had become conventional in American treatises by the early decades of the nineteenth century: "A Definition of Taste"; "Sensibility as Connected with Taste"; "Standards of Taste"; "Taste as Affected by Intellectual Habits"; "Connection of Taste with the Imagination"; "Different Qualities of Taste Explained"; and "Literary Taste" (43–66).

Theoretical attention to the doctrine of taste was a typical feature in treatises that imitated Blair's *Lectures* (Jamieson, Newman, Quackenbos) as well as in theories that addressed the nature and function of taste in combination with "scientific" accounts of the philosophy and principles of rhetoric.[14] In *Elements of the Art of Rhetoric* Day argues that the principles of discourse must conform to the "laws of taste" because such laws outline how eloquence can be designed to "affect another mind . . . in accordance with the aesthetic character of the communicating mind." Day is more concerned with the epistemological foundations of conviction and the nature of proof than with an extensive explication of literary taste; however, his review of the major principles of taste is conventionally belletristic: he defines specific aesthetic principles and promotes the view that the rhetorical process must be informed by an attention to how the "various elements of Beauty . . . Absolute Beauty, Grace, and Propriety" awaken emotions pertinent to the communication of thought (19–25). Similarly, Bain's treatment of "Qualities of Style" in *English Composition and Rhetoric: A Manual* recapitulates essential belletristic principles regarding the appeal of the sublime to the faculty of taste. Bain's approach to style represents the type of synthetic theoretical method that distinguishes Day's treatise. Epistemological precepts derived largely from Campbell and Whately are combined with belletristic dictates regarding rhetorical principles and technique. In treating "strength" as a quality of style synonymous with the "sublime," Bain refers directly to Campbell's theory of "vivacity" but also recapitulates typical belletristic pronouncements on the nature and function of the sublime in keeping with his general definition of rhetorical practice as the "art . . . of polish, elegance, or refinement" (xii). Bain's tendency to illustrate rhetorical principles with literary illustrations is also typical of the belletristic stance:

> Strength is the name of the quality of style that elates us with the pleasurable feeling, called the sense or sentiment of Power. The highest form of strength is the Sublime. . . . The poems of Sir Walter Scott exemplify this characteristic. Fervour supposes a great intensity of passion in the writer, made apparent in the language. Loftiness scarcely differs from Sublimity. Bril-

liancy implies an ornate or figurative style well sustained. (58–59)

Whether advanced in a distinctly belletristic theoretical format, addressed as part of a wider inquiry into the philosophical foundations of rhetoric, or incorporated in the treatment of specific principles and canons, the belletristic doctrine of taste contributed substantially to nineteenth-century theory. Equally influential on nineteenth-century theory was the belletristic assumption that rhetoric has a critical function. From the eighteenth-century belletristic point of view, criticism is the means by which the principles of taste, already known and understood, are applied to the evaluation and appreciation of works that embody artistic intention and craft. In the *Lectures* Blair defines rhetoric as that study which formally accounts for the principles of "taste and good sense" and which teaches the best method of applying these principles to criticism and to communicating thought. By conflating traditional notions of rhetoric as a useful art with belletristic notions of rhetoric as an "elegant art," Blair designates the study and practice of rhetoric as an enterprise relevant to society not only in the most obvious pragmatic sense but also in its unique role of fostering an acquaintance with the principles of art and a deeper insight into the philosophy of human nature. In the nineteenth-century tradition, numbers of influential treatises reasserted the case for the role of rhetoric in the cultivation of taste and promoted the ideal that the study of rhetoric and the practice of criticism confer rhetorical expertise as well as moral and intellectual virtue. In fact, a faithfulness to belletristic idealism is one of the marked features of the evolving tradition in North America, a tradition that continued to assign a critical and moral function to the study and practice of rhetoric well into the early decades of the twentieth century.

A measure of the powerful authority that belletristic theory exerted over the development of the North American tradition between 1800 and 1900 is the frequency with which theories of rhetoric elaborated on the taste-rhetoric dynamic and treated criticism as a requisite art of rhetoric. In

Nineteenth-Century Rhetoric

The Elements of Rhetoric (1878) James De Mille summarizes the notion of the "literary" or critical function of rhetoric that had become a normative view by midcentury:

> While, therefore, a knowledge of rhetoric is of great importance to the writer, it may be shown to possess a still higher value as a means of culture and educational discipline. By culture is meant the refining and humanizing influence of art or letters, through which one attains to a more delicate sensibility of taste, and a higher and purer stage of intellectual enjoyment. As a means of culture, literature is at once more accessible, more effective, and more enduring than art. In order to obtain the full benefit of our literature, it should be studied in accordance with some system. In this way the effort after culture may be combined with an educational discipline not inferior to any which may be derived from the ancient classics. . . . the rhetorical [mode] has to do with the style of various works, their excellences and defects, together with the principles upon which they are constructed.[15] (iv–v)

Genung's account of the "adjustments of Style, and the Culture that promotes them" in *Working Principles of Rhetoric* also represents this same theoretical tendency to embrace belletristic idealism under the pedagogical assumption that the study of taste provides insight into compositional principles and improves the habits of the mind:

> The culture necessary to the perfect adjustment of style to thought is the culture of taste. Taste is to writing what tact and good breeding are to manners. Much of it may be native, the goodly heritage of ancestry and refined surroundings; but much of it is imparted, too, by one's companionship with cultivated people and with the best literature. By his daily habits of reading and conversation, if these are wisely cared for, a man may acquire insensibly a literary instinct which enables him to feel at once what is false in expression and what is true. . . . To profit by such culture is the real joy of literature. (21)

Accepting without qualification the belletristic assumption that to acquire critical insight is to achieve greater mastery over discourse and a

Legacy and Synthesis

deeper aptitude for the profound, Genung represents rhetoric as a study that
aids the development of taste, the quality of thought, and the skill of
constructing discourse in terms of rhetorical laws and principles. Similarly,
David J. Hill's treatment of taste in *The Elements of Rhetoric and Composition* (1878) is designed to explain how aesthetic qualities bear on "the laws
of effective discourse, or the art of speaking and writing effectively" (1).
Hill reviews taste in terms of a comprehensive insight into how "rhetoric
teaches us . . . to add to mere correctness and consistency such force and
attractiveness as to make our thoughts clear and interesting to others"; he
thereby affirms the belletristic assumption that the study of taste is necessary
to the development of rhetorical excellence. Hill also presumes the importance of taste to the development of critical sensibility, a sensibility indispensable to the development of the powers of eloquence:

> Literary criticism is the art of judging of the merits and defects of
> a written composition. . . . It is a common error to suppose that
> criticism is the art of fault-finding. Its true function . . . is judi-
> cial. The critic is a judge. . . . He is to point out excellences as
> well as defects, and balancing all to decide upon the value of the
> production. In this he will necessarily be guided by his own prin-
> ciples and tastes; hence it is important that these should be correct
> and pure. As criticism is thus dependent upon personal views and
> feelings, it cannot claim scientific certainty for its results, except
> as these are founded upon universally admitted principles. The
> value of criticism is two-fold: 1) to the writer in composing; and
> 2) to the reader in enjoying literary works. (134)

The value that nineteenth-century theorists awarded to the critical
function of rhetoric is affirmed further by their consistent attention to
imitation and the importance of studying an exemplary canon. Blair insists
that the study of rhetoric enhances the sensibility of taste by defining the
"proper models for imitation and the principle beauties that ought to be
studied"; an essential assumption of the belletristic approach is the premise
that the study of exemplary models encourages excellence in writing and
public speaking (x). This pedagogical stance, which stresses the relationship

between the development of rhetorical expertise and the critical study of a literary canon, is advocated in numbers of nineteenth-century treatises that promote the belletristic view. The belletristic emphasis on imitation (which can be understood as a recovery of the classical doctrine of *imitatio*) is prominent in nineteenth-century theory not only in explicit statements outlining the integral function of criticism but also in a systematic tendency to rely on literary examples to illustrate rhetorical principles and techniques. In *The Principles of Rhetoric* A. S. Hill refers to a number of British and American authors whose works are cited frequently by nineteenth-century rhetoricians as models of rhetorical excellence: Edmund Burke, Thackeray, Irving, Browning, Shakespeare, Macaulay, Arnold, Cardinal Newman, Emerson, George Eliot, Ruskin, Swift, Hawthorne, Pope, Dryden, Ben Jonson, Dickens, Scott, Cooper, De Quincey, Trollope, Coleridge, Stevenson, Wordsworth, Milton, Twain, Austen, and Daniel Webster. Hill's use of excerpts from Thackeray's *Virginians,* Dickens's *David Copperfield,* Eliot's *Daniel Deronda,* and Irving's *The Sketch Book* to illustrate how descriptive details can "stimulate the imagination" is typical of the way in which nineteenth-century rhetoricians relied on a representative sampling of literary examples to demonstrate the skillful adaptation of rhetorical principles:

> The monarch is a little, keen, fresh-coloured old man, with very protruding eyes, attired in plain, old-fashioned, snuff-coloured clothes and brown stockings, his only ornament the blue ribbon of his Order of the Garter. [Thackeray]

> "A slight figure," said Mr. Peggotty, looking at the fire, "kiender worn; soft, sorrowful, blue eyes; a delicate face; a pritty head, leaning a little down; a quiet voice and way—timid a'most. That's Emily." [Dickens]

> One moment had been burnt into his life as its chief epoch—a moment full of July sunshine and large pink roses shedding their last petals on a grassy court enclosed on three sides by a Gothic cloister . . . a boy of thirteen, stretched prone on the grass where

it was in shadow, his curly head propped on his arms over a book, while his tutor, also reading, sat on a camp-stool under shelter. [Eliot]

The animal he bestrode was a broken-down plough-horse, that had outlived almost everything but his viciousness. He was gaunt and shagged, with a ewe neck and a head like a hammer; his rusty mane and tail tangled and knotted with burrs; one eye had lost its pupil, and was glaring and spectral; but the other had the gleam of a genuine devil in it. [Irving] (262–63)

Literary sources were conventionally cited as examples of rhetorical excellence in texts that promoted the critical rationale. M. B. Hope's *Princeton Text Book in Rhetoric* (1859), a treatise modeled extensively on the theoretical approach of Day's *Elements of the Art of Rhetoric,* follows the belletristic pattern of providing illustrative examples of principles from what would have been a familiar canon of literary favorites (Shakespeare, Spenser, Sydney, Byron, Pope, Coleridge, etc.) and recommending the authors of "English Literature" as models: "The school of poetry founded, respectively by Burns, and Cowper, and the Lake Poets, has taught us, that Common words may be poetic—even the somewhat rugged, but strong, manly, Saxon words of our noble native tongue,—when presided over by good taste,—are good enough to entertain even the angels of poesy" (on "the force of style," 200). In *A Practical System of Rhetoric* Newman outlines the merits of English authors in an appendix, "Historical Dissertation of English Style," in which he recommends several authors for study and imitation: "Herbert, Hobbes, Boyle, . . . for precision and accuracy"; "Lilly, Bacon in his Essays, Donne, Ben Jonson, Burton, and other writers of the reign of James I" for liveliness of fancy, vivacity and sprightliness; Milton, Barrow, and Sidney for strength, force, and manliness; and Bacon, Milton, and Dryden for "elevation, richness, and every noble quality of style" (309–11).[16]

The assumption that the study and imitation of an exemplary literary canon is a crucial means of acquiring a command of eloquent communication was incorporated in nineteenth-century theory as a normative premise.

Nineteenth-Century Rhetoric

So was the closely related notion that the study of an exemplary canon and the principles of rhetorical criticism improve thought and character. In allegiance to the New Rhetoric's formulation of a modern variant of *arete,* nineteenth-century theory preserved the idealism of the eighteenth-century belletristic tradition, a tradition that conflated the development of aesthetic instinct with the evolution of moral virtue and ascribed an edifying function to the study of rhetoric and belles lettres. Such belletristic idealism pervaded nineteenth-century theory and imposed a moral accent on the North American tradition: rhetorical expertise was equated with highly evolved intellectual processes and a sensitivity to the profound and the good. Nineteenth-century treatises that promoted a belletristic program typically offered some variant of this idealistic orientation, particularly in recommendations for the virtues conferred by the study of criticism. Quackenbos describes the benefits of studying the principles of taste and the "standard masterpieces of literature" as an awakening of finer sensibilities; his discussion is typical of the way in which nineteenth-century belletristic theory promoted a Blairian attitude toward the idealistic role of rhetoric:

> These studies, however, do more than entertain and please; they improve the understanding. To apply the principles of sound criticism to composition, to examine what is beautiful and why it is so, to distinguish between affected and real ornaments, can hardly fail to improve us in the most valuable department of philosophy, the philosophy of human nature. Such examinations teach us self-knowledge. They necessarily lead us to reflect on the operations of the judgement, the imagination, and the heart; and familiarize us with the most refined feelings that ennoble our race. Beauty, harmony, grandeur, and elegance; all that can soothe the mind, gratify the fancy or move the affections,—belong to the province of these studies. They bring to light various springs of action, which, without their aid, might have passed unobserved; and which, though delicate, often exercise an important influence in life.[17]
> (155)

Legacy and Synthesis

In this paraphrase of Blair, Quackenbos outlines what was conventionally taken as one of the "great advantages" of the study of rhetoric—an insight into the "refined" dimensions of thought and feeling. Explicitly equating the development of such a state of mind and heart with moral character, Quackenbos ascribes an overtly ethical function to the study of rhetoric and belles lettres:

> The cultivation of taste has in all ages been regarded as an important aid in the enforcement of morality. Let the records of the world be canvassed, and we shall find that trespasses, robberies, and murders, are generally not the work of refined men. . . . Nor does the study of rhetoric operate as a preventive to the more heinous offences only; it elevates the tone of the mind, increases its sensibility, enlarges the sphere of its sympathies, and thus enables it to repress its selfishness and restrain its more violent emotions. To a man of acute and cultivated taste, every wrong action, whether committed by himself or another, is a source of pain; and, if he is the transgressor, his lively sensibility brings him back to duty, with renewed resolutions for the future. . . . Noble sentiments and high examples, constantly brought before the mind, can not fail to beget in it a love of glory, and an admiration of what is truly great. Though these impressions may not always be durable, they are at least to be ranked among the means of disposing the heart to virtue. (155–56)

Quackenbos's philosophical conflation of "taste" with the "noble" and the "great" is characteristic of the deep ideological relationship between the aesthetic and the ethical in belletristic theory, a relationship that Blair's *Lectures* successfully popularized. Aesthetic sensibility was presented in nineteenth-century theory as an intellectual and emotional state on which true eloquence relies: Newman describes the practical consequences of the study of taste as allowing the rhetorician to "throw a higher interest . . . over the thoughts he communicates, and increased influence over the minds of his readers" (*Practical System* 82); Day insists that the development of

elegance, "that property of style by virtue of which the discourse is com-
mended to the taste of the hearer," depends on "acquiring those moral
habits and associations which are necessary for the expression of right
sentiment" and "the study of art," which "is directly beneficial in creating
that sense of propriety which is the condition of beauty; as well as in
forming the sentiments and in developing power of expression" (*Elements*
285–90); Bascom similarly defines elegance as "all in a composition that
gives pleasure to taste, both in the matter brought forward and in the method
of presentation" and observes that elegance "rests chiefly on richness and
delicacy of feeling. . . . The more diversified and sensitive one's emotional
nature, the more rapid and certain will his judgment be in questions which
ultimately make their appeal to feelings. Moral problems are often interpreted and solved by generous, just feeling, quite as quickly and surely as
by unimpassioned speculation" (207–8). Genung defines eloquence by
reiterating "Daniel Webster's famous definition": "When public bodies are
to be addressed on momentous occasions, when great interests are at stake,
and strong passions excited, nothing is valuable in speech further than as
it is connected with high intellectual and moral endowments" (*Working
Principles* 644).[18] The doctrine of taste and the critical rationale for rhetoric
it promotes rely on the assumption that principles of taste embody "natural"
inclinations brought to greater conscious awareness. Essentially eschewing
the notion of the artificial per se, belletristic theory insisted on the "natural"
dynamics by which rhetorical modes and forms enhance natural intellectual
responses to the beautiful and inclinations to virtue in the rhetor and in
those who experience the discourse. As Hunt observes in *The Principles of
Written Discourse* (1884), one of the major objectives of rhetoric is "to
make emphatic . . . the Moral Element. . . . The processes involved in the
expression and impression of our thought are ethical as well as intellectual.
The discourser is bound by every consideration to show all that is elevating
and to dwell upon the highest levels of thought and emotion" (11).

  Nineteenth-century theoretical allegiance to an idealistic view of the
edifying consequences of the study and practice of rhetoric perpetuated one
of the most explicit principles of eighteenth-century belletristic theory

Legacy and Synthesis

(and one of the implicit assumptions of the epistemological rationale that belletristic theory presupposes): the exercise of taste and its application to composition and discourse confer particular virtues on the rhetor, including a liberal mind, a sensitive moral nature, and an ability to reinforce "elevated" thoughts and feelings in others. Nineteenth-century theory reinforced yet another principle of the New Rhetoric: an expanded concept of the scope of rhetoric. In the New Rhetoric, both belletristic and scientific treatises advocated an expansion of the theoretical and pragmatic concerns of rhetoric to include the modes of public speaking and the major genres of prose; the nineteenth-century tradition continued this practice of defining rhetoric as the general study of communication. The primary theoretical interest of the New Rhetoric was in reconstituting rhetoric as an enterprise that reveals, and depends on, basic principles of human nature. The belletristic tradition specifically explored the aesthetic dimensions of human nature and treated those rhetorical dynamics implicated by these dimensions; it also offered a more extensive treatment of all the forms of communication. In nineteenth-century theory, both the general theoretical disposition to extend the scope of rhetoric to include all forms of oral and written discourse and the particular belletristic interest in outlining those principles and techniques appropriate to written composition and public speaking are obvious.

An explicit account of the modern scope of rhetoric was a typical feature of nineteenth-century treatises that imitated the Blairian system of treating the major divisions of rhetoric as the major modes of public speaking and the formal genres of prose; in fact, Blair's systematic approach to the divisions was standard in the majority of nineteenth-century treatises that offered a general theory of rhetoric, whether of a distinctly belletristic or scientific orientation. Alfred H. Welsh's *Complete Rhetoric* (1885) and Quackenbos's *Advanced Course of Composition and Rhetoric* offer treatments of the "departments of expression" that indicate the degree to which nineteenth-century treatments of the divisions were influenced by eighteenth-century belletristic concepts of the scope of rhetoric. Welsh and Quackenbos offer explications of those divisions of oratory and prose that figure so prominently in Blair's *Lectures:* judicial, deliberative, and secular oratory; the epistle; the essay; historical and philosophical writing; fiction; and poetry. Bain's treatment of the divisions in *English Composition and Rhetoric* (1866) embodies this view of rhetoric: Bain examines the expository essay as the major mode of scientific and philosophical writing, treats judicial, political, and pulpit oratory and debate as forms of persuasion, and examines the "species of poetry" and prose fiction. Similarly, Genung (*Working Principles*) treats description, narration, history, biography, fiction, exposition, oratory, and debate as "the literary types" of rhetoric in addition to treating critical topics such as "poetic traits in poetry and prose" and "rhythm in poetry and prose" (x–xii).[19]

So conventional within nineteenth-century theory was this expanded view of the scope of rhetoric that explicit statements regarding the "proper" realm of rhetoric appeared in influential lectures and treatises throughout the century. In *A Practical System of Rhetoric* (1842 edition) Newman's definition of the "different kinds of composition" as didactic, persuasive, argumentative, descriptive, and narrative relies on the epistemological rationale of understanding the function of discourse in terms of the "end" in view. While Newman's designation of the types of composition is in keeping with the general philosophical orientation of nineteenth-century theory, it also promotes a New Rhetorical view of the range of rhetoric by discussing prose writing and "discourses addressed to assemblies" (28). Day's *Art of Rhetoric,* a typically synthetic work, co-opts Campbell's philosophy of rhetoric, Whately's approach to argumentation, and Blair's doctrine of taste and criticism, defining the scope of rhetoric as "covering the entire field of pure discourse as address to another mind" (Day v). Channing affirms the same view of a comprehensive rhetoric in his lecture "General View of Rhetoric" (representative of the type of theoretical account of rhetoric offered at Harvard between 1819 and 1851). Channing observes that while rhetoric was originally intended to instruct in the composition and delivery of orations, it should properly be understood as a system of rules addressing all forms of communication: "It does not ask whether a man is to be a speaker or writer,—a poet, philosopher, or debater;

Legacy and Synthesis

but simply,—is it his wish to be put in the right way of communicating his mind with power to others, by words spoked or written" (31). In *A Manual of Composition and Rhetoric* (1870) John S. Hart introduces his discussion of rhetoric with precepts that appear to have achieved the status of theoretical maxims by 1870: "1. *Rhetoric* is the science which treats all discourse. 2. By *Discourse* is meant any expression of thought by means of language. 3. Discourse may be either *oral or written*" (17; Hunt's italics).[20] Hart's treatment of the species of rhetoric imitates Blair's examination of oral and written genres and further expands the catalogue of belles lettres by supplementing standard treatments of poetry (epic, dramatic, lyric, elegiac, pastoral, didactic) and oratory with an expanded list of prose forms, adding editorials, reviews, news writing, and travel writing to the typical coverage of letters, essays, historical writing, and philosophical treatises (261–304). In *The Principles of Written Discourse* Hunt lists theoretical maxims similar to Hart's, maxims that proceed from the assumption that "we treat the subject of Discourse in its comprehensiveness as the expression of our thought in language. We study its laws and processes; its qualities and objects applicable alike to the writer and the orator" (15). The maxims are as follows:

1. Discourse includes both Prose and Poetry.
2. Discourse includes Oratory and Composition. It may be both Oral and Written.
3. Discourse is both a Science and an Art. It has a body of rational principles in systematic form and these are applied to visible production.
4. Discourse is the expression of thought. The excellence of the form will depend on that subject matter. (20)

Some nineteenth-century treatises were less explicit in their theoretical affirmation of a comprehensive range for rhetoric or did not identify the literary genres as divisions of composition. A. S. Hill's *Principles of Rhetoric,* for example, treats "kinds of composition" under four divisions based on epistemological aims of "description, narration, exposition, argument, and persuasion" (x). However, in discussing "the special principles that apply to each kind," Hill identifies many of the standard belles lettres categories, alludes frequently to literary genres that embody different aims, and continues the refinement of the genres of prose composition. In his discussion of description, Hill distinguishes between "scientific description" and "artistic description," alluding to "works of science" (e.g., Edward A. Samuels, *Ornithology and Oology of New England*) as well as various poems by Wordsworth, Pope, and Oliver Wendell Holmes to illustrate how description secures the attention of the mind (249–90). Similarly, exposition is examined in terms of an extensive range including prose and oral discourse produced under a variety of circumstances: "the results of observation, or reflection on observed facts" expounded by the scientist; the lecture by the teacher that "unravels knotty questions or clears up doubtful points"; the summary of a lawyer's argument, the case analysis of a physician, the journalist's article, the critic's review of a book or essays or a play; and the correspondence of "the man of affairs" (300–302). Under "Persuasion" Hill discusses examples of political, legal, and ceremonial oration and cites a host of public documents, literary works, tracts, and well-known orations as examples of how to move the will to action: "the report of the arguments before the Supreme Court of the United States in the recent income-tax cases," the *Autobiography* of Benjamin Franklin, the legal arguments of Daniel Webster, Edmund Burke's essay "Reflections of the Revolution in France," "a treatise on the evils of slavery" by "Mrs. Stowe," and Lord Brougham's defense of Queen Caroline in *Speeches on Social and Political Subjects* (386–400). Hill's treatment of the species or divisions of rhetoric under epistemological headings is in keeping with the theoretical inclination of the nineteenth-century tradition to affirm the epistemological rationale. Hill's method, like Hart's, is typical of the way nineteenth-century theorists increasingly extended the arts of rhetoric and belles lettres to include an ever-increasing variety of writing and speaking occasions, artistic and otherwise. Nineteenth-century theorists preserved the belletristic principle that rhetoric is a comprehensive study and took the principle further by acknowledging the proliferation of conventional rhetorical occasions that had come to characterize the field of formal communication by the end of the nineteenth century.

Nineteenth-century theory was indebted to belletristic approaches to the canons as well as to the idealism and comprehensive definition of rhetoric that belletristic doctrine popularized; this indebtedness is especially obvious in treatments of style. Particularly important to the general philosophical foundations of the New Rhetoric was a theoretical correspondence between the "rhetorical" and the "natural"; belletristic theory paid special attention to how the "natural" functions of the imagination and the passions are facilitated by intellectual and emotional appeals that rely on aesthetic qualities or the natural principles of taste. Such a theoretical conflation of the natural and the aesthetic informs Blair's discussions of the doctrine of taste, the value of criticism, and the scope of rhetoric and his treatments of traditional canonical issues such as arrangement, style, and delivery. In examining these issues Blair is particularly interested in outlining how effects associated with the function of taste (beauty, elegance, the sublime) can be created or emphasized through rhetorical devices and strategies (see chapter 1). Treatments of style in North American rhetorics from the early decades of the century to 1900 reiterated such overtly belletristic interests and also relied on the epistemological point of view that both Blair and Campbell imposed on a neoclassical scheme of elements. Relying as Whately did on a synthesis of New Rhetorical approaches to style, nineteenth-century theorists reviewed a number of belletristic elements of style, elements conventionalized quite early in the century: a designation of beauty or elegance as a major quality of style (in addition to perspicuity and force); an attention to the aesthetic impact of diction, sentence structure, and sentence arrangement; and a treatment of figurative language in terms of appeals to the imagination and the feelings.[21] Welsh's *Complete Rhetoric* offers an account of style typical of both the epistemological and belletristic explanations of canonical principles and techniques.[22] Affirming the epistemological importance of perspicuity and energy to comprehensibility, Welsh discusses the quality of elegance with a clear debt to Whately, who uses the term "Elegance" for what Blair treats under "Beauty":

91

Nineteenth-Century Rhetoric

Elegance is in discourse what refinement is in manners. . . . It is
that quality which gives pleasure, as distinguished from that which
gives instruction or impressiveness or force. . . . Minds are influenced by what is agreeable, as well as by what is reasonable; and
in proportion as those addressed have richness and delicacy of
feelings, matter and manner combine to make the product beautiful. Elegance of expression implies refinement in the choice and
arrangement of words. It depends upon: Euphony . . . Rhythm
. . . Harmony . . . Variety . . . Imagery. (109–19)

Quackenbos's similar discussion of figurative language stresses that
figures "enrich language by increasing its facilities of expression," "dignify
style," and provide the mind with the "pleasure" of "detecting and tracing
resemblances" (231). This characterization reiterates the aesthetic interest
in ornament and its impact on the faculties promoted and popularized by
Blair. Adhering closely to Blair's model of treating a select number of
figures, Quackenbos lists those figures treated in nineteenth-century theory
as principal figures of rhetoric: simile, metaphor, allegory, metonymy,
synecdoche, hyperbole, vision, apostrophe, personification, interrogation,
exclamation, antithesis, climax, irony, apophasis, and onomatopoeia (234–
54). In keeping with the method of the New Rhetoric, nineteenth-century
explanations of the general and specific effects of figures drew on the
epistemological assumption that the mind is predisposed toward resemblances and the belletristic premise that the imagination and the feelings
have special roles to play in facilitating such connections:

[On "figurative energy":] Here we find the explanation of the fact
that the same discourse pleases an imaginative mind skilled in the
use of language and accustomed to refer the words to the sensible
object which they originally represented, that, to another mind,
seems wholly destitute of beauty. Here, too, is found the explanation of the peculiar energy and beauty of that species of style
which puts the imagination of the reader constantly in the way of
making this reference. (Day, *Elements* 266)

Hyperbolical expressions are of frequent occurrence in common
conversation; we often say, *as cold as ice, as hot as fire, as*

white as snow, &c., in all which phrases the quality is exaggerated beyond the bounds of truth. Their frequency is to be attributed to the imagination, which always takes pleasure in magnifying the objects before it. (Quackenbos 240)

The metaphor is evidently a bolder and more lively figure than the simile. As it results from a more intensely excited imagination, so it conveys a more forcible conception. A metaphor is more like a picture than a simile is, and hence the graphic use of metaphor is called "word painting." (David J. Hill, *Elements* 83)

The climax possesses two principal merits: it prevents mental fatigue by continually increasing the pleasure of mental exertion; and it supplies means of measuring the value of the final assertion, as the lower Alps help the eye to measure the height of Mont Blanc. (A. S. Hill, *Principles* 193)

These belletristically oriented comments illustrate the degree to which nineteenth-century approaches to style were shaped by the aesthetic and critical concerns of the New Rhetoric. These concerns also influenced nineteenth-century treatments of other elements; for instance, both eras preferred the "natural delivery" as the more beautiful and aesthetically appealing approach to moving the passions, the imagination, and the will. Nineteenth-century works that incorporated the doctrine of taste, a belletristic concept of the range of rhetoric, and the aesthetic and critical interests of the belletristic approach treated other systematic features of theory from a distinctively belletristic orientation:

—Definitions of rhetoric that stipulate the relationship between effective rhetoric and the exercise of taste or aesthetic principles (Hunt 8; Day, *Elements* 4, chap. 3; Quackenbos 156)
—Treatments of qualities of taste (sublimity, beauty, euphony, harmony, melody) as major qualities of style and/or discourse (Hunt, chap. 11; Quackenbos 151–323)
—Treatments of the divisions of rhetoric as the modes of conviction, the species of poetry, and the forms of persuasion or oratory (Bain, *English Composition* [1866] 147–227; De Mille 456–518)

Nineteenth-Century Rhetoric

—Treatments of the pathetic as a quality of beauty and a necessary appeal in persuasion (De Mille, part 5; Hope 89–110)

The number of significant belletristic principles and theoretical presumptions conventionalized in nineteenth-century theory testify to the far-reaching impact of the eighteenth-century belletristic movement on the theoretical substance and orientation of the nineteenth-century tradition, a tradition that inherited the belletristic point of view through various methodological venues: primary imitation of Blair's treatises and/or adherence to the critical rationale that Blair and other belletristic critics expounded; secondary imitation of belletristic approaches through the use of Whately's *Elements* as a model; and the inclusion of select belletristic elements (the doctrine of taste, the nature of criticism, oral and prose divisions, style) in a synthetic theoretical base featuring other formal elements of the New Rhetoric such as Campbell's philosophy of the aims of rhetoric and Whately's outline of types of arguments.

Day's *Art of Rhetoric* relies on exactly this kind of synthetic foundation and is typical of the treatises that began to develop at midcentury. While often citing Blair, Campbell, and Whately as authoritative sources on particular elements, such treatises relied primarily on a hybrid theoretical structure that brought together doctrinal assumptions and theoretical commitments foregrounded by all three major treatises of the New Rhetoric. The tendency of nineteenth-century theory to incorporate principles of the belletristic and epistemological rationales in these ways points to another major similarity between the nineteenth-century and eighteenth-century traditions—a dependence on a composite of modern and neoclassical principles and elements. Campbell's *Philosophy of Rhetoric* and Blair's *Lectures* articulate "modern" philosophies of rhetoric and subject traditional principles and systematic elements to a review in terms of the implications of that philosophy. Campbell and Blair, and later Whately, do not dispense with classical principles and attitudes but rather recast these in the light of their particular theoretical interests, reexamining and thus reinscribing a number of classical presumptions as principles of theory: the conventional status of the divisions and the canons; the theoretical and pragmatic maxim that the rhetorical process can be understood in terms of the interplay of purpose, audience, and occasion; and the pedagogical assumption that eloquence can be acquired through the study of rhetorical principles, practice in the rhetorical genres, and imitation of works of genius. In addition to assimilating these classical assumptions in the theoretical fabric of their work, Campbell and Blair also make frequent references to classical rhetoricians as authoritative sources on matters of principles and practice, promoting the view that the teachings of Cicero and Quintilian are more than relevant to their "modern" examinations of rhetorical theory. As Whately's work draws heavily on the established norms of the New Rhetoric, *Elements of Rhetoric* presumes many of the same neoclassical presumptions and further reinscribes these traditional precepts as normative principles of theory. Whately, too, frequently cites classical sources as authorities. The New Rhetoric was quite self-conscious of the classical tradition on which it relied and took a respectful theoretical stance toward it, preserving a good many traditional principles and elements in its general revisionist efforts.

As a body of theory that relied on the treatises of the New Rhetoric as authoritative sources, nineteenth-century theory presumed many of the same neoclassical perspectives implicit in the New Rhetoric. Therefore, nineteenth-century theory depended not only on a synthesis of epistemological and belletristic elements for its theoretical substance but also on certain neoclassical presuppositions already incorporated in the New Rhetoric: an emphasis on the purpose-audience-occasion dynamic as an overriding rationale for practice; a systematic focus on the discussion of the canons and the divisions of rhetoric; and a recapitulation of the study-practice-imitation creed for acquiring expertise. In addition to reinscribing these neoclassical principles, nineteenth-century theory also incorporated and thus conventionalized the revisions of traditional precepts effected by Campbell and Blair. The most significant of these revisions were the reconstitution of the canon of invention as the discovery of materials and proper evidence and the subsequent conflation of the boundaries of the canons of invention and arrangement. As Whately reiterated these alterations as well as those neoclassical features retained by the New Rhetoric, nineteenth-century theoretical and systematic dependence on *Elements of Rhetoric* constituted a secondary imitation of Campbell and Blair's neoclassical concerns.

Nineteenth-century theory emphatically reinforced the theoretical principle that the rhetorician must adapt discourse to the requirements of the audience and the governing context. Nineteenth-century theory also reinforced the general philosophical view of the New Rhetoric that the rhetor, whether speaker or writer, must understand the epistemological dynamics at work as well as the conventional expectations and circumstantial constraints. A variety of theorists recapitulated this traditional point of view in their definitions of the nature of rhetoric and its function as an art. Genung's definition of rhetoric as "the art of adapting discourse, in harmony with its subject and occasion, to the requirements of a reader or hearer" summarizes the nineteenth-century view that the rhetorician's art is inextricably involved with the subjective varieties of human nature and the characteristic features of discourse scenes. Genung's self-consciousness of traditional conceptions of the dynamics of rhetorical communication reveals the degree to which the nineteenth-century tradition regarded its efforts as extending classical traditions:

This idea of adaptation is the best modern representative of the original aim of the art. Having at first to deal only with hearers, rhetoric began as the art of oratory, that is, or convincing and persuading by speech. Now, however, as the art of printing has greatly broadened its field of action, rhetoric must address itself to readers as well, must therefore include more forms of composition and more comprehensive objects; while still the initial character of the art survives, in the general aim of so presenting thought that it shall have power over men, which aim is most satisfactorily defined in the term adaptation. (*Practical Elements* 1)

Legacy and Synthesis

In *The Principles of Rhetoric* A. S. Hill stresses the principle of adaptation in a definition of rhetoric that explicitly claims parallels with classical assumptions:

> Rhetoric, being the art of communication by language, implies the presence, in fact, or in imagination, of at least two persons,—the speaker or the writer, and the person spoken or written to. Aristotle makes the very essence of Rhetoric to lie in the distinct recognition of a hearer. Hence its rules are not absolute, like those of logic, but relative to the character and circumstances of the person or persons addressed; for though truth is one, and correct reasoning must always be correct, the ways of communicating truth are many. (v–vi)

Hill and Genung present the principle of adaptation as the essence of the rhetorical process and the major challenge of rhetoric as an art; such explicit attention to the purpose-audience-occasion dynamic emerges consistently in nineteenth-century treatises. Day stresses the principle of adaptation with regard to invention, reiterating guidelines that recapitulate classical advice regarding the "relative" nature of rhetorical materials and appeals as well as the importance of the rhetor's command of knowledge:

> The principles which regulate this process regard either the mind of the speaker himself, the occasion of speaking, the mind addressed, or the object of the discourse. There is obviously . . . a necessity of consulting the character of the audience; the extent of their information, their peculiar habits of thought, their feelings, also, and their relations to the speaker. . . . The character of the theme and the particular view that is taken of it as well as the general mode of developing it will also be affected by the particular object which the writer may wish to accomplish in his discourse. (*Elements* 39–41)

The theoretical importance that Day awards to the principle of adaptation in the process of invention illustrates that the purpose-audience-occasion dynamic was an explicit consideration in nineteenth-century discussions of rhetorical modes and canons. As a conspicuous theoretical element in treatments of persuasion and oratory, adaptation is presented as affecting the nature of rhetorical materials as well as predisposing the potential impact of the discourse. In *A Treatise on the Preparation and Delivery of Sermons* (1870) John A. Broadus points out the importance of the principle of adaptation in his discussion of how to achieve "application" in a sermon. Quoting Webster's adage that the preacher should make the subject of a sermon "a personal matter" to the audience, Broadus stresses that the "application" of the sermon entails showing the hearer how the truths of the sermon "apply" to him through the selection of materials and illustrative methods: "It is obvious that while some subjects may be applied to the congregation as a whole, others will be applied only to particular classes, or will have to be applied to distinct classes separately, as converted and unconverted, old and young. . . . What men apply to themselves, without feeling that it was aimed at them, is apt to produce the greatest effect" (230–31).[23]

The theoretical affinity between what Broadus discusses here as application, a conventional topic in homiletics, and what Day and others discuss as adaptation is an intimate one: the importance of adapting to audience is defined as a crucial consideration in the development of suitable rhetorical materials for specific scenes. The attention that the principle of adaptation received in nineteenth-century theory was a consequence of the fact that nineteenth-century theorists, like the New Rhetoricians, followed tradition in awarding theoretical status to this principle. The promotion of the principle of adaptation was also reinforced by the fact that nineteenth-century theorists supported the same epistemological aims for rhetoric that Campbell and Blair claimed and thus asserted the importance of understanding human nature and the ways of the mind. The New Rhetoric defined the purpose-audience-occasion relationship as a prerequisite concern in persuasion and also in terms of the selection of rhetorical materials and proof in address to the understanding. In treating conviction, Campbell points out that it is crucial that the logical substance of discourse addressed to the understanding be conceived in terms of what hearers would perceive as consistent with their experience and common sense. Clearly, a knowledge of the subject matter and the audience becomes crucial in such an inventional process. Campbell and Blair (also Whately) observe that in the process of persuasion (address to the will), the "fitness of arguments" must be adjusted to the "different orders of men" addressed and the "sphere" of their knowledge (see chapter 1). Recommendations that the nature of the audience and their circumstances be considered in devising appeals to the understanding and the will were also a standard part of nineteenth-century treatments of conviction and persuasion. In keeping with the tendency to echo the advice of Campbell, Blair, and Whately, Hunt's treatments of conviction and persuasion in *The Principles of Written Discourse* recapitulate standard advice regarding requisite knowledge of the state of mind of those addressed, methods of awakening feelings, the nature of human motives, and the affective conditions that constrain persuasion (220–83). Such discussions assume that the principle of adaptation is not only a maxim of rhetorical theory but also a dictate governing communication in general: "The personal tastes and sentiments of men are consulted, their likes and dislikes, their hopes and their fears, and the problem is, how to run the object to which we would incite them parallel with such views and feelings. Society and the State take full advantage of this principle" (287).

Day too affirms this maxim when he calls attention to the importance of the speaker's understanding of the diverse mental states of his hearers: "As in explanation, so still more in confirmation it is requisite that the speaker regard the taste, the opinions and the feelings of his hearers; not merely in the exordium and the peroration, but also in the general conduct of the discourse" (*Elements* 89). Similarly, Bain's definition of the nature of oratory affirms the importance of the principle of adaptation by stressing the importance of "Knowledge of the Persons Addressed" in moving the will:

Oratorical persuasion endeavors to obtain the co-operation of . . . free impulses for some proposed line of conduct, by so presenting it in language as to make it coincide with them. . . . If all men were constituted exactly alike, and were always in the same mood, a speaker would need only to judge for himself how to move others. But such is the disparity of human characters, that no small time is expended in knowing thoroughly any considerable number of men. . . . The young do not comprehend the feelings of the old; the one sex is often at fault in judging the other. The rich and the poor, the noble, and the plebeian, the educated and the uneducated, the professional worker and the manual worker, the members of distinct professions have each their peculiarity. . . . For Oratorical ends, knowledge of character must descend into minute details, and flow from personal experience. An acquaintance with human nature in general, as obtained by mental science, or by maxims laid down in books, is good so far; but we cannot operate with effect on individual men or masses, without the further knowledge given by actual intercourse with these men or with others like them. . . . It is well to have in the view a systematic scheme of man's nature,—of the mind's activities, feelings, and thinking powers . . . such a systematic view instructs us what to look for, and how to arrange the facts coming under our observation. . . . The practical maxims acquired by men in the course of their education and experience, are their principles of action, or rules of procedure trusted for gaining their ends, individual or social; these are the *data* of the orator, his medium of persuasion, the major premises of his reasoning. (*English Composition* [1866] 171–77; see also David J. Hill, *Science* 63–65)

Bain's treatment of adaptation reiterates traditional wisdom regarding the importance of understanding human character and the various ways that station and profession impinge on affective response; Bain also draws attention to the epistemological dimensions of adaptation by stressing that an insight into human impulses relies on the study of "mental science" and the deductions of common sense and experience. Bain's conflation of a neoclassical perspective on adaptation with an epistemological perspective is typical of the way in which nineteenth-century theorists followed the lead of Campbell, Blair, and Whately in reinscribing the purpose-audience-occasion dynamic as a basic principle of the art of rhetoric. As a marked theoretical feature in treatments of conviction, persuasion, and canonical elements, the principle of adaptation was discussed in nineteenth-century treatises under a number of conventionalized neoclassical and epistemological headings: "Style must be adapted to the Subject and the Capacity of One's Readers"; "First to conciliate the good Will of the Hearers"; "Regard to the Mind Addressed"; "Adaptation to the Intelligence of the Audience"; "Judicious Selection of the Occasion for Speaking"; "Relation of the Speaker to his Audience"; and "Principle of Adaptation."

Nineteenth-century theory embodied a number of elements that addressed the fundamental importance of the principle of adaptation either in terms that were overtly neoclassical or revised neoclassical (with an added epistemological viewpoint). The neoclassical dimension of nineteenth-century theory is also observable in the overall systematic architecture of nineteenth-century treatises, which characteristically provided formal treatments of the canons and divisions of rhetoric. While nineteenth-century theory expanded the classical range of the divisions by treating prose composition and the literary genres in addition to public speaking, its general tendency was to preserve the traditional disposition of rhetorical theory toward a systematic configuration organized in terms of analyses of the canons and divisions of rhetoric. Quackenbos offers a description of the process of "prose composition" that is typical of the way in which nineteenth-century theorists stressed the importance of gaining a mastery of the canons and a command over rhetorical genres:

> The process of Invention, which furnishes the thoughts to be clothed in a dress of words, and which constitutes the most difficult if not the chief branch of the art, is first considered. The young composer is shown how to analyze his subject, and to amplify the thoughts successively suggested into a well-connected whole. The different parts of an exercise are taken up in turn; various forms and models of introductions are presented; description, narration, argument, &c., are treated, and the peculiarities of each

pointed out, as well as the styles which they respectively require.
. . . Thus made acquainted successively with Letters, Narratives,
Fiction, Essays, Argumentative Discourses, and Orations, and fur-
nished with subjects in each department and suggestions as to their
proper treatment, the student is next led to the consideration of
Poetry. (4–5)

Quackenbos reiterates two extremely important neo-Ciceronian assumptions: (1) the pedagogical notion that the acquisition of rhetorical
expertise necessarily involves the study of the canonical procedures and the
mastery of the particular nature of individual modes of rhetoric; and (2) the
more implicit but more significant theoretical presumption that the art of
rhetoric can be treated in terms of these issues. The formalization of a
course of study in invention, the development of a "well-connected whole"
and appropriate introductions (arrangement or *dispositio*), style, and the
"peculiarities" of various forms of prose and oratory is one of the major
ambitions of nineteenth-century theory, which consistently combined a
canons-modes configuration with accounts of the philosophy of rhetoric,
the doctrine of taste, and abbreviated treatments of the history of rhetoric
and the English language (in imitation of Blair).

The major treatises of the New Rhetoric treat the canons and the
divisions as major features of theory while offering revisions of certain
features of that scheme. So, too, nineteenth-century theory reinscribed the
canons-divisions component as a conventional theoretical and pedagogical
commitment while preserving the alterations to this scheme mandated by
the philosophical interests of the New Rhetoric. De Mille displays a conventional regard for the canons-divisions rubric in *The Elements of Rhetoric,*
in which he defines rhetoric as a term with a twofold meaning, referring
both to the subject-matter and to the mode of its presentation. Arranging
his treatise around the subjects "Style, or the choice and arrangement of
words; Method, or the choice and arrangement of subject-matter; The
literature of the Emotions; and the General Departments of Literature," De
Mille offers a treatment of the canons-divisions element of theory influenced
by a belletristic interest in the psychology of taste as well as by neoclassical

presumptions. De Mille's treatment of inventional processes and arrangement under the topic "Method" indicates the degree to which New Rhetorical revisions of invention and arrangement shaped the view of nineteenth-century theory toward the "choice and arrangement of subject matter."

Similarly, Channing is convinced that the study of rhetoric necessarily involves an understanding of the processes of invention and composition and the particular nature of various genres of discourse. He affirms the traditional assumption that the study of rhetoric and its application to conventional forms of discourse provide insight into recurrent intellectual principles and generic elements of form. Defining the "offices" of rhetoric in "General View of Rhetoric," Channing observes that rhetoric investigates "the style and method of persuasion . . . the finding and arranging of arguments . . . and instruction in speaking" (32–39). In defending this general theoretical scope, Channing reveals an overtly neoclassical regard for the study of the canons and the divisions as "fundamental instruction for all cases":

> The most important elements and characteristics of argumentative composition belong equally to all argumentative works, and . . . the least important things are the distinctions that separate one class from others. Yet so true is this, that you can not teach [a student] the proper way of collecting and stating his arguments for a sermon, a debate, or a philosophical treatise, without teaching him nearly everything that belonged to that matter universally.
> . . . it is of consequence to save the learner from the false and narrowing notion, that what is most important in any one kind of argumentative composition is peculiar to it, yet he must not be ignorant of what *is* peculiar to each, and a little study and experience will soon inform him. (36–37).

Although it is important to observe, as we have, that certain transformations of the divisions and canons of rhetoric were embodied in nineteenth-century theory, it is also necessary to note the consistency with which nineteenth-century treaties reconstruct the canons-division schemes. The prominence of neoclassical presumptions during this period also extended to dominant pedagogical rationales, such as the governing assumption that the development of rhetorical skills entails the study of rhetorical principles, practice in technique and genres, and the imitation of exemplary writers and orators. Although nineteenth-century theorists promoted the belletristic rationale for imitation as a means of acquiring insight into critical standards, they also reiterated the neoclassical stance of the New Rhetoric regarding the importance of the formal study of a system of principles, the necessity of experience in writing and speaking, and the benefits of imitation. Treatments of the study-practice-imitation process were often modeled on Blair and Whately, whose discussions of how to improve in composition and eloquence affirm the importance of studying "a system of rules" and the value of "exercises," "the habit of application," and "attention to the best models." Frequently stressing the importance of a general foundation of knowledge, nineteenth-century theorists paid a good deal of attention to the traditional notion that even the greatest natural aptitude can be improved through study and practice. Recapitulating the belletristic principle that the composition of effective discourse requires "good sense accompanied with a lively imagination," Jamieson's "Directions for Forming Style" presuppose that the study of "rules" must be supplemented with "frequent practice of composing" and draws particular attention to the "assistance that is to be gained from the writing of others" (242–43). In his introduction to *A Practical System of Rhetoric* Newman argues that students must be instructed in the governing principles of composition and the formation of a "good style" as well as in the "philosophy of rhetoric"; he also insists on the importance of "reading good authors in connexion with rhetorical studies" (iii–ix). In his reflections on the nature of rhetoric as an art or a system of rules by which we reach a practical end, Bascom offers an account of the means by which the art of rhetoric can be acquired, which is typical of the manner in which nineteenth-century theory reinscribed neoclassical pedagogical assumptions:

Skill arises from a practical familiarity with rules. It is the acquisition by muscle and mind of the quickness, the ease, which arise from habit. Both the mind and body are greatly dependent for rapidity and precision of action on practice. To this the artisan and the orator owe their facility and power of exertion. . . . It depends wholly on familiarity, on a protracted use of rules. . . . Elegance of manners, ease of expression, and even the highest virtue, arise from forgetfulness of rules in their perfect and unconscious application. (9–11)

In discussing the advantages of developing "rhetorical discipline" through the study of the art of expression, Genung echoes Bascom's argument (and the classical view of the function of art) that excellence in rhetoric is achieved only by first acquiring the "self-conscious" grasp of standards and technique that aids natural genius: "One does not think of stopping with mere native aptitude, but develops and disciplines all his powers so that they may be employed wisely and steadily; so in the art of expression one needs by faithful study and practice to get beyond the point where he only *happens* to write well, or where brilliancy and crudeness are equally uncontrolled, and attain that conscious power over thought and language which makes every part of his work the result of unerring skill and calculation" (*Working Principles* 6–7). Genung also observes that not to apply the rules of the art of rhetoric is to disavow what traditional "experience" has taught regarding this "difficult art." Promoting a similar point of view, Welsh's recommendation is more prescriptive: as the "rules of rhetoric" are a "teacher which inspired men cannot reject, to which ordinary men must attend. . . . He who will not answer the rudder will answer to the rocks" (4).

Genung and Welsh's insistence on the importance of studying and practicing the rules of rhetoric in order to avoid error and develop skill represents a standard emphasis in nineteenth-century theory and an emphatic neoclassical affirmation of the importance of systematic study and application of the principles of rhetoric. A similar affirmation of the necessity of imitation was also commonplace in discussions of what the art of rhetoric is founded on and how a "good style" can be acquired and received even more attention in treatises favoring belletristic interests in the develop-

ment of critical abilities. Day's summary of the means by which the art of
rhetoric can be acquired embodies the typical nineteenth-century neoclassical stipulation that the study-practice-imitation sequence represents the
fundamental processes by which the skills of rhetoric are acquired and
"improved":

> The means by which every art seeks its development and improve-
> ment are twofold: by a study of the nature and principles of the
> art, and by exercise. . . . The knowledge of the nature and princi-
> ples of the art of rhetoric is attained chiefly in two ways; by the
> study of rhetorical systems, and by the study of models of elo-
> quence. . . . It is hardly practical for the human mind to obtain a
> clear and familiar knowledge of any art without illustrations. . . .
> This great means of training the ancients denominated *imitation*.
> . . . No knowledge of principles . . . no study of models, how-
> ever extended, will make an artist without exercise. Exercise in
> rhetoric, in order to be most beneficial, must be intelligent, sys-
> tematic, critical, and abundant. (15–18)

The distinctly neoclassical elements of nineteenth-century theory
constitute a third major component in the synthetic disposition of nineteenth-century theory (epistemological/belletristic/neoclassical). Although
neoclassical elements and attitudes often were mediated by the influence of
belletristic and epistemological assumptions and aims, nineteenth-century
theory displayed a debt to the rhetorical tradition that paralleled the neoclassical dimension of the New Rhetoric. Affecting large-scale systematic
structures such as treatments of the canons and divisions and pedagogical
rationales as well treatments of the canons of style, delivery, arrangement,
and discussions of the forms of oratory, neoclassicism influenced a number
of conventional systematic elements in nineteenth-century theory:

—Reviews of the history of rhetoric with particular attention to
   the theories of Aristotle, Cicero, and Quintilian
—Treatments of invention (albeit revised) as the most fundamental rhetorical process, involving the identification and structur-

ing of evidence and materials—a process that presupposes the
anterior function of logic
—Treatments of style that retained a number of traditional elements such as attention to diction, word order, sentence structure, the use of figures, and the overall qualities of clarity, distinctiveness, and ornament
—Treatments of arrangement that retained the traditional distinctions between the functions of the introduction and subsequent
components of the discourse and that stress the principle of arrangement by strength
—Treatments of delivery that retained the traditional obligations
of management of the voice and gesture
—Treatments of the forms of oratory that retained traditional attention to discrete characteristics of particular forms of public
speaking (judicial, political, sermonic)

    The neoclassical consciousness of the nineteenth-century tradition
was in keeping with the theoretical stance of the New Rhetoric, which
considered the classical tradition and its teachings exemplary but in need
of reinterpretation and revision in terms of the philosophical insights and
pragmatic needs of modern times. The nineteenth-century supported Blair's
view that "the ancient models may still, with much advantage, be set before
us for imitation; though, in that imitation, we must, doubtless, have some
regard to what modern taste and modern manners will bear" (44–45).
Although nineteenth-century theorists tended to follow the example of
Campbell, Blair, and Whately in citing classical precepts and authorities,
nineteenth-century theorists devoted more commentary than did their predecessors to documenting the changing circumstances of rhetoric and identifying exactly which classical traditions and attitudes contribute to the study
of rhetoric in modern times. Revealing a self-consciousness of a long-
established but evolving tradition, nineteenth-century commentators inves-
tigated exactly what it meant to assess the "ancient" rhetoricians with "a
wise regard to the altered condition of society" (Channing 10).[24] In "The
Orator and His Times" Channing elaborates on the "circumstances in the
state of society, which distinguish the modern from the ancient orator,"

arguing that the difference in social and political climates between the past and the present does not erode the function of oratory but affects the type of eloquence "suited to our state of society." Channing observes that "improvements of the age" such as "the stable foundation and ample protection of government, and the general diffusion of knowledge and a spirit of inquiry" have changed the nature of modern oratory, making it a more temperate and egalitarian form of communication (12–14):

> Strange as it may seem to us, after hearing so much lofty declamation about the power of great speakers, whom nations listened to and obeyed, it is nevertheless true, that the orator is the creature of the circumstances in which he is placed. A modern debate is not a contest between a few leading men for a triumph over each other and an ignorant multitude, the orator himself is but one of the multitude, deliberating with them upon common interests, which are well understood and valued by all. . . . They are not assembled to be the subjects upon which he may try the power of his eloquence, but to see what eloquence can do for the question. (16)

Aware of the nature of classical rhetoric and its function in what he assesses to be a very different type of society, Channing insists that the sociological conditions that support rhetoric have changed dramatically and imposed changes on the nature and manner of discourse. The contention that modern political and cultural conditions have promoted different standards and techniques for eloquence was reiterated in a variety of forms in nineteenth-century works ranging from explicit commentary on the sociological function of rhetoric to disclaimers regarding the applicability of all "ancient" standards and techniques to modern practice. Quackenbos defines the range of modern rhetoric against what it "originally" comprehended and comments specifically on the changes in theoretical assumptions since the classical period:

> The word Rhetoric is derived from the Greek verb . . . to speak, and in its primary signification had reference solely to the art of

Legacy and Synthesis

oratory; in this sense, moreover, we find it generally used by ancient writers. As, however, most of the rules relating to the composition of matter intended for delivery are equally applicable to other kinds of writing, in the course of time the meaning of the term was naturally extended; so that even as early as in the age of Aristotle it was used with reference to productions not designed for public recitation. At the present day, Rhetoric, in its widest acceptation comprehends all prose composition; and it is with this signification we here use the term. . . . The ancients thought it necessary for one who would master this subject to study with care everything connected with the great object proposed, the conviction of the hearer or reader; and with this view some rhetoricians introduced into their system Treatises on Law, Morals, Politics, &c., on the ground that no one could write or speak well on these subjects without properly understanding them. . . . This, however, is assuming too much. . . . a knowledge of the subject of which the orator or essayist is to treat, constitutes no part of the art of Rhetoric, though essential to its successful employment. (149–52)

Quackenbos displays a characteristic stance in nineteenth-century theory toward the classical tradition—a desire to align the modern discipline with the the traditional authority of the "ancients" and to co-opt principles and attitudes from classical theory in a highly selective manner. An understanding of the self-consciousness of this selective dependence on the classical tradition is important to an acknowledgment of the highly synthetic dynamic of nineteenth-century methodology, a methodology that was the consequence of the formal dependence of nineteenth-century theory on both the innovative and the reinscriptive consequences of the New Rhetoric. The unique theoretical characteristic of nineteenth-century theory was this synthetic method, this characteristic tendency to integrate major principles from the epistemological, belletristic, and classical traditions into a new theoretical hybrid that, while substantially derivative, was unprecedented in its combination of elements. In a revealing summary of the many invocations that nineteenth-century theory made to the classical tradition and the commitments of the New Rhetoric, Welsh provides a litany of the ambitions of a "complete rhetoric," a litany that in and of itself embodies the elaboration of the New Rhetoric that was the project of the nineteenth-century tradition:

> To exercise the imagination and improve the taste, with their attendant happy effects on life, by bringing into view the chief beauties that ought to be imitated and the leading defects that ought to be shunned; to unlearn bad habits; to substitute the best models for the worst of the indifferent; to cultivate accurate thinking, as well as accurate speaking, by the careful practice of putting our sentiments into words according to law; to enable the person of brain and emotion to put himself in communication with the minds and hearts of others under the most favorable circumstances; to guide and develop; to shorten the time and the uncertainty of walking in the dark; such are the utilities, subjective and objective, on which we rest the dignity and merit of the present study. Let us define Rhetoric, therefore, as *the art of enabling those who have something to say, to say it to the best advantage.* (5)

*An Oration is a discourse intended for public delivery, and written in a
style adapted thereto. At the present time, this term is generally applied
to discourses appropriate to some important or solemn occasion. . . . It
is a speech of an elevated character.*

G. P. Quackenbos, *Advanced Course of Composition and Rhetoric*

*Besides a perfect mastery of his subject, he [the orator] must have a
deep and sustained interest in what he is saying. He must believe that
what he is uttering is what others ought to hear and take to heart. . . .
Whatever be the subject, he must have his points fixed and always visible, his statements almost laboriously distinct, the strain of the discourse unbroken; and by all the power of the imagination he possesses,
he must try to keep up a gentle, steady, cheering flame from the opening to the close.*

Edward T. Channing, *Lectures Read to the Seniors in Harvard College*

*In no point is public sentiment more united than in this, that the use-
fulness of one whose main business is public speaking, depends greatly
on an impressive elocution. This taste is not peculiar to the learned or
the ignorant; it is the taste of all men.*

Ebenezer Porter, *Analysis of the Principles of Rhetorical Delivery*

4

The Art of Oratory

The nineteenth-century rhetorical tradition in North America displayed a steadfast allegiance to the vision of rhetorical practice promoted by the New Rhetoric. In the theoretical climate of nineteenth-century theory, competence in the various rhetorical arts was equated with the acquisition of an overall rhetorical sensibility. Deploying the principle advocated by Campbell and Blair that rhetoric was to be understood as the general study of discourse, the nineteenth-century tradition defined the rhetorical arts on the basis of what types of expertise embody a complete understanding of "the art of efficient communication" (A. S. Hill, *Principles* v). Oratory, prose composition, and literary analysis were designated as the significant rhetorical arts during this century, and the nineteenth-century disciplines in both the United States and Anglo-Canada adhered to the notion that a rhetorical education was not complete until mastery of these arts had been achieved through practice, performance, and the study of theory.

Like their eighteenth-century predecessors, nineteenth-century theorists assumed that different modes of expression relied on those natural laws and processes that constrain the dynamics of the mental faculties and predispose intellectual and emotional response to discourse. Deriving the governing principles of the rhetorical arts from the philosophy of rhetoric, nineteenth-century rhetoricians stressed *adaptation,* or the appropriate application of fundamental rhetorical principles to specific uses, as the key to developing the arts of rhetoric. As a consequence, nineteenth-century explications of the rhetorical arts stood in an intimate and self-conscious

Nineteenth-Century Rhetoric

relationship to the authority of formal theory. Treatments of the principles of oratory, composition, and literary analysis drew on a synthesis of epistemological, belletristic, and classical principles. This dependence on major theoretical elements of the New Rhetoric in treatments of the rhetorical arts is another significant instance of how the nineteenth-century tradition in North America extended and transformed the theoretical force of the late eighteenth-century tradition.

In introducing his treatise on homiletics, *A Treatise on the Preparation and Delivery of Sermons,* John A. Broadus explains the importance of the study of rhetoric to the preacher: "In respect of skill, preaching is an *art;* and while art cannot create the requisite powers of mind or body, nor supply their place if really absent, it can develop and improve them, and aid in using them to the best advantage. To gain skill, then, is the object of rhetorical studies, skill in the construction and in the delivery of discourse" (25). Broadus views homiletics as a "branch of rhetoric; he recommends the study of what he calls rhetorical "principles," because "those fundamental principles which have their basis in human nature are of course the same in both cases, and this being so, it seems clear that we must regard homiletics as rhetoric applied to this particular kind of speaking" (30).[1]

Broadus's insistence on the importance of the formal study of rhetoric is typical of nineteenth-century theorists' tendency to define oratory as an art dependent on the application of fundamental rhetorical principles to oral modes and contexts. As Edward T. Channing observes in his discussion "General View of Rhetoric," in *Lectures Read to the Seniors in Harvard College,* "A thorough preparation for an orator,—that is of one who is to deliver orations of whatever kind,—includes a large amount of instruction that will do equally well for every other class of speakers and writers" (29).

Supporting a view of rhetoric as a comprehensive art of communication that formalizes all the principles that a good writer or speaker must understand and utilize, nineteenth-century rhetoricians treated the art of oratory by establishing the relevance of general philosophical principles to the aims and methods of oral discourse. Elements of the art of oratory were

114

defined primarily in discussions of the nature and strategies of argumentation and persuasion and the characteristic nature and conduct of oratory as
a genre of discourse. The theoretical disposition of such discussions was
synthetic: general aims and inventional techniques of oratory were defined
in epistemological terms (with reference to laws of the mind and the
dictates of human nature); neoclassical views influenced discussions of
arrangement, delivery, the divisions of oratory, and the qualifications of
the orator; and belletristic values regarding the importance of the imagination and taste influenced characterizations of oratorical style and the importance of oratory as a genre.

Epistemological Foundations of Oratory in Argumentation and Persuasion

Throughout most of the nineteenth century, theoretical discussions
of the principles of oratory were predisposed by the assumption that the
aims of oral discourse can be understood in terms of epistemological
dynamics: the requisite nature of any speech is constrained by whether the
orator seeks to influence the understanding, move the will, or engage the
passions. Nineteenth-century rhetoricians equated gaining "mastery over
minds" through eloquence with the use of argumentative and persuasive
strategies that the orator employs "to produce a change in the sentiments
and conduct of other men" (Theremin 69). In *Philosophy of Rhetoric* John
Bascom expresses the popular nineteenth-century view of public speaking
as a mode of rhetoric that influences "action and opinion" by constraining
the mind through persuasion and argument:

> The means and method appropriate [to oratory] are determined by
> this practical end of immediate influence. . . . Thoughts and emo-
> tions are considered only in their bearing on the proposed action,
> and are made, with light and heat, to converge at this point as a
> perfect focus. The mind must be convinced, but convinced of the
> value and practicability of the action proposed; the heart must be

aroused, but aroused to the motives of duty, profit, and pleasure which press upon it. By true oratory the whole soul is thrown into a single current, setting outward effort,—this effort becoming more protracted and thorough in proportion to the deep inclusive character of the desired end. The highest oratory can only be called forth when the energies of the whole nature, with its fundamental forces are to be aroused. (36–37)

Bascom's assumption that oratory functions under epistemological constraints reveals how powerfully theories of "natural intellection" influenced nineteenth-century treatments of the fundamentals of public speaking. Bascom assumes that the procedures and forms of rhetoric must be compatible with the principal channels of perception and action in the mind. This point of view affirms key tenets of the epistemological rationale for rhetoric: interaction of the faculties of the understanding and the passions is necessary to move the will ("thought and emotions considered in their bearing on the proposed action"); evidence must be presented in common-sensical forms or in ways that invite the mind to infer plausibility or probability by drawing on experience ("the mind must be convinced of the value and practicability of the action proposed"); and emotional impressions enhance the intelligibility of ideas through liveliness and sympathy ("the emotion has sprung up everywhere in the track of truth"). In affirming these principles, nineteenth-century accounts of the dynamics of oratory presume the founding philosophical assumptions of the New Rhetoric: first, that ideas develop in the mind as a consequence of the associative nature of mental activities; and second, that the mental processes are linked together in an animated, interdependent chain. An insistence on founding the principles of oratory on such laws of the mind was a typical stance in nineteenth-century treatments of oratory, a stance that affirmed one of the most characteristic claims of nineteenth-century theory: the rhetorician must understand the dynamics of the faculties in order to compose discourse that will have immediate influence over the minds of the audience.

Nineteenth-century theorists consistently stressed that the successful orator utilizes a combination or sequence of argumentative and persuasive strategies to appeal to the "mental condition" of the audience. In *The Princeton Text Book in Rhetoric* (1859) M. B. Hope observes that when presenting an argument, the orator must keep in mind that the listener is not simply guided by "conviction" (commonsense notions derived from the function of the understanding) but is also affected in the process of judgment by the passions: "the passions in the generic sense of the word, i.e., as descriptive of the emotional and active principles of our nature,—are the normal motors of the will. . . . To induce action—i.e., to move the will— the orator must bring some end into view, adapted to secure attention. The end of action, apprehended as desirable, is its only motive" (77). Day stresses the importance of addressing "the feelings and affections as a distinct class of mental phenomena" in the composition of "funeral and triumphal" orations and "a considerable part of pulpit oratory," modes of oratory which are dependent on excitation (*Elements* 133–50). Similarly, A. S. Hill characterizes species of forensic oratory in terms of how each appeals to the understanding:

> Argument, like exposition, addresses the understanding; but there is an important difference between the two. Exposition achieves its purposes if it makes the persons addressed understand what is said; argument achieves its purpose if it makes them believe that what is maintained is true; exposition aims at explaining, argument at convincing. The difference between an argument and an exposition may be shown by a comparison between the address of an advocate to the jury and the charge of the judge. The advocate tries to convince the jury that his client has the right on his side; the judge, if he has the truly judicial spirit, tries to make the jury understand the question at issue exactly as it is. (*Principles* 327)

These treatments of oratory followed the lead of the New Rhetoric by assuming that the aims of particular types of oratory are linked necessarily to predominant epistemological appeals. Skill in public speaking was equated with a command over the specialized modes of appealing to the mind that are implicit in argumentation and persuasion. Argumentation, or appeal to the understanding, is used when decisions, conclusions, or changes in opinion are sought. Persuasion, or appeal to the will, is used when it is appropriate to move the feelings, as an end in itself or as a means of engaging the will. Because nineteenth-century theorists presupposed that the aims and methods of oratory depend on the rhetorical processes of argumentation and persuasion, their analyses of oratorical invention coincided with explications of the epistemological foundations and inventional obligations of argumentative and persuasive discourse.

Argumentation

Nineteenth-century rhetorical treatises typically treated argumentation in terms of how appeals to the understanding are best made through the materials and form of arguments (written and oral). This theoretical orientation was a dominant influence on North American treatments of argument, which were indebted particularly to Whately's analysis of argument in *Elements of Rhetoric*. Whately offers his outline of the principles of argumentation as a general account of "compositions . . . of the Argumentative kind" He treats the following issues as major elements of argumentation: the classes of arguments suited to conviction (arguments from cause to effect; arguments from sign, example, and testimony); the nature of presumptions and the identification of burden of proof; the function of refutation; the arrangement of arguments for best effect; and the conduct of arguments (see chapter 1). Whately formulates the rules of argumentation as general maxims and verifies these with references to a variety of rhetorical situations. Frequent references to the "argumentative writer" and to the circumstances of formal speaking (e.g., the courtroom, the parliament, and the pulpit) confirm that Whately intends his explication of the nature of conviction and the formal structure of argument to be viewed as general guidance for preparing oral as well as written arguments (111). For example, Whately defines the aims of conviction in terms of general epistemological aims (satisfaction to a candid mind, instruction, and the compelling of assent), yet he cautions that one of the most typical limitations of "persons unaccustomed to writing or discussion" is an inability to justify appeals to the understanding with sound reasoning (111–12). Similarly, in discussing the arrangement of types of arguments, Whately defines a rhetorical dictum by analyzing the response of an audience:

> When Arguments of each of two formerly-mentioned classes are employed arguments from example and arguments from cause to effect, those from Cause to Effect (Antecedent-probability) have usually the precedence. . . . Men are apt to listen with prejudice to the Arguments adduced to prove anything which appears *abstractly* improbable . . . and this prejudice is to removed by the Argument from Cause to Effect, which thus prepares the way for the reception of the other arguments. (137)

Nineteenth-century theorists upheld the view of the New Rhetoric that rhetorical principles address the invention and conduct of all forms of discourse; as a consequence, they adopted Whately's methodological habit of defining the "rules" of argument and illustrating such principles with references to effective speeches or written arguments. The invention of argumentative oratory was covered implicitly in discussions of how the "mental capacities" are to be engaged in discourse (oral and written) that addresses itself to the understanding. Alexander Bain's treatment of argument in *English Composition and Rhetoric* (1866) is indicative of the typical nineteenth-century method of offering explications of the scientific foundations of argument in which the techniques of argumentative oratory are implied. Bain discusses the principles of argumentative reasoning under topics standard in nineteenth-century theory by midcentury: "deductive arguments, inductive arguments, and arguments from Analogy" (classes of arguments), "Number and Order of Arguments," "Refutation or Reply," and "Burden of Proof" (187–99).[2] Bain presents his discussion of these particular issues as a general account of how "we may establish truth, and bring home conviction to a rational mind," yet frequent references to how "hearers" evaluate proof leave little doubt that Bain intends his explanation as a guide to the composition of all argumentative modes, including the oration. For example, Bain's analysis of refutation proceeds from a theoretical definition of the principle of "Disproof" and cites effective orations as illustrations:

> The mode of refuting a general affirmation is to produce excep-
> tions, or other admitted principles contradicting it. The refutation
> is effective in proportion as these incompatible facts and principles
> are well known and understood. . . . Earl Montague's defence of
> the Court of the Lord High Steward for trying Peers is a good ex-
> ample of rebutting a general charge by particulars. . . . Probably
> the best way of dealing with a mystifying and confused opponent
> is to select a specimen of his arguments for a full and minute ex-
> posure. In controversial warfare, opponents of this kind are not
> uncommon; and there are a few illustrious examples of the method
> of replying to them. We may adduce Locke's controversy with
> Stillingfleet; Hobbes's defence of his theory of the will against
> Bishop Bramhall; and, in our time, the reply of Robert Hall King-
> horn on the subject of "Free Communion." (196)

Henry N. Day's treatment of argument also establishes the nature of argumentative oratory by implication. In this discussion of the function of sign and example in "a priori reasoning," Day defines a principle of rhetorical logic and proceeds to apply that rule to the argumentative structure of political oratory:

> What is often called *a priori* reasoning not unfrequently includes
> in itself not only an antecedent probability argument, but also a
> sign, or an example. From the falling of the barometer, we infer *a
> priori* that there will be a change of the weather; not because we
> suppose the fall of the mercury to be the cause of the change. We
> in this case, in truth, first argue by a sign, to the existence of a
> cause, and then by an antecedent probability argument, to its ef-
> fect, viz: a change of the weather. . . . Lord Chatham in his
> speech "on removing the troops from Boston," argues the contin-
> ued and determined resistance of the Americans to an arbitrary
> system of taxation from the spirit of liberty which animated them
> in common with all Englishmen; and the existence of this spirit is

proved by *an example*—the proceedings of the General Congress
at Philadelphia. This would ordinarily be called an *a priori* argument, inasmuch as the force of it rests mainly on the existing
cause to produce the continued resistance. But an "example,"
which is of the nature of an *a posteriori* argument, is introduced
to prove the existence of the cause, and the intermediate step of
the argument, the cause itself, is not expressed but only implied.
(*Elements* 112)

Day's assessment of Chatham's speech as a successful instance of
a priori reasoning draws its theoretical authority from the epistemological
principle that argumentative strategies must engage the functions of the
understanding. "The validity of this species of proof rests ultimately on
the principle, received unhesitatingly by every mind, that every effect
presupposes a cause and an occasion its operating" (103). Like Bain and
Whately, Day discusses the strategies of argument in terms of the philosophical principles on which rhetorical processes rely. This epistemological
orientation represents the major philosophical influence on both Day's
and Whately's treatments of argumentation, as well as the rationale that
predisposed nineteenth-century rhetoricians to define the process of argumentation in terms of a standardized set of general principles intended as
guidelines for the invention of the argumentative oration as well as the
argumentative treatise. These guideline may be summarized as follows:

—The theme of an argument must be expressed in a logical proposition which embodies the truth that is to be established in the
  hearer's mind.
—The determination of presumption or burden of proof is necessary before proofs can be selected.
—Proofs should be either analytic or empirical (drawn from experience, antecedent probability [cause and effect], sign, and testimony).
—Arrangement of arguments should rely on the placement of
  "strong" arguments, analytic proofs, and antecedent probability
  before arguments from sign and testimony.

—Refutation should be used to overthrow opposing arguments and refute objections but should never be placed to make the first or last impression.[3]

The highly normative status of these guidelines is confirmed by the fact that homiletic treatises, which extrapolated specific rules for preaching from general rhetorical principles, typically identified these same topics in discussions of how the preacher can best use argument to stir the conscience. In explaining argumentation as one of the major "materials" of preaching, Broadus addresses topics that parallel those stressed in popular rhetoric manuals: "1. Preliminaries to Argument—Burden of Proof, Etc. 2. Principal Varieties of Argument. A. A Priori. B. From Testimony. C. Induction. D. From Analogy. E. Deduction from Established Truths. F. Certain Forms of Argument 3. Refutation. 4. Order of Arguments. 5. General Suggestions as to Argument" (*Treatise* 158).

The homogeneity between treatments of argument in homiletic treatises and popular general rhetorics of the period reflects the consistency with which nineteenth-century rhetoricians treated the invention of argumentative oratory as a relatively straightforward matter of applying fundamental principles regarding the formation of a plausible proposition and the selection and management of proofs or evidence.[4]

Persuasion

Nineteenth-century treatments of persuasion are similar to discussions of argumentation in that a substantial portion of the analysis of the principles of persuasion was devoted to the explication of mental processes. Persuasion was defined as having "special reference to the Will and Conscience . . . that object being, to secure an immediate effect, more or less permanent, upon the will and conduct—to lead to present and personal action" (Hunt 278). However, analyses of persuasion typically differed from treatments of argumentation in that more explicit attention was given to outlining how the orator is to adapt substance, form, and manner to best move the will. Theoretically dependent on the epistemological view of persuasion outlined by Campbell, Blair, and Whately, nineteenth-century rhetoricians associated persuasion more exclusively with the venues of "impassioned" oratory and discussed it primarily in terms of the orator's obligation to stimulate the passions and engage the will by appealing to the "active principles" of human nature. A. S. Hill takes this approach in his analysis of how persuasion differs from argumentation: "persuasion . . . includes all those processes that make the persons addressed willing to be convinced or ready to carry conviction into action" (*Principles* 386). Hill's treatment of the "processes" of persuasion confirms the importance of strategies that engage the emotions: (1) the creation of sympathy through direct impressions on the imagination and sincerity; (2) knowledge of the persons addressed; and (3) adaptation of what is said to the character and the circumstances of the persons addressed (394–98).[5] Like most nineteenth-century treatments of persuasion, Hill's discussion of persuasive strategies affirms the fundamental epistemological principle of Whately and Blair's treatments—the faculties must be engaged in particular ways and in a set sequence.

> Persuasion . . . is addressed to the feelings, its methods must be those which lead to success in reaching the feelings. . . . What we may do is to express our own feeling and trust to the contagion of sympathy; or we may take our readers or hearers to the sources of feeling and thus bring them, as far as is possible, under the influence by which we have ourselves been moved. . . . "The heart is commonly reached, not through the reason, but through the imagination, by means of direct impression, by the testimony of facts and events, by history, by description." (394)

Hill's analysis identifies those methods generally treated in discussions of how persuasion must function; however, his outline does not offer the elaborate philosophical analysis of human motives standard in Campbell and Whately's analysis of persuasion. Whately discusses these motives as those "active principles" that affect the passions (184–86). Hill's highly condensed and abbreviated treatment of the philosophy of persuasion is more typical of the approach offered in treatises appearing after 1880. Texts circulating from 1850 through the 1880s, such as M. B. Hope's *Princeton Text Book in Rhetoric* (1859), Day's *Elements* (1866), Bain's *English Composition and Rhetoric* (1866), and David. J. Hill's *Science of Rhetoric* (1877), offered treatments of the "psychology" of persuasion that imitated Campbell and Whately's extensive analyses of the emotions and how to produce them.[6] David J. Hill's explanation of how the feelings are to be engaged demonstrates how thoroughly the epistemological grounds of persuasion were explained in treatises that recapitulated the natural laws governing the emotions:

> We may excite a feeling of a certain kind by presenting the stimulating objects to the mind. To arouse the emotion of beauty, we must present a beautiful object; to excite pity, we must present a scene or person that will call it forth. Several circumstances are specially adapted to the production of feeling. (1) Probability. . . . (2) Verisimilitude. . . . (3) Ideal Presence. . . . imaginative realization of relations. . . . (4) Minute Details. . . . (5) Proximity of Time. . . . (6) Proximity of Place. . . . (7) Personal Relation. . . . (8). Indirectness. . . . (9) General Importance. . . . (10) Connection with the Consequences. (55–59)

Such accounts of the topoi of persuasion are usually offered in conjunction with an analysis of characteristic emotional responses, or the "active principles tributary to persuasion." These active principles of the emotions are defined as the affections, the desires, self-love, and the moral faculty (or disposition toward the good). Such "sentiments" influence the will and, as such, constitute those "motives" that the orator must engage in order to move an audience to action.

Nineteenth-century treatments of the motives and the conditions of persuasion indicate the degree to which nineteenth-century theorists followed the lead of the New Rhetoricians in addressing the traditional principles of pathos and ethos as epistemological issues. Campbell, Blair, and

Oratory

Whately stress that "knowledge of those addressed" is crucial to inspiring sympathy, or the sensation of felt experience on which persuasion relies. The epistemological orientation of nineteenth-century definitions of persuasion implicitly addressed pathos as a dynamic to which all strategies of persuasion are committed. Bain's discussion of "oratorical persuasion" illustrates this epistemological interpretation of the importance of appealing to the emotions:

> Men are variously moved. Outward compulsion may determine their conduct. As free beings, they follow their natural activity, their sense of good and evil, their passionate excitement, and the lead of others by imitation and sympathy. Oratorical persuasion endeavors to obtain the co-operation of these free impulses for some proposed line of conduct, by so presenting it in language as to make it coincide with them. (*English Composition* [1866] 171)

Bain assumes that emotions are natural manifestations of mental life; the orator must appeal to the faculties (in this case, the passions) in ways that engage the hearers' experiential and intuitive responses. Only knowledge of the emotional responses of the audience can ensure the success of this type of appeal; consequently, knowledge of the persons addressed was a fundamental principle of persuasion. Discussion of this principle was prominent in both condensed and elaborate analyses of the foundations of persuasive oratory. The advice offered to the orator stresses what many nineteenth-century theorists referred to as the "Principle of Adaptation," or the ability "to read and adapt to human nature."[7]

Another principle of persuasion, *ethos,* or the speaker's impression, was viewed as essential to the creation of sympathy. Discussed under headings such as "Sympathy as An Instrument of Power in Eloquence" and "Qualifications for an Orator," ethos was treated as yet another crucial strategy for engaging the hearers' emotions (Hope 102; De Mille 504). Hope's explanation of how ethos affects the persuasive speech stresses its role in securing the attention of those emotions that motivate the will. Citing the principle that "an orator can seldom speak better than he is," Hope examines what classical rhetoricians discussed as "sincerity" from a distinctly epistemological perspective:

> There are means by which he the orator establishes a relation with his audience, embracing what we term collectively as Sympathy; and by which, the will, of an audience is controlled, through their passions, without the logical apprehension of any other ground for such control, than its felt *presence, in the orator*. This is a law of human nature. . . . A rational ground for this familiar law, may be found, no doubt, in the obvious consideration, that whatever grounds for emotion an orator may profess to furnish *by means of his discourse,* they are fatally discredited by the *natural signs of emotion* in himself. . . . This great principle or law, ruling in the propagation of passion,—i.e. the power of eloquence,—is the true foundation for the requisition . . . that in order to [achieve] the fullest effect of an orator upon his audience, he must possess their unqualified confidence. (102–4)

Nineteenth-century discussions of the function of the speaker's impression reiterated classical wisdom regarding ethos by pointing out that it is wise to appear friendly and honest when trying to persuade; however, the greater proportion of theoretical attention was awarded to warning the orator that an artificial impression blocks emotional dynamics that must exist between speaker and hearers if persuasion is to be achieved. When the speaker displays a thorough understanding of the subject and emotional involvement in the issue, this "natural channel of truth" is enhanced (Genung, *Working Principles* 656).

A concern for the function of ethos in facilitating communication along this "natural channel " is indicative of nineteenth-century views of the nature of persuasive oratory. Like all rhetorical processes, persuasion relies on the engagement of the faculties in an interactive chain through which "truth" is recognized and acknowledged. Fairly uniform in their reiteration of Whately's formalization of the epistemological foundations of persuasion, nineteenth-century treatments of persuasion offered a standard set of guidelines to the orator regarding the invention of speeches that aim to influence action and beliefs:

—Persuasion depends primarily on moving the will by engaging the passions. Appeal to the understanding is also needed: the mind has to be assured that the proposed object is possible as well as desirable.

—In order that the will be engaged and the passions addressed, the orator must have an understanding of the sentiments that move human nature and how these are produced, including the major sentiments and motives (appetites, affections, self-love, moral-faculty) and the circumstances of producing the sentiments (probability, plausibility, proximity of place and time, personal relation, importance, connection with the consequences).

—The orator must have knowledge of the persons addressed in order to identify those motives that will move the group to action or by which the group will identify themselves.

—The orator who would persuade must feel deeply.

—Direct impressions and vivid detail engage the imagination and thus excite the feelings.[8]

Arrangement

Nineteenth-century theories of persuasion and argumentation were dominated by a theoretical interest in how rhetorical processes can best appeal to those aspects of human nature that govern intellectual and emotional response. This epistemological point of view also influenced nineteenth-century theories of arrangement and the conduct of oratory, discussions that also adhered to a host of prominent classical assumptions. The advice typically offered in North American treatises regarding the arrangement of a speech reiterated the approach of the New Rhetoricians to this canon: neoclassical principles regarding the structure of the oration were reviewed with an emphasis on how arrangement facilitates the dynamics of the faculties. Conventional nineteenth-century methods of treating arrangement were influenced significantly by the approaches of Blair and Whately. Blair defines the "natural constituent parts of a regular Oration" as the exordium, the division, the narration, the argument, the pathetic, and the conclusion. His neo-Ciceronian analysis of the conduct of discourse stresses fundamental rules of arrangement and how these are to be applied to various types of oratory (see chapter 1). Whately also relies on a recapitulation of classical wisdom in his discussion of argumentative introductions and conclusions; however, his analysis pertains to the conduct of argumentative discourse in general and not to the structure of oratory alone. Both Blair and Whately comment on the proper arrangement of arguments, but their methods of handling this topic differ: Blair treats the arrangement of arguments in his general discussion of arrangement; Whately treats this issue along with analyses of argumentative introductions and conclusions in his discussion of conviction. Nineteenth-century treatments of arrangement depended on the theoretical and methodological examples of both Blair and Whately. Typically relying on a combination of systems for treating arrangement, nineteenth-century theorists offered advice regarding oratorical arrangement under more than one heading. Under discussions of the conduct of discourse, nineteenth-century rhetoricians imitated Blair's neoclassical approach of outlining each part of the oration and explaining how to conduct each division in specific types of oratory. In imitation of Whately's method, nineteenth-century theorists treated the arrangement of arguments and the conduct of argumentative introductions and conclusions under discussions of argumentation; these discussions promoted Whately's assumption that advice regarding the order of argumentative elements is applicable to both oral and written arguments. Although neoclassical principles were fundamental to the theoretical core of these discussions, nineteenth-century rhetoricians gave priority to the epistemological principle that the proper arrangement of discourse can enhance intellectual and emotional response.

Blair's neo-Ciceronian scheme provided the theoretical model for discussions of arrangement in popular general rhetorics such as G. P. Quackenbos's *Advanced Course of Composition and Rhetoric,* M. B. Hope's *Princeton Text Book in Rhetoric,* and David J. Hill's *Elements of*

Oratory

Rhetoric and Composition. Oratorical arrangement was treated under a variety of headings including "Of the Parts of a Discourse" and "The Plan and Division of an Oration" (Quackenbos 386). Adherence to the Blairian six-part model of arrangement was characteristic of most North American treatises circulating between 1840 and 1870. In *A Practical System of Rhetoric* Newman summarizes Blair's account of arrangement in his recommendation that a "performance" be arranged in terms of a formal introduction, statement of the subject, a plan or division, and the conclusion of reasoning (30–36). Similarly, Quackenbos, who presumes that an argumentative thesis "intended for delivery, or written in suitable style for that purpose becomes an oration," defines the divisions of the oration as "the Exordium or Introduction, the Division, the Statement, the Reasoning, the Appeal to the Feelings, and the Peroration" (389). Like the majority of nineteenth-century theorists who affirmed the six-part scheme, Newman and Quackenbos reiterate a number of traditional assumptions regarding the requisite nature of each division:

—The function of the introduction is to make a good impression, engage the hearer's attention, and enlist interest in the subject.
—The function of the division is to make known the method that is to be pursued and announce the topics or "heads" to be discussed.
—The function of the statement or narration is to set out the facts of the case or issue in clear and forcible terms.
—The function of the reasoning or argument is to present those arguments that will induce conviction. Arguments should be treated distinctly; strong arguments should be arranged first and last for greatest effect.
—The function of the appeal to the feelings is to excite feelings through the skillful management of the emotions.
—The function of the peroration or conclusion is to sum up the argument and leave a forceful impression on the hearers' minds. The peroration should be brief, clear, definite, and full of feeling.

Treatises circulating after 1870 reiterated these same principles but tended to define the disposition of the oration in terms of three or four fundamental units: "the Exordium, the Discussion, and the Conclusion"; or "the Introduction, the Statement, the Main Discourse, and the Conclusion" (David J. Hill, *Elements* 190–91; Kellog, 304–5). The abbreviated scheme, popularized by Day, David J. Hill, Brainerd Kellog, and A. S. Hill among others, reorganized the six divisions into fewer, more complex units while maintaining a traditional overview of what arrangement must achieve. In his discussion of the "parts of a composition," David. J. Hill notes that "the ancient rhetoricians regarded an oration as having six essential parts. . . . this division is mechanical and arbitrary. The more natural and fully conformed to the subject-matter and the purpose the division is, the better. Sometimes no exordium is needed. Often a formal division is undesirable. A statement is occasionally unnecessary. . . . An appeal to the feelings is sometimes wholly improper" (*Elements* 17).

Hill argues that since not all of the divisions are appropriate to every subject or occasion, a more "usual" scheme for arrangement is an introduction, a discussion, and a conclusion:

> The usual parts of a composition are three: (1) *There should be an Introduction*. This . . . is usually required to bring the discussion into connection with the occasion. (2) *There must be a discussion*. By this is meant that we cannot establish anything in the mind of another without using facts, illustrations, or arguments to assist us. (3) *There must be a conclusion*. When we invite others to accompany us in our thoughts, we are under an obligation to conduct them to some new state of mind. Unless there is some *end* to be attained, there is no use of writing or speaking. We should always have some definite state of mind in view to which everything should tend. (16–17)

The systematic innovation that Hill's treatment represents can be traced to two theoretical precedents: Blair's pronouncement that strict adherence to the six-part scheme can often be unsuitable and unnatural (e.g., formal introductions are not always needed; the "division" and the "pathetic" are not necessarily appropriate to every speech) and Whately's view that argumentative discourse (oral or written) consists of three major parts, the introduction, the argument, and the conclusion.[9] Hill's stipulation that arrangement should reflect the "natural" status of the subject echoes Blair's insistence that arrangement should embody a "natural train of Speaking" and not adhere to "pedantic and stiff" procedures (157); the formalization of three components as the "usual" structure of discourse recalls Whately's method of dealing with arrangement in terms of disposition suitable to both oral and written discourse.

The three-part scheme was promoted by Hill and others because it represented a more versatile approach to arrangement. Even theorists who called attention to classical principles in their explanations of arrangement plans favor the abbreviated scheme. De Mille's treatment of arrangement illustrates how nineteenth-century theorists adapted traditional assumptions to the explication of the three-part scheme. Defining the three major divisions as the introduction, the presentation of arguments, and the conclusion, De Mille reviews a number of neoclassical assumptions in his discussion of the introduction and the conclusion:

> The introduction in oratory is called the exordium. It is of more importance here than in any branch of composition, and requires more careful handling. Its object may be stated as follows: To prepare the hearer to listen readily to what is to be said by seeking to gain his good-will, his attention, and the desire for further information. . . . The introduction may serve to prepare the mind for that which is to follow. . . . In oratory the conclusion is called the peroration. Its importance here is greater than in any other department of literature. The following are the leading characteristics: Ist. A brief summing up of the heads of the arguments. 2d. The speaker enlarges upon some topic that has already been brought forward. . . . 3d. An appeal, exhortation, or other expression of emotion. (369, 376)

Like the majority of nineteenth-century theorists who outlined the shorter arrangement scheme, De Mille collapses the function of division with that of the introduction and reiterates Blair's advice that "the pathetic" is most often a part of the conclusion.[10] De Mille's conspicuous neglect of narration reveals another of the theoretical assumptions underlying the promotion of a three-part arrangement scheme for oratory. Encouraged by Whately's method of treating narration as part of framing the proposition, De Mille relegates "statement of the facts" to the argumentative portion of discourse and elects to treat the conduct of argument within a general analysis of argumentation. The allocation of narration to the "discussion" section of discourse, division to the introduction, and the pathetic to the conclusion (if it appears at all) was conventional by 1880; by then, the three-part scheme of introduction–argument (discussion)–conclusion had become the standard approach to arrangement.[11]

The most important systematic feature of nineteenth-century treatments of arrangement was the conventional formulation of principles of arrangement in discussions of the conduct of discourse (both oral and written) and in discussions of the nature and conduct of conviction and persuasion. In imitation of Whately's treatment of conviction, a number of nineteenth-century rhetoricians discussed arrangement in their analyses of the nature and form of argumentation.[12] Intending such treatments of the conduct of argument as advice applicable to both oral and written arguments, nineteenth-century theorists reiterated a number of maxims regarding the proper order of an argument:

> 1. In proof there are two chief modes [of order]. The ideas are sometimes arranged in an ascending series and go on increasing in strength until the end. . . . 2. Where the strongest argument is still reserved till the last, but the first one presented is of great weight and force, and the weaker ones are introduced in the middle. Here the forcible opening argument is adapted to arrest the attention and impress the mind of reader or hearer at the outset, and then, after the weaker ones have followed, the strongest of all concludes. (De Mille 330–31)

> [A]nalytic proofs precede all others; antecedent probability arguments precede examples and signs. . . . The example, introduced after the antecedent probability argument, will serve both to illus-

trate and also to confirm it. Indeed, in this order, they reflect light on each other. Mr. Burke, in his speech on the Nabob of Arcot's debts, in endeavoring to prove that India had been reduced to a condition of extreme want and wretchedness, first presents the *causes* in operation to produce it; then, *examples* of the operation of those causes; and finally particular *signs* of the fact. (Day, *Elements* 117–18)

Another inquiry relates to the proper place for introducing the refutation of objections. On this point, the general rule is given, that objections should be considered near the commencement of a composition. . . . Often, however, it is necessary to bring forward some views of the subject, preparatory to the examination of objections; in these instances, their refutation is found in the midst, or deferred to the close of the composition. (Newman, *Practical System* 37)

Should a reasoner begin by stating the proposition to be proved or disproved, or should he lead up to it through proof? . . . If the proposition is familiar to the persons addressed, there will usually be some advantage in beginning with what is novel in the proof; for an old conclusion acquires fresh interest when regarded from new point of view or approached by a new path. If the proposition . . . is likely to awaken hostility, it should not be announced until steps have been taken to procure for it a favorable reception. (A. S. Hill, *Principles* 381)

It is desirable to arouse interest by the character of the introduction. Adaptation to its purposes requires that the introduction vary with the character of the composition. A few varieties are enumerated by Dr. Whately: 1) Inquisitive.—The inquisitive introduction aims to arouse interest by asking some question, or showing the importance of what is to be treated; 2) Paradoxical.—When one is perfectly sure of his proofs, it may stimulate interest to state the conclusion to be reached in some paradoxical way, or to represent it as strange or unusual. 3) Corrective. (David J. Hill, *Elements* 129)

If the specific object of the discourse be persuasion proper, it is evident that those motives which lie in perceptions and convictions of the intellect should precede; and when the understanding is properly enlightened and convinced, the way will be open for the addresses to the feelings. (Day, *Elements* 162)

These treatments draw directly from Whately's discussion of the precedence of cause-effect arguments (antecedent-probability), the proper position of the proposition and refutation, the placement of pathetic appeal in an argument, and the varieties of argumentative introductions (see chapter 1). These commonplaces regarding the preferred order of distinct and strong arguments represent those rules normatively defined in nineteenth-century treatments of the arrangement of arguments. For example, Hope is faithful to Whately's treatises in his coverage of "The Comparative Weight of Arguments," "the relative order of the proposition and the proof," and "Place for refutation" (53–66). Day treats these same topics and also offers an analysis "Of Arrangement in Persuasion," a discussion in which he reiterates Whately's point that impassioned appeal should be made only after the understanding of the hearers has been properly satisfied (116–19, 163). A. S. Hill's analysis of "general rules for arrangement" indicates how conventional such summaries of Whately's rules for argumentative arrangement had become by 1878. Hill observes that "the importance of arranging the several parts of an argumentative composition that they may render effective support to one another can hardly be overestimated"; his discussion addresses the position of the proposition, the order of types of arguments, and the proper placement of the refutation (*Principles* 380–85). John F. Genung covers these same principles in *The Working Principles of Rhetoric* under the headings "Order of Arguments," "As Regards Kind of Argument," "As to Relative Strength of Argument," and "Order of Refutation" (639–42). Genung's discussion indicates that Whately's approach to arrangement was still extremely popular at the turn of the century.

Such treatments of arrangement are not strictly neoclassical. By adopting Whately's method, theorists like Hill and Genung broke with Blair's neo-Ciceronian method of treating the conduct of argumentation within a comprehensive discussion of arrangement. Blair imitates the classical approach (exemplified in the *Ad Herennium*) of defining the canon of arrangement in terms of the proper structure of "the whole speech" (introduction, statement of facts, division, proof, refutation, and conclusion) and in terms of the order of "individual arguments" (proposition, reason, proof of the reason, embellishment, and resume).[13] Nineteenth-century theorists covered these two traditional aspects of the canon but did so within a conventional systematic approach that treated the arrangement of arguments and the disposition of the speech and the written treatise as related but distinct topics. Although nineteenth-century treatments of the arrangement of arguments did not adhere strictly to classical systems, these discussions did reinscribe the same classical principles that Whately and Blair affirm in their analyses of the order of arguments:

—Strongest arguments should be placed at the beginning.
—Arguments of medium force and those that are strong only when combined with other proofs should be placed in the middle.
—Refutations should be placed near the beginning of an argument if strong objections have been lodged by the opponent; when this is not the case, refutation should be placed nearer the middle.
—Arguments should be amplified but never extended beyond the bounds of reasonable illustration.
—Arguments should not be too numerous; this can imply that the case is weak.

Nineteenth-century stipulations regarding the proper arrangement of the oration were influenced as well by the epistemological stance that predisposed how the New Rhetoricians defined the aims of arrangement. Blair reiterates traditional advice when he describes the functions of the introduction, yet his rationalization for why it is important to "begin well" is based on the assumption that it is necessary to engage the immediate attention of the understanding by making "a favourable impression at first setting out; when the minds of the hearers, vacant and free, are most disposed to receive any impression easily" (Blair 158–61). Similarly,

Blair's justification for the descriptive function of narration or statement of facts assumes that the understanding cannot be convinced unless presented with details that create "probable" impressions that coincide with the hearer's experience or common sense (175). Nineteenth-century theorists also relied on such combinations of classical principles and epistemological rationalizations in their discussions of the conduct of oratory. Assuming that the logical order of discourse is "organic" or founded on a "rational ground in nature," they stressed the epistemological conditions that allow arrangement to be effective. Hope promotes this view when he explains that the discrete divisions of arrangement are aligned with the dynamics of "the intercourse of mind with mind." Hope argues that all divisions need not be utilized in a "fixed order," but he maintains that "in every complete speech, these elements can be found; and commonly the more clearly they lie in the mind of the speaker, the more conclusive will be their effect upon the mind of the hearer" (134–35). Hope's advice regarding the function of the introduction, the division, the narration, the argument, and the conclusion adheres closely to the Ciceronian slant of Blair's treatment, yet he makes frequent references to requisite appeals to the faculties as he explains the function of discrete divisions. For example, in justifying the importance of establishing good will and confidence in the introduction, Hope claims that the "*precise object and function of the Introduction*" is the engagement of sympathy, which cannot be said to already exist when mind meets mind "on the field of oratory" (136). Hope also observes that an effective narration depends on "verisimilitude or credibility" (establishing clear causal relations) and a powerful appeal to the hearer's imagination by rendering reality in vivid detail (160). This type of commentary, which rationalizes rules of arrangement in terms of the processes of the mind, was a conventional feature of nineteenth-century treatments of the conduct of oratory from the first appearance of indigenous North American texts well into the early decades of the twentieth century.

The most fundamental epistemological assumption governing treatments of the conduct of oratory was the notion that arrangement establishes order, unity, and proportion, which in turn make discourse intelligible.

Oratory

Like their eighteenth-century predecessors, nineteenth-century theorists considered intelligibility to be a quality of discourse created by the presentation of distinct ideas in logical or "natural relations." This type of presentation engages the understanding and "pleases" the imagination by incorporating elements that the imagination recognizes as beautiful, such as order, unity, and proportion. Broadus explains the consequences when the arrangement of a speech fails to conform to "the natural laws of human thinking":

> The audience keep nothing of the discourse; they carry away, in retiring, an indistinct mass of remarks, of assertions, of appeals, which nothing co-ordinates in their memory, and the impressions received are summed up in the saddest criticism that can be made by a devout person who came to hear with attention: I do not know exactly what the preacher preached about. We must strive not merely to render it possible that the people should understand us, but impossible that they should misunderstand. (*Treatise* 245)

In the context of nineteenth-century theory, "hearing with attention" was considered equivalent to an intense state of engagement between the mind of the speaker and the mind of the hearer, a state unfettered by any form of conceptual chaos that would limit the hearer's ability to exercise the powers of the understanding (experience and common sense) and the imagination (recalling the beauty implicit in empirical experience). Combining traditional advice regarding the function of each division of the speech with recommendations on how to engage and intensify this state of "attention," nineteenth-century treatises typically addressed a number of issues regarding the "natural" conduct of oral discourse:

1. Introductions are necessary because hearers have a natural aversion to abruptness and are pleased by a gradual approach that defines what is at issue and what is to be discussed. An effective way to introduce the subject is to establish its relation to a subject or issue already known. This approach engages the mind in its natural inclinations toward analogic, metonymic, and metaphoric thinking.

137

Nineteenth-Century Rhetoric

2. The division should announce the plan of the speech. This plan engages attention by showing the logical character of the speaker's mind and by securing initial belief in the probability of the general conclusion to be pursued by modeling the deductive process. The topics should be announced in similar forms of expression; this parallelism underscores the symmetry of the plan, rendering it more pleasing.

3. The narration prepares hearers for understanding the argument by establishing the reality of absent circumstances. The characterization of circumstances in terms of cause and effect is extremely appealing to the understanding; also, the presentation of sensuous impressions moves the imagination and the emotions and enhances the empirical reality of facts.

4. In the argument, arguments from cause to effect should generally be placed first. These arguments establish a logical principle with which the case in point can be linked through the operation of common sense. The proofs should be arranged so the argument seems to rise in importance. In this way the attention of the understanding is engaged through the appeal to novelty and will continue to be held.

5. Conclusions or perorations work toward unity by gathering the various components of the discourse and moving toward a general conclusion or dynamic emotional moment. Appeals to the affections and the will are the major aims of perorations; consequently, the use of elegant figures is appropriate.

The epistemological constraints implied by these rules of arrangement were understood to influence not only the conduct of oratory but the structure of all rhetorical genres. This points once again to one of the most significant systematic characteristics of nineteenth-century theory: rhetorical processes were examined in terms of fundamental principles assumed to apply to all types of discourse. In keeping with the basic philosophical presumption of nineteenth-century theory that laws of the mind predispose the nature of all rhetoric, the epistemological dynamics governing arrangement were assumed to apply to oratory and prose. This conventional theoretical stance explains why nineteenth-century rhetorical treatises did not treat the arrangement (and invention) of oratory as a unique

138

process. Although several popular rhetorics did analyze the conduct of oral discourse per se, such discussions implied that the six-part or three-part scheme is applicable to both speeches and written treatises. Similarly, nineteenth-century rhetoricians assumed that in outlining the proper disposition of arguments, they were defining rules governing the organization of the parts of all genres of argumentative discourse.[14]

The methodological habit of defining the principles of oratory in terms of rules that apply likewise to the strategies of prose is observable as well in discussions of oratorical style. Assuming that the principles of style are governed by natural laws that dominate strategies of expression in all modes of communication, nineteenth-century rhetoricians treated style in terms of rules intended for both the orator and the writer. Day, for example, makes frequent mention of "the speaker or writer" in his explanations of style; so too does De Mille, whose entire treatment of style is predisposed by the assumption that the principles governing the choice and arrangement of words apply to all classes of literature (15). In introducing his lecture on style, Channing expresses the widely held view that style embodies a "medium of human thought" intrinsic to all forms of rhetoric:

> Since words are representations, however imperfect, of what passes in the mind, and are suggested and warranted by its operations and wants, we need not be surprised that they are used and spoken of as if they were themselves the things they stand for, and that they should be applied as tests or proofs of our thinking clearly and correctly. They are mental expressions; and in studying them we are studying the mind and human nature itself. Hence, for the practical purposes of rhetoric, we insist that a part of our training should direct us to inquire into the full force of words *as such*. (233)

Channing assumes that mastery of an effective style resides in understanding what "readers and hearers" require from "words." Hunt is even more explicit in his claim that the mastery of major qualities of style applies to all "composers": "Though it has been said 'that the Scientist may stop at Clearness; the Orator, at Force; and the Poet, at Beauty,' we shall find that to the model discourser each is essential. No one of them can exist alone in the typical Discourse" (164). Hunt and Channing assume, as did the majority of their nineteenth-century colleagues, that all discourse must evidence "essential" qualities of style and that all those who would communicate must master the abilities to use words clearly, forcefully, and elegantly.

As in treatments of arrangement, nineteenth-century discussions of style synthesized elements of the New Rhetoric: Whately's framework for defining the major qualities of style as perspicuity, energy, and elegance was adapted as a basic formula; Campbell, Whately, and Blair's advice regarding grammatical purity, perspicuity, and force (vivacity) was retained; and Blair's belletristic treatment of ornament and the aesthetic effects of style was reiterated as a basic consideration in the merits of the eloquent style.[15] By 1860, nineteenth-century treatments of style addressed the following issues as a matter of course:

—*Grammatical purity* or *correctness* is maintained through appropriate diction and grammatical sentence structure.
—*Perspicuity* or the clear presentation of thoughts relies on the selection of words, the construction and arrangement of sentences, and the use of clear transitions.
—*Energy* or *force* results in impressive expression and is created through connotation, sentence structure and arrangement, and the use of figures that intensify representation of objects and ideas—metaphor, synecdoche, metonymy, personification, ellipsis, simile, contrast, allegory, allusion, prosopopoeia, apostrophe, interrogation.
—*Elegance* or *beauty* in style is created through selection of subject, diction, arrangement, and use of the figures that appeal to the imagination and the passions.

The usual method employed by authors of general rhetoric manuals (e.g., Day, Hope, Bain, David J. Hill, De Mille, Welsh, A. S. Hill, and Genung) was to define these elements of style and illustrate how they can be achieved in oratory and prose. Welsh's discussion of style in *Complete Rhetoric* illustrates how nineteenth-century rhetoricians co-opted the analysis of oratorical style under treatments of the major qualities of expression pertinent to all modes of discourse. Although Welsh makes frequent mention of "writers" throughout his analysis of "Methods of Expression," he introduces his examination of "Energy" with an anecdote stressing the importance of the forceful style in oratory:

> Sheridan, returning one morning from the meeting of a Parliament, and being asked by a friend for the news of the day, replied that he had enjoyed a laugh over the speeches of Mr. Fox and Lord Stormont, the latter of whom began by declaring in a slow, solemn, nasal monotone, that "when—he—considered—the enormity—and—unconstitutional—tendency—of the measures—just—proposed, he was—hurried—away in a—torrent—of passion—and a whirlwind—of im-pet-u-os-i-ty." Mr. Fox was described as springing to his feet, and beginning, lightning-like, thus: "Mr. Speaker, such is the *magnitude* such the *importance* such the vital *interest* of the question that I cannot implore I cannot but *adjure* the House to come to it with the utmost *calmness* the utmost cool ness the utmost *deliberation*." Each manner is here significant of the real state of the writer's mind: but the one is characterized by immobility, which is death; the other by movement, which is the effect and evidence of life. Both are clear, but the former is crawling, colorless, feeble; the latter is anxious, active, and hence communicative. A thought may be expressed clearly in the highest degree, yet be capable of more effective presentation. . . . Energy may therefore by defined as the force, vigor, or strength of expression, whereby the mind addressed is more or less powerfully influenced or interested. (94)

This particular citation stresses the virtues of Fox's deliberative style and makes the point that the effective political speaker relies as much on stylistic force as do essay writers, historians, and scientific writers. Welsh's reference to an exemplary orator is characteristic of the manner in which nineteenth-century theorists referred to prominent speakers or to extracts from speeches in the course of outlining qualities of style. Likewise, Welsh's citations to exemplary addresses and sermons are combined with references to a number of prose works, including the essays of Carlyle, Macaulay, Arnold, Hume, and Lowell (16–141).[16] Such an effort to address the style of prose texts in combination with an analysis of the decorum of public speaking is indicative of the general tendency of nineteenth-century rhetorical theorists to apply the rules of style to all major modes of rhetoric. Excerpts from a selection of popular rhetoric manuals illustrate how customary it was for nineteenth-century theorists to equate general rules regarding grammatical purity, perspicuity, energy, and beauty with guidelines for the development of stylistic excellence in oratory:

[On "the advantage of short sentences":] The advantage of the short sentence is that it gives to the style simplicity, directness, and rapidity. This is well illustrated in President Lincoln's Gettysburg Address. Here the short sentences, simple and vigorous, lead up to a single long sentence, which sums and completes the whole thought. (Carpenter 94)

[On the detrimental effect of "technicalities on perspicuity":] As specimens of faulty use of technical language, take the following: "God begins his cure by caustics, by incisions and instruments of vexation, to try if the disease that will not yield to the allectives of cordials and perfumes, frictions and baths, may be forced out by deleterics, scarifications, and more salutary, but less pleasing physics" (Jeremy Taylor's Sermons). Such language might be entirely clear and very forcible addressed to a congregation of surgeons, . . . but, certainly, nowhere else. (Hope 181)

[On creating clarity and force through word choice:] If . . . a writer wishes to say something about a class of objects, he will be as well understood if he speaks of the class as if he presents a single object as a sample of the class; but the latter method will be the more likely to arrest attention. . . . [An] example is furnished by the following passages: "In large bodies, the circulation of power must be less vigorous at the extremities. Nature has said it. The Turk cannot govern Egypt and Arabia, and Curdistan, as he governs Thrace; nor has he the same dominion in Crimea as Algiers, which he has at Brusa and Smyrna." (From Burke's *Speech on Conciliation,* qtd. in A. S. Hill, *Principles* 114)

[On the use of apostrophe as a device of energy:] "This figure abounds in the orations of Cicero. Thus in his first against Cataline: ". . . There is a camp formed in Italy at the entrance of Etruria, against the State; our enemies increase daily but we see the commander of the camp and general of the enemies within our walls, in the very senate, contriving some intestine ruin to the State. . . . If now, Cataline, I should order you to be seized and put to death . . . " (Day, *Elements* 278)

[On "poetical beauty" in style:] Bates, in a sermon on "Heaven," thus speaks of the pleasures that spring from knowledge in the regions of the blessed: "When the soul opens its eyes to the clear discoveries of the first truth, in which is no shadow of error, and its breast to the dear and intimate embraces of the supreme good, in which is no mixture of evil, and beyond which nothing remains to be known, nothing to be enjoyed, what a deluge of the purest and sweetest pleasure will overflow it!" (Newman, *Practical System* 304)

Although some theorists provided more of these references than others (e.g., Day and Welsh provide more commentary on oratorical examples and circumstances than do A. S. Hill, Newman, and Quackenbos), nineteenth-century rhetoricians generally made explicit links between the general principles of style and the decorum of public address. Serving to define the epistemological and belletristic rationale for style as well the rules for word choice, the construction and arrangement of sentences, and the use of ornament, treatments of the canon of style offered the student of oratory a primer in the grammatical and rhetorical principles of expression.

Although treatments of style provided the most extensive information on language use typically provided by nineteenth-century rhetoric manuals, it was not uncommon for treatises to provide supplementary information on oratorical style in discussions of the distinctive characteristics of oral discourse as a type of literature or class of belles lettres. (As noted above, it was under such headings that the arrangement of oratory received attention when treated as a distinct topic.) Adopting Blair's belletristic view that discourse can be categorized under numerous generic headings (public speaking, historical writing, philosophical writing, poetry, drama, and comedy), many nineteenth-century rhetoricians discussed oratory as a discourse genre and analyzed its distinguishing characteristics. Discussions of oratorical style presented under headings such as "Kinds of Discourse" and "Orations" were more abstract than illustrative and presumed an understanding of the basic principles of style.[17]

Predisposed theoretically by the assumption that orations are typically either argumentative or persuasive in intention, theorists stressed that certain qualities of style have priority over others depending on how the speaker wishes to affect the hearers' minds: (1) when the orator is appealing to the understanding, perspicuity and force are the most important qualities of style; (2) when appealing to the will, clarity and force must be combined with ornament in order to ensure an appeal to the imagination and the emotions; (3) when vivid impressions must be made, the use of figures that appeal to the imagination and the understanding should be applied. In taking this view of stylistic strategies, nineteenth-century theorists showed an essential faithfulness to the classical principle of adaptation and also reiterated a fundamental premise of the New Rhetoric: the orator should adjust style to the needs of the occasion (chapter 2). Genung expresses this view when he advises the orator to choose stylistic techniques in keeping with the effect sought:

> Oratorical diction . . . may be as plain and familiar as conversation; but also it rises freely with its theme and answers to the glow of emotion or sublimity or imagination that enters into it. The ideal of oratorical style, in its general compass and effect, is called eloquence. . . . Eloquence is not grandiloquence; not synonymous with ambitious or pretentious style. It is simply wise to respond to occasion. When the occasion itself is eloquent, then its best expression may be silence; and it knows when plainness and even bareness of statement works with the occasion to have power

on men. . . . When on occasion eloquence rises into splendor of style, rhythm, imagery, as it has full liberty to do, still its basis of structure and phrase remains as plain as ever. (*Working Principles* 644–55)

In urging the orator to consider the requirements of "occasion," Genung promotes the traditional notion that a consideration of subject matter and the nature of the audience is crucial to the development of an appropriate style. Nineteenth-century characterizations of oratorical style emphasized that the orator must adjust style to argumentative and persuasive intentions as well as to the particular type of hearer addressed:

—The obligation of the preacher is to fix the attention of the congregation and overcome the listeners' inertia and indifference through exhortative appeals to the emotions and the use of figurative impressions that "bestow on what is common the charm of novelty" (Welsh 297).

—In parliamentary debate, in which "all the intellectual forces are put forth," an effective style relies on "great command of language, together with all the resources of wit, humor, and pathos; the sharpness of epigrammatic statement, the vehemence of denunciation, the keenness of the quick retort, sharp repartee, or biting sarcasm" (De Mille 473).

—In judicial oratory, the speaker selects and arranges words to reveal the logical order of reasoning in "the best light " and relies on a style that is "earnest and impressive; but is also temperate and even subdued" (Channing 111).

—When persuading political and public assemblies, the orator must employ a simple style that derives its reserved force from imaginative appeals to the heart and the use of "a language level with the ear of his audience" (Emerson, qtd. in A. S. Hill, *Principles* 398).

In addition to promoting the notion that stylistic techniques should be selected in terms of how best to achieve "power" over the minds of the audience in any given situation, nineteenth-century rhetoricians associated oratory with what was generally defined as the impassioned or eloquent style. Because of the immediacy of oral circumstances and the social and moral significance of the usual subjects of the various forms of public speaking, oratory was defined as that form of discourse which has the most immediate and the most profound effect on the human mind. A number of rhetoricians, including Genung, Newman, Day, Quackenbos, Bascom, and Welsh, pointed to the development of an impressive and tasteful style as one of the obligations of any speaker who hopes to exert powerful ethical influence.[18] This expectation was applied particularly to speakers seeking to persuade individuals to action or profound passions, as in the case of pulpit oratory and address to political and public assemblies.

Nineteenth-century rhetoricians were influenced in their formulations of what constitutes the eloquent style primarily by belletristic assumptions regarding the function of the imagination and the power of taste. Theorists reiterated the notion that eloquence depends on energetic and beautiful impressions that strike at the hearer's most sublime thoughts and sentiments. Hunt observes that the "sacred form" of oratory requires a style that "rises above the sphere of the merely verbal and aesthetic to the higher and broader planes of the mental and spiritual" (299). Quackenbos insists on the importance of the "stately" style in speeches of "elevated character": "The style of an oration should be elevated and forcible. It should not lack ornament; and whatever embellishments are introduced must be of the most exhalted character" (393). Defining the oration as a popular address on "some interesting and important subject," Newman observes that "the style of orations should be elevated and elegant; the forms of expression . . . characterized by force and vivacity. The ornament should be of a high kind—such as ennobles and exalts the subject" (218). Franz Theremin's discussion of style reflects the popular nineteenth-century view that the eloquent style develops naturally when the orator understands the hearers' sentiments and motives:

Oratory

> There may be many forms of expression suitable to the thought,
> and intelligible to the hearer; but there is perhaps still another in
> particular, by which a region of his mind enveloped in darkness
> may be suddenly filled with light, and which at least strikes some
> of the manifold threads of which the web of his feelings consist;
> this latter form the orator should know how to find, and he will be
> enabled to find it by means of that study of his hearers which is
> grounded in an interest for their well being. . . . The style of ex-
> pression which spontaneously associates itself with the silent emo-
> tions of our heart, when they come forth into consciousness, is al-
> ways as noble at it is simple. (169–71)

Theremin's comments reveal the degree to which rhetorical theorists
in this period associated oratory with a profound social and moral calling;
the eloquent style was considered to have a direct effect on the cultivation
of elevated thinking and the higher sentiments. If the orator was to inspire
profound reactions, the eloquent style was a necessity. A measure of the
significance awarded to the eloquent style is the fact that analyses of
oratorical style were frequently conjoined with discussions of how eloquence can be acquired. These discussions, offered under headings such as
"Culture of Eloquence" and "The Forming of Style," subscribed to the
belletristic principle that an eloquent style develops only if the orator
acquires a high standard of taste, appreciates and imitates model orations,
and engages in frequent practice (Hope 112; Quackenbos 311). In his
discussion of how the speaker can develop a style suited to the exhibition
of "high and pure associations," Day outlines a typical set of rules regarding
the acquisition of the eloquent style. Day's advice is conventional in two
respects: he reiterates the belletristic assumption that taste influences the
orator's ability to generate the "right sentiments," and he reasserts the
traditional precept that imitation and practice are fundamental to the development of eloquence in expression: "In the acquisition of this property of
style . . . three means are essential; First, mental culture; Secondly, study
of art, including both its principles and its exemplification in models; and
Thirdly, exercise with judicious criticisms" (*Elements* 289). Day's rules

reiterate Blair's formula for improving in eloquence: good sense, knowledge, industry, study of models, and practice (226–45). This basic formula was recommended throughout the century by a number of prominent nineteenth-century theorists, including Newman, Quackenbos, Bain, Genung, Kidder, and Broadus, who stressed the particular relevance of the eloquent style and the proper effects of oratory.

Delivery

Nineteenth-century rhetoricians considered the art of delivery essential to achieving eloquent effects in oratory; however, most theorists of this period regarded elocution as an ancillary art. In *The Princeton Text Book in Rhetoric* Hope defines elocution as a "collateral" art "tributary to the end sought in Rhetoric" and offers an extensive analysis of the use of the voice and gesture that parallels Whately and Blair's treatments (228–89). While nineteenth-century rhetoricians generally shared Hope's view that elocution is an important auxiliary art, most declined to include it in their analysis of rhetorical principles on the basis that it relates only to oral expression and not to the laws of discourse in general. David J. Hill expresses this stance in his account of what constitutes the proper nature of rhetoric. Defining rhetoric as "the whole theory of effective discourse," he continues, "Elocution has long been regarded as a part of Rhetoric, but it is by itself too important and extensive a subject to be treated as a division of rhetorical science. It does, indeed contribute to render spoken discourse more effective, but so does elegant chirography or clear typography improve the effectiveness of written thought. Rhetoric treats of discourse in general, not of written or spoken discourse in particular" (*Science of Rhetoric* 5). Hill assumes that the primary objective of the rhetorician is to develop an understanding of human nature and a mastery over the types of intellectual and emotional appeal that allow thoughts to be conveyed from mind to mind. The art of delivery becomes useful to the rhetorician only when this broader knowledge is adapted to the particular requirements of oral expression. Although elocution was not awarded canonical stature in nine-teenth-century treatises, a number of theorists, including Hope, Hill, Chan-ning, Day, and Bain, acknowledged the importance of delivery to the public speaker and affirmed the importance of mastering this skill.[19]

The ancillary status of delivery is corroborated by the importance generally accorded to elocution in nineteenth-century culture. Elocution was considered an art of expression necessary for all persons hoping to achieve recognition in civic and polite society. Several elocution treatises achieved wide circulation in Canada and the United States between 1800 and the early decades of the twentieth century and were recognized by the academy and the literate public alike as authoritative works on the proper delivery of speeches and public readings and the rules of pronunciation and conversation. Works such as Ebenezer Porter's *Analysis of the Principles of Rhetorical Delivery as Applied to Reading and Speaking* (1827), William Russell's *American Elocutionist* (1844), and Alexander Melville Bell's *Principles of Elocution* (1878) provided a course in the rudiments of deliv-ery for the scholar and the "private learner."[20] Influential homiletic treatises such as Daniel P. Kidder's *Treatise on Homiletics* (1864) and Austin Phelps's *The Theory of Preaching* (1882) offered general principles of delivery as well as particular hints for pulpit elocution.[21] Elocutionists and homileticians alike stressed the fundamental dependence of oratory on effective delivery and promoted the notion that no public speaker could hope to achieve the effects of true eloquence without having first mastered the skills of elocution. Introductions to discussions of delivery usually included specific commentary on the interdependence of good oratory and the art of delivery:

> Delivery, in the most general sense, is the communication of our thoughts to others, by oral language. The importance of this, in professions where it is the chief instrument by which one mind acts on others, is so obvious as to have currency to the maxim, that an indifferent composition well delivered is better received in any popular assembly, than a superior one, delivered badly. In no point is public sentiment more united than in this, that the use-

fulness of one whose main business is public speaking, depends greatly on an impressive elocution. This taste is not peculiar to the learned or the ignorant; it is the taste of all men. (Porter 2)

Who are the men that in our great republic are now attracting universal attention? Who are they, to hear whom our Senate Houses, our Halls of Justice, and our Churches are thronged to overflowing? Who are they, whom assembled multitudes, in our public halls, in the crowded squares and streets of our cities clamor for, and whose voices they will hear? They are not always the most learned men among us, nor are they always the most profound thinkers. Generally speaking, they are men of good sound common sense, who have a good Elocution. (Caldwell 15–16)

The value of the study of spoken language can scarcely be overrated. The human voice is a great power among men. It is human nature to want to hear truth presented in the most interesting and, if may be, the most vivid manner; and although the daily papers have become the medium of conveying to the masses current news and general information, it is still the province of the public speaker *to convince men and move them to action*. This can be done through the living voice and manner.[22] (Fulton and Trueblood 5; authors' italics)

Offering similar advice regarding how the orator develops an "interesting and vivid manner," homiletic treatises and popular elocution manuals reviewed a standard set of principles regarding properties of the voice and management of gesture. As a rule, homiletic treatises and academic texts discussed these principles from a philosophical point of view and offered fairly elaborate theoretical treatments of these issues. Elocutionary manuals intended for the general reader tended to offer brief outlines of rules and numerous exercises for practice in the proper use of the voice and the body.

This difference is exemplified in the contrast between Porter's *Analysis of the Principles of Rhetorical Delivery* and Bell's *Principles of Elocution*. Although viewed as a general reference work on delivery, Porter's text was prepared initially to instruct "young men, who are preparing for the sacred ministry, how to preach the gospel." In contrast with elocutionists appealing to a popular audience, Porter provides more detail regarding the epistemological dynamics governing particular strategies of delivery. For example, Porter defines the principle of *time* as control over the pace at which single words, clauses, and sentences are uttered, and he makes the traditional observation that if "every word and syllable were uttered with the same length, the uniformity would be as intolerable as the worst monotony." In addition to reiterating this basic rule, Porter goes on to explain that "rate" can facilitate emotions in the speaker that affect eloquence:

> But *time* in elocution, has a larger application than that which respects words and clauses, I mean that which respects the general rate of delivery. . . . I refer rather to the difference which emotion will produce, in the rate of the same individual. . . . Narration is equable and flowing; vehemence, firm and accelerated; anger and joy, rapid. Whereas dignity, authority, sublimity, awe—assume deeper tones, and a slower movement. Accordingly we sometimes hear a good reader or speaker, when there is some sudden turn of thought, check himself in the full current of utterance, and give indescribable power to a sentence, or part of a sentence, by dropping his voice, and adopting slow, full pronunciation. (113–14)

Porter's account of how time serves the "good speaker" represents the approach of elocutionists who explained the principles of delivery with explicit attention to how epistemological conditions affect successful delivery. Bell defines *time* more narrowly as a simple matter of control over five degrees of pace—rapid, quick, ordinary, slow, adagio (112). Mainly interested in pointing out the relationship between pace and force, Bell identifies the various types of pace but does not explain the effects of time except to note that it contributes to variety. Bell's approach in this instance is characteristic of the method of "popular" elocutionists who focused primarily on naming and illustrating techniques. Although the theoretical complexity of accounts of elocution varied from manual to manual, most elocutionists defined the principles of delivery in terms of the traditional two-part scheme of voice and action and favored the inclusion of readings for practice.[23] This rubric was reiterated throughout the century in elocution manuals that conferred normative status on a particular sets of rules for the delivery of speeches and public readings. One set of rules concerned properties of the voice:

Articulation. A good articulation or pronunciation allows the orator to be clearly heard and secures the attention of the audience. Correct articulation depends on the pronunciation of every syllable, the distinctiveness with which vowel sounds and consonant sounds are uttered, and the clear pronunciation of prefix and suffix syllables, auxiliaries, etc. The orator must be careful not to slide over unaccented vowels or give undue distinctiveness to accented syllables. Articulation should appear graceful and natural at all times.

Inflection. If the orator wishes to convey sentiments with clarity and force, natural inflections of the voice must be employed according to the form and sense of various sentences. Four types of inflection are involved in public speaking: monotone, when the voice sustains a sameness of sound on successive syllables; rising, when the voice rises or ascends upwards; falling, when the voice falls or slides downwards, and circumflex or compound, when the the rising and falling inflection is combined in the same word. The nature of a sentence is conveyed in how inflection signals the affirmative (falling), the negative (rising), the interrogative (rising), and the imperative senses (falling).

Accent. Accent is the stress put on particular syllables and is determined primarily by custom. Accent confers variety on discourse and certain qualities of rhythm. Every word of more than one syllable has an accented syllable; many words of three and four syllables, and all longer words, have a secondary accent or accents. The accent is generally on the root syllable. Prefixes, affixes, and "common terminations" are usually unaccented (Bell 9).

Emphasis. Emphasis consists of giving deliberate accent to certain words to best convey the sense or meaning of the utterance. Every phrase, clause, or sentence has a principal word or cluster of words that conveys the principal idea to be expressed. This word or group of words should be distinguished from the subordinate and accessory words through emphasis

Oratory

or stress. In phrases and sentences, words that express ideas new to the context should be distinguished by emphasis. Words used in contrast to preceding terms should also be rendered prominent through emphasis.

Pause. The pause is to the speaker what punctuation is to the writer. Pauses allow the speaker to draw breath but also perform the important rhetorical functions of retaining the interest of the audience and substantiating the grammatical sense of the utterances. Pauses consist of three types: the smaller or short pause, which corresponds to the comma; the greater or middle pause, which corresponds to the semicolon; and the greatest or rest, which corresponds to the period or full stop. Placement and length of pauses depend on the speaker's sense of how sentiment is best conveyed: e.g., in the case of the emphatic pause the speaker follows a striking thought with a rest to fix the idea in the memory (Porter 114–16; Carpenter 8–11).

Force. Force or power in the voice is crucial to the speaker because it ensures that the speech will be heard. Force is also necessary to the expression of certain sentiments and to creating an appearance of sincerity and self-reliance. The speaker should have control over a range of force and be able to vary the volume of the voice along a range of degrees from the vehement and energetic to the moderate and soft. Great force is not always required.

Time. Time or rate of utterance confers variety and expressiveness on speech. The time of a syllable depends on the length of the vowels and the nature and arrangement of succeeding consonants. The time of the sentence depends on the taste of the speaker and his understanding of the sense and intended effect of the sentence. There are five degrees of time: rapid, quick, moderate, slow, and adagio (very slow). Explanatory clauses and parenthetical sentences are pronounced in a quicker time than predicates. Sentiments of which the speaker approves should be conveyed in a slower time than those he disregards; veneration and awe are delivered in slow time; grief is slow, joy is quick, passion is rapid, meditation is slow, and decision is quick.

Pitch. Control over pitch is necessary in conveying emotion. The voice has three distinct pitches or tones—high, low, and middle. The most used is middle pitch, the tone of common discourse. The orator should use this pitch whenever strong passions are absent—e.g., in narration, descriptive statement , or moral reflection. The high key is proper for all the strong passions or elevated feelings: rage, threatening, denunciation, invective, joy, and exaltation. Low pitch is reserved for the expression of grief, melancholy, veneration, deep thought, and hate (Carpenter 15).

Other guidelines concerned properties of action or gesture:

Attitude of the body or stance. The normal position of the body in speaking should be erect, facing the audience, the chest expanded, the head evenly balanced (a slight inclination of the head at the opening is acceptable), the arms and hands at the sides, and the feet a short distance apart (Broadus, *Treatise* 249).

Gestures of the hands. Expressions of the hands are almost equal to the expressive force of the face and eyes. The hand should express variety and animation. The right hand should be most used. After any gesture, the arm and hand should return to the normal position at the side of the body. The positions of the hand depend on the disposition of the fingers, the presentation of the palm, double gestures using both hands, and the parts of the body on which the hands can be placed. The orator should guard against monotonous gestures as well as excessive gestures that weaken the effect of sense.

Gestures of the arm. Graceful movements of the arm confer simplicity and power on the action of the orator. The action of the arm should always be free and unconstrained, proceeding from the shoulder rather than the elbow. The arm should always be moved in curved lines. The curve is the line of beauty in the action of the arm and should be observed consistently. Errors to be avoided include using the arm in an inward rather than outward sweep, using the arm in indefinite sweeps with no specific termination point, overusing any particular arm gesture, and moving the arm in straight lines or angles.

Position of the feet and lower limbs. Dignity and grace of the standing figure depend on the position of the lower limbs. The weight of

Oratory

the body should be supported on one leg, with the other placed to balance the body. In this position one foot is firmly planted. Positions best suited to oratory are: (1) the right foot is firmly planted; the left foot forms a right angle; (2) the right foot is advanced; the left foot "shaded"; (3) the left foot is firmly planted (the reverse of number 1); and (4) the left foot is advanced (the reverse of number 2). Common errors in the position of the feet include throwing the weight of the body forward on the ball of the foot, placing the feet too close together, and pacing up and down (Caldwell 221–30).

Expressions of the face and eyes. There is natural sympathy between the feelings and the expression of the countenance. The orator must pay attention to expressions conveyed through the eyes, the eyebrows and eyelids, the forehead, and the mouth. Orators must avoid distracting expressions such as excessive smiling or frowning, overworking the eyebrows, biting the lips, and retracting the corners of the mouth. The orator should direct a steady gaze to the audience and establish eye contact with various listeners as if engaging them in conversation. The eyes should not wander or stare. Tears should be reserved only for the expression of serious sentiments such as grief and joy.

In their discussions of these principles, nineteenth-century elocutionists drew on the teachings of Cicero and Quintilian as well as the work of prominent eighteenth-century elocutionists Thomas Sheridan, John Walker (*The Melody of Speaking,* 1787), and Gilbert Austin (*Chironomia,* 1806).[24] The authority of Cicero and Quintilian endured throughout the century as did the influence of Austin's *Chironomia;* however, by midcentury the exclusive theoretical influence of Sheridan and Walker on theories of the voice had been supplemented by James Rush's *Philosophy of the Human Voice* (1827). Rush's views shaped the theories of a number of influential American elocutionists, including William Russell, James E. Murdoch, Jonathan Barber, and Merritt Caldwell, who shared Rush's interest in how expressive use of the voice enhances emotional appeals and the clarity of utterances addressed to the understanding.[25] The general theoretical debt of nineteenth-century treatments of delivery to such epistemological

155

assumptions is observable throughout the century and marks yet another example of the extent to which traditional and modern perspectives shaped nineteenth-century treatments of rhetorical technique.

The Species of Oratory

In addressing the characteristic features of the major species of oratory, nineteenth-century theorists paid particular attention (1) to identifying the appeals to the faculties that are most appropriate to different types of public speaking and (2) to outlining how the qualifications of the speaker can predetermine the impact of oratorical strategies. Along with treatments of arrangement and style, definitions of the modes of oratory were a standard feature of discussions of oratory as a rhetorical genre and were usually introduced under headings such as "Kinds of Discourse—Oratory" and "Special Forms of Composition: Oratory" (Day, *Elements* 25; David. J. Hill, *Elements* 186). Early nineteenth-century treatises were modeled directly on Blair's division scheme: eloquence of the pulpit, the bar, and popular assemblies. (In Blair's system, eloquence of popular assemblies is understood to include both political oratory and addresses to public gatherings.)[26] In the last decades of the century, rhetorical theorists began to designate popular oratory as a distinct mode of secular oratory separate from political speaking. The formalization of popular oratory as a species extended the range of oratory beyond the three-mode scheme outlined by the New Rhetoricians to a four-mode scheme: judicial, deliberative, popular, and sacred oratory. The creation of this new division—popular oratory—reflected the prominence that public lecturers and platform speakers had achieved by the latter part of the nineteenth century and the proliferation in nineteenth-century North American society of communal occasions at which platform speaking was a central activity.[27] By 1880 rhetoricians had begun to take note of the rapid expansion of popular oratory by identifying those subspecies of oratory for which the public speaker could likely be responsible: campaign speeches, after-dinner speeches, "lectures to lyceums and lecture associations," and college addresses (Hart 301–3; Kellog 233–35).

Throughout the century, accounts of the divisions retained a number of the neoclassical stipulations obvious in Blair's treatment of the divisions. At the level of overall theoretical stance, the neoclassical debt of nineteenth-century treatments of the divisions is most obvious in the formulaic attention given each division in terms of subject matter, aim, audience, and appropriate form. Like Campbell and Blair, nineteenth-century rhetoricians combined traditional guidelines with explanations of how the faculties of the mind can best be engaged in the modes of speaking. This theoretical orientation is obvious in the rhetorical strategies assigned to each species. The three-mode scheme, dominant from 1800 to 1880, paralleled Blair's treatment:

Judicial oratory
—Subject: accusation and defense before judge and/or jury
—General aim: to secure decisions regarding guilt or innocence
—Dominant rhetorical strategy: argumentation; persuasive techniques usually required
Deliberative oratory
—Subject: debate and consultation regarding national or civil matters before members of a legislative or popular assembly
—General aim: expedient adoption of resolutions or dissuasion from a course of action
—Dominant rhetorical strategy: persuasion; argumentation often required
Sacred oratory
—Subject: explication of sacred texts and lessons on moral conduct before a congregation
—General aim: instruction in scriptural truth and exhortation to moral conduct
—Dominant rhetorical strategy: persuasion; argumentative techniques of exposition, narration, and description often required

The four-mode scheme dominant during the period 1880–1900 both resembled and departed from the three-mode scheme that it had supplanted:

Nineteenth-Century Rhetoric

Sacred oratory
—As above
Judicial oratory
—As above
Deliberative oratory
—Subject and general aim narrowed to context of legislative assembly
Popular oratory
—Subject: all topics affecting the public interest: trade, national elections, morals, education, scientific advances, and historical commentary; commemorative addresses and eulogies on famous figures
—General aim: to move the will of the people, to sway the masses
—Dominant rhetorical strategy: persuasion; techniques of argument and explanation often required

Although not associated exclusively with conviction, judicial oratory was defined as a type of oratory relying primarily on the engagement of understanding in the consideration of facts of law and the circumstances of injury and justice. Reiterating Blair's observation that the first principle of judicial eloquence is close reasoning, nineteenth-century rhetoricians stressed the importance of adapting basic steps of the argumentative process to the composition of the judicial address: clear statement of the question or point at issue; concise narration of the facts of the case; and presentation of irrefutable evidence. Channing's summary of the major characteristics of "the properties of law eloquence" illustrates how nineteenth-century theorists equated excellence in judicial oratory with the dynamics of argumentative force:

> Generally, as might be expected, it is marked by calmness, by a firm, steady march to its object, by a composure which a mastery of the subject and the gravity of such investigations would ordinarily inspire. It is marked by distinct order. It observes relations and dependencies among the successive details of proof, till the

158

great proposition which they are establishing is reached. So natural is the disposition of every part, that both the speaker and his hearer always feel secure that they are moving in the direction they started with and towards the object they set out for. (99–100)

Channing's presumption that the "steady march" of logic embodies the ideal constitution of the judicial oration was a common one. Nineteenth-century theorists frequently referred to theoretical maxims regarding "logical method" when addressing the content and arrangement of the legal oration: David. J. Hill observes that "arguments should be disposed according to the nature of the theme proposition, but so as to bring the strongest last" (*Elements* 191); De Mille cites the use of "artificial and inartificial" proofs as major modes of proof or disproof in "accusation and defence" (470); and Bain defines "The Oratory of the Law Courts" as an "endeavor" in which "Argumentative Oratory must bear a chief part" (*English Composition* [1866] 172). Such advice presumes that the principles of argumentation provide the rationale for the nature and structure of the judicial oration. As nineteenth-century rhetorics normatively treated the principles of argumentation as a major theoretical issue, discussions of judicial oratory usually offered only references to theoretical maxims or brief recapitulations of argumentative principles.

The application of principles of argumentation was also stressed in discussions of deliberative and sacred oratory; these forms of oratory were perceived to rely on appeals to the understanding in the overall process of moving the will to action. As Bain explains, the satisfaction of the understanding is crucial to moving the will, and moving the will is one of the "twofold aspects" of political oratory: "the art of persuading some society, or body of people, or a nation at large, to adopt, for the good of the society, one line of policy rather than another" (*English Composition* [1866] 172). In addressing the uses of argument in deliberative oratory, nineteenth-century theorists again employed a "referential" method of naming principles of argumentation that they assumed to be well understood. For example, De Mille simply lists devices of argument that the speaker can use to "make opinions acceptable" to assemblies: statement of the necessity of a case; preparation for what is to follow; unexpected or surprising statement of the topic; explanation; answers to objections; and anticipation of objections (474–85). Illustrating these devices with a variety of excerpts from well-known deliberative speakers such as Earl Chatham, Patrick Henry, and Henry Clay, De Mille affirms the theoretical presumption that the successful political speaker inevitably depends on such fundamental techniques of conviction.

Although not all nineteenth-century rhetoricians offered the review of oratorical tactics presented by De Mille, most theorists affirmed the maxim that the deliberative speaker must present ideas in a logical way in order to achieve success. A similar expectation was stipulated for the preacher. Like their eighteenth-century predecessors, nineteenth-century rhetoricians defined pulpit oratory as a mode partially dependent on appeals to the understanding. The sermon was defined as a genre that utilizes the methods of conviction in an effort to persuade a congregation to higher levels of moral conduct. Discussions of pulpit oratory stressed that appeals to the understanding are necessary if the preacher is to succeed in providing instruction in the scriptures and moral lessons. Most nineteenth-century theorists advised the preacher to make use of the fundamental expository methods—explanation and illustration—when explicating and applying the meaning of the scriptures. Typical in both substance and emphasis of how nineteenth-century rhetoricians discussed the expository methods of the sermon, Quackenbos's treatment of explication stresses the importance of explaining the "sense" of terms and propositions and of giving "a clear and full view of the subject":

> Explication . . . consists of explaining the terms used, or the subject, or both. There are two sorts of explications: the one, simple and plain, needs only to be proposed, and agreeably elucidated; the other must be confirmed, if it speak of fact, by proofs of fact; if right, by proofs of right; if of both, by proofs of both. . . . In all cases, illustrate by reasons, examples, comparisons of the subject; their relations, conformities, or differences. You may do it

by consequences; by the person, his state, &c., who proposes the subject; or the persons to whom it is proposed; by circumstances, time, place, &c. (397)

Quackenbos stresses the dependence of instruction on the explication of terms and the illustration of ideas. This approach to what constitutes the proper methods of discussion in preaching presumes that the understanding will accept a proposition as "true" if experience and common sense have been satisfied by examples, comparisons, and established relations to known experience. No matter that the preacher's ultimate aim is moral persuasion; the hearers must first be made to understand the sense of the scriptural text and be offered an account of the significance of the subject that correlates with their own circumstances. Promoting Blair's maxim that facts must be understood before a truth can be believed, nineteenth-century theorists advised preachers and deliberative speakers alike to lay the groundwork for persuasion by employing the methods of argument.

Nineteenth-century discussions of pulpit and deliberative oratory stressed that the speaker's major goal in these modes is to engage the emotions and thereby move the will. Already in the sphere of the feelings and the will by virtue of their special subjects (moral conduct and the general welfare), the preacher and the political speaker depend on skillful management of the emotions for success. As with recommendations regarding the use of logical methods in judicial oratory, formal characterizations of pulpit and deliberative oratory presumed on a theoretical acquaintance with the principles of persuasion and rarely offered more than brief references to persuasive techniques. For example, in providing an overview of the role of the orator before a congregation, Welsh reminds the would-be preacher that persuasion requires the speaker to engage natural sympathy through an understanding of the views and motives of the audience:

Before a congregation of worshippers, he the orator is a preacher, endeavoring to influence man in his strictly personal life, not superficially and transiently, but profoundly and permanently. His appeal is not to carry a point connected with his own ambition or

gains, but to advance their spiritual good. He regards his hearers
in every relation and condition of life—as members of the family
and subjects of the state, as laboring and professional, as poor and
rich as ignorant and enlightened. His themes are noble, important,
sublime. (297)

Welsh perceives the aim and the "noble" subject of the sermon to
necessarily involve the preacher in the process of influencing the heart. In
the theoretical context of the nineteenth-century tradition, apprehension of
the sublime in any form was understood to depend on the engagement of
the higher sentiments. Although nineteenth-century theorists rarely re-
hearsed the doctrine of taste or outlined the psychology of the sentiments
in their treatments of the sermon, characterizations of pulpit oratory in this
period overtly assumed the belletristic principle that the preacher must
move the higher passions in order to establish "profound" influence over
the hearer's personal and spiritual conduct. The ultimate impact of pulpit
eloquence is measured in how successfully the preacher utilizes persuasive
strategies to "converse with every man's heart" (Channing 139).[28]

Nineteenth-century theorists considered deliberative speaking to be
another form of oratory that depends on persuasion. Although the deliberative speaker is under the general obligation to present ideas in a convincing
manner, addresses to assemblies on matters of civil or national welfare
primarily seek to move the audience to action. Definitions of the nature and
scope of deliberative oratory characteristically stressed the persuasive aims
of political speaking:

This wide department [political oratory] may be defined as the art
of persuading some society, or body of people, or a nation at
large, to adopt, for the good of the society, some one line or policy rather than another. Such is the Oratory of the Parliament, and
of all deliberative assemblies, whether great or small, national or
local, whether for general well-being or for narrow or special objects. (Bain, *English Composition* [1866] 173)

Deliberative oratory includes most political and parliamentary discussion. Its themes are war, supplies, finance, and improvement.

Oratory

Its aim is to dissuade from certain measures, and exhort to others. It looks toward the expedient. (David J. Hill, *Elements* 187)

[The forensic form] takes its name from the Roman Forum. It is Ciceronian in origin. As a modern type, it is Parliamentary or Congressional. Its general aim is, to unfold, maintain and enforce the laws of the state as expressed in codes and constitutions. Its specific aim is, to persuade a legislative body to adopt or reject a given code or resolution. It seeks to affect the public will as represented in its national legislators. (Hunt 293)

These definitions of deliberative speaking take for granted, in a theoretical sense, that the rhetorical characterizations "persuasive" and "exhortative" indicate which techniques of managing the feelings are called for. Nineteenth-century theorists presumed a similar pragmatic connection when they characterized popular oratory as a mode of discourse that seeks "to move the will of the people." The popular orator was viewed as a speaker who seeks to persuade a public assembly that the greater good lies in a particular course of action; nineteenth-century theorists stressed that the platform speaker must understand and appeal to the sentiments and tastes of the audience and inspire sympathy by evincing desirable sentiments. As Genung observes, it is the obligation of the popular speaker to approach men according to their motives and sentiments, "to enter their sphere of ideas, to appreciate their standards of life, to strike the chord of their sympathies and interests in accordance with their station, intelligence, or pursuit. Thus the orator finds them, and makes the connection between their interests and his cause" (*Working Principles* 649). In support of this advice, Genung cites the wisdom of Emerson on the art of persuading the popular assembly:

Him we call an artist who shall play on an assembly of men as a master on the keys of a piano,—who, seeing the people furious, shall soften and compose them, shall draw them, when he will, to laughter and to tears. Bring him to his audience, and, be they who they may,—coarse or refined, pleased or displeased, sulky or savage, with their opinions in the keeping of a confessor, or with their opinions in their bank-safes,—he will have them pleased and humored as he chooses; and they shall carry and execute that which he bids them. (*Working Principles* 649)

Emerson's point that the platform speaker must possess exceptional sensitivity to audience in order to compel action is indicative of the widely held nineteenth-century view that the orator who seeks to persuade must have a keen insight into how emotions move the will. Like the preacher who exhorts the congregation to elevated moral conduct, the popular speaker often excites an assembly to action or immediate change. Day explains that such attempts to persuade the public depend on engaging those feelings that directly affect volition:

Where . . . the object of the discourse is to produce a merely temporary effect, as that of a general exhorting his soldiers on the eve of a battle, those motives which respect more directly the feelings as the the immediate incentives to action, will have the preference. It will often be the case that . . . the speaker will aim to bring his hearers not only to adopt a general course of conduct or pursuit, but also to commit themselves to it at the moment by some particular act. The Temperance reformers, thus, in seeking to induce and secure a permanent reform, press the inebriate to an immediate committal by some particular act, as signing a pledge or the like. (*Elements* 152)

Day's emphasis on the importance of appealing to "incentives to action" is founded on a philosophical assumption shared with his colleagues: the success of each mode of oratory depends on the engagement of one or more of the faculties in a particular combination. The popular orator's success is based on understanding those sentiments that motivate action: the appetites, the affections, self-love, and the moral faculty. Nineteenth-century rhetoricians took the view that the success of all forms of oratory depends primarily on an accurate assessment of what type of appeal to the faculties is suited to the subject matter and conventional nature of the rhetorical situation. This viewpoint reinscribed the classical principle that form evolves from a consideration of aim, audience, and occasion and also promoted the New Rhetoricians' presumption that the orator must engage the mind's natural inclinations.

Nineteenth-century treatises typically included discussions of the requisite qualifications of various types of public speakers. Recommendations for preachers, lawyers, political speakers, and platform speakers alike stressed how certain qualities of the orator can facilitate the argumentative or persuasive aims appropriate to each rhetorical context. These comments appeared either in the form of particular characterizations within definitions of each division or within more general discussions of the "Qualifications of the Orator" that comprised one of the customary topics in treatments of oratory as a genre. Nineteenth-century rhetoric manuals offered a standard list of qualifications for all orators: cultivated moral qualities (probity, candor, humanity, sympathy, reverence, modesty and courage); taste (a sensibility to the beautiful and good in nature and in art); earnestness or sincerity of feeling (honest enthusiasm for the subject and point of view argued); confidence (certainty of self and cause); logical power (ability to reason and arrange ideas); command of the subject (versatile and detailed knowledge of subject addressed); imagination (the ability to present familiar materials in a vivid and novel manner by creating images that affect the senses and feelings); knowledge of the persons addressed (insight into human nature sufficient to assess the intellectual interests and emotional motives of the hearers); and command of the language (mastery of diction and the principles of style).[29]

Assumed to be the qualities that foster the development of eloquence, these traits distinguish the speaker who aspires to grace and influence. Without these qualities, the orator cannot engage the reason, the imagination, the emotions, or the will of the audience. Without such engagement, the aims of oratory cannot be fulfilled. Context, aim, and the nature of the audience dictate how these qualities should be manifested. The deliberative speaker must be confident of his opinion: "a man cannot be long in doubt if he would have wide and firm influence among freemen."

Nineteenth-Century Rhetoric

The judicial speaker must have general knowledge of the law and special knowledge of the case in hand; the jurist must have "clear conceptions, deep convictions, and forcible expression." The popular speaker must understand all manner of issues that shape public opinion, and the preacher must evince modesty, sincerity, earnestness, and self-control (Channing 78; Hunt 293; Welsh 302–3).

When outlining the qualifications of those speakers who seek to persuade, nineteenth-century rhetoricians reiterated the classical maxim that it is the good person speaking well who is best able to persuade. This principle was stressed in nineteenth-century discussions of the qualifications of the orator not only because classical wisdom on this issue was highly regarded but also because rhetoricians in the period adhered to the epistemological assumption that moral character and sincerity conjoin to create a natural path of communication from mind to mind. Only the moral person can be earnest, and only the earnest or sincere speaker can generate sympathy. In discussing requisite traits, nineteenth-century theorists reiterated the classical adage that judicial and political orators must have extensive command of their subject matter as well as broad background knowledge. However, equal stress was given to the point that such qualities alone cannot ensure success if the orator is not "a man of right feelings" (Channing 108). Sincerity and moral character are crucial to the lawyer, the political debater, and the public orator, who must convince an audience that matters of truth, justice, and the public welfare are implicated in the cause at issue. For orators in these arenas, moral character evidences itself in a deep devotion to the national and public good; in the preacher, moral character is represented in piety and a concern for the spiritual welfare of others.

The importance that nineteenth-century rhetoricians awarded to prerequisite moral character in the speaker is confirmed by the view that oratory plays a crucial role in moral edification, civil education, and communal debate regarding social values. Oratory was represented as a mode of rhetoric that facilitates the proper workings of the political process, the disposition of justice, and the maintenance of the public welfare and social

Oratory

conscience. Such concepts of the civil and cultural importance of oratory
built on the neoclassical commitments and belletristic values of the New
Rhetoric: the eloquent speaker exemplifies the finest qualities of mind and
heart and thus promotes the influence of taste as well as civil harmony and
integrity. The belletristic view of oratory assumed that the promotion of
taste furthers the development of moral virtues and vice versa; the speaker
promotes taste in the aesthetic technique of oratory and by addressing the
moral and civil conditions of society in such a way that the finer sentiments
and emotions are engaged and encouraged to develop. This view of oratory
was highlighted by rhetoricians such as Channing, Newman, Quackenbos,
Newman, De Mille, and Genung, who drew heavily on Blair's *Lectures*
and stressed the critical function of rhetoric. Even those nineteenth-century
rhetoricians who stressed the philosophical nature of rhetoric upheld the
view that oratory is a significant cultural and moral force: Day observes
that the end of all proper oratory is "moral in its character . . . viz: the
right, the good, and the beautiful or noble" (*Elements* 31); Theremin
characterizes eloquent oratory as the "development of the Ethical impulse
itself" (71); and Bascom insists that in advocating social well-being, oratory
has an "ulterior reference to the moral conditions of society—a subservience
of immediate to remote good, of individual to general good" (61–62).

Often interpreting the "general good" in the light of democratic
idealism, nineteenth-century rhetoricians assigned the orator a special role
in the preservation of freedom: the orator helps to safeguard liberty by
exercising the right to individual expression and by engaging peers in the
free debate of issues and circumstances that affect the common good. A
number of nineteenth-century American rhetoricians promoted the notion
that the moral ends of oratory are synonymous with the "liberal" principles
of American culture, a culture that nurtures the spirit of democratic exchange in which oratory can best flourish:

You need not fill your imaginations with glorious forms of ideal
perfection in the arts, only ask yourself what must be the power of

167

an orator who is perfectly fitted for an age like this; of one thoroughly prepared to do all that eloquence can do among the enlightened and free, I would set no bonds to his power; it is only for truth and freedom and justice to do it. (Channing 25)

In some parts of the world, it is true, eloquence is of no great use, because men are controlled by force; and freedom even of speech, is not allowed. Of what use, e.g., is eloquence in Italy, where no one dare advocate other opinions than those of the dominant authorities; and *they* need not *eloquence* for their support. . . . The fires of freedom must be, not only guarded, but prohibited, like fire in a powder mill, lest some spark struck out by eloquence should blow up the old edifice, of intellectual, spiritual and social depostism; and so bury the owners in the ruins. In our own country, however, it is far otherwise. (Hope 118)

We note that the Popular Form is eminently, the Liberal or Democratic Form. It could not exist in an Absolute Monarchy, or exist in its best expression in any other than a Free State. In such countries as England and France, it is rapidly increasing, owing to the increasing strength of the popular element in politics. It is the American form. As written, it is found in the Press. Potent, however, as the influence of the Press is in Public crises, the living oratory is demanded. (Hunt 296)

Where men are convened for debate or consultation, the orator is one of the assembly, every member of which has equal right with himself to the expression of opinion. He, at least theoretically, is to think less of bringing a majority to his side than of ascertaining which side is the true one for all. (Welsh 296)

Democratic idealism never supplanted the philosophical influence of neoclassical and belletristic views of the aims of oratory in nineteenth-century American theory; however, references to democratic ideals and the particular circumstances of American culture in discussions of oratory increased after midcentury. These references indicate that as the century progressed, American theorists made more and more an effort to discuss the nature and aims of oratory in terms of an American context.[30] In this

168

Oratory

subtle "Americanization" of the function of oratory we see one of the very few differences between American and Canadian approaches to oratory in this era. Few Canadian treatises were published in the nineteenth-century; however, De Mille provides a typical Anglo-Canadian view of the function of oratory. Predictably, De Mille relates the aims of oratory to the pertinent circumstances of Canadian life and discusses the civil function of oratory primarily in terms of how debate serves the parliamentary process. Although stipulations regarding the "Liberal and Democratic Form" of oratory and the purpose of egalitarian debate among the "enlightened and free" are absent from his account of the conduct of parliamentary debate, De Mille acknowledges the importance of oratory and calls parliamentary debate "the greatest blessing which a nation can enjoy, for in this way it can best win and maintain its liberties" (473). Clearly, De Mille shares with his American colleagues a regard for the interrelationship between free speech and liberty; however, he credits the cultural integrity of the "English-speaking race" in general and the development of "the English Parliament" specifically for forging this bond.

> [Parliamentary debate] has grown up in the free representative as-
> semblies of the English-speaking race, and has developed by them
> to its present state. . . . The form of parliamentary debate is mod-
> ern. It was created and developed in England. It was born in the
> English Parliament, and has spread thence to other parliaments,
> and also to other public assemblies which have no connection with
> politics. So useful is it that it is employed even where there is no
> debate proper, but only discussion. . . . Debate is of more impor-
> tance than formerly , since there is a larger audience. This is the
> result of a free Parliament and press. The members of Parliament
> represent the people to discuss; but the reporters of the press rep-
> resent the people to listen. Thus the whole nation is present to de-
> bate and to hearken by proxy. (472–73)

De Mille defines parliamentary debate as the most highly evolved form of debate and assumes that the practice of oratory is linked inextricably to the proper conduct of representative governments and the well-being of societies that value liberty. Despite differences as to whether the virtues of free speech are defined as typically "American" or "English," nineteenth-century North American rhetoricians generally affirmed the importance of oratorical practice in democratic states and credited the public speaker with the role of representing the interests of the general citizenry. By extending the moral obligations of oratory to include the preservation of democratic culture in its modern forms, the nineteenth-century tradition in North America affirmed the ideological significance of oratory in far more political terms than did the New Rhetoricians, who placed the greatest value on the personal and civic virtues that rhetoric encourages by nurturing the faculty of taste.

The truth is that in rhetoric, as distinguished from grammar, by far the greater part of the questions that arise concern not right or wrong, but better or worse; and that the way to know what is better or worse in any given case is not to load your memory with bewilderingly innumerable rules, but firmly to grasp a very few simple, elastic general principles. . . . [T]hese principles, I believe, are observed by thoroughly effective writers.

Barrett Wendell, *English Composition*

The four kinds of composition . . . are: Description, which deals with persons or things; Narration, which deals with acts or events; Exposition, which deals with whatever admits of analysis or requires explanation; Argument, which deals with any material that may be used to convince the understanding or to affect the will. The purpose of description is to bring before the mind of the reader persons or things as they appear to the writer. The purpose of narration is to tell a story. The purpose of exposition is to make the matter in hand more definite. The purpose of argument is to influence opinion or action, or both.

A. S. Hill, *The Principles of Rhetoric*

Great importance is attached to the practical use of the laws of discourse both in criticising the works of others and in original composition. After mastering the principles of Rhetoric, the student is prepared to examine literary productions with intelligent discrimination. He will be gratified to find that all truly effective writing and speaking are in accord with the laws he has learned, and that compositions which ignore these laws are faulty in the degree of their departure from them. He will find also that his own efforts will increase in real value in proportion to his observance of these laws. Each day's practice in criticism and production will contribute somewhat to the improvement of the faithful student, until he will at length become a master of accurate, methodical and effective composition.

David J. Hill, *The Science of Rhetoric*

5

The Arts of Composition
and Belles Lettres

Throughout the nineteenth century, rhetorical expertise was equated with an understanding of fundamental rhetorical principles and an appreciation of the aims and form of conventional genres. In treating the art of composition, nineteenth-century rhetoricians gave prominent attention to the traditional maxim that effective technique follows on an understanding of rhetorical theory and its application. Like the orator, the writer depends on "a very few simple, elastic general principles" (Wendell 2). Nineteenth-century rhetoricians defined invention, arrangement, and style as the principles on which both composition and oratory rely; discussions of these canons focused on how the writer (as well as the speaker) can utilize rhetorical strategies to appeal to the readers' understanding, emotions, will, and imagination. In addition to outlining the application of fundamental principles of rhetoric to composition, nineteenth-century rhetoricians analyzed the different modes of developing content (description, narration, explanation, and argument) and explained the aim, subject matter, and form of the major prose genres. These accounts of the principles of composition and the species of prose relied on a theoretical synthesis of Blair's belletristic approach to style and formal genres with Campbell and Whately's explanations of rhetorical invention and arrangement. By addressing the principles of rhetoric in terms of a synthetic analysis of the New Rhetorical canons, nineteenth-century theorists established the art of writing, like the art of oratory, as a process involving the invention and management of ideas and evidence, the orderly arrangement of the treatise, mastery over style and grammatical correctness, and command over the genres of prose.[1]

Discussions of the principles of composition and the prose genres proceeded on two significant assumptions of the New Rhetoric: (1) dynamic responses of the mental faculties predispose the effects that content, arrangement, and style will have on a reader; and (2) generic elements of prose form and style enable the writer to engage the type of intellectual, emotional, or aesthetic response appropriate to the aim of the discourse. Epistemological and belletristic perspectives were the dominant theoretical influences on nineteenth-century treatments of composition; an epistemological stance shaped rationales for invention and arrangement and a belles lettres perspective predisposed discussions of qualities of style and the formal genres of prose. Neoclassical views were affirmed in discussions of the conduct of prose and the constituents of style (grammatical purity, sentence structure, and figurative language) and in the canonical status awarded to invention by those nineteenth-century rhetoricians who affirmed invention as "the uniform method of the ancient rhetoricians" (Day, *Elements* 32). The importance that nineteenth-century rhetoricians assigned to imitation and critical study in the development of the art of composition also affirmed the classical tenet that the study of an exemplary canon confers greater mastery over technique and deepens intellectual and moral acumen. This classical notion was confirmed in the nineteenth-century tradition by the widely held belletristic attitude that the cultivation of taste through imitation and literary analysis improves and elevates abilities in composition.

Invention in Composition

Nineteenth-century treatments of the art of oratory were predisposed by a consideration of what formal strategies are best suited to the speaker's intention to convince or persuade in the course of deliberative, judicial, and popular speaking. Similarly, treatments of the principles of composition proceeded on the general assumption that the writer must develop subject matter in accordance with epistemological constraints and the particular aims of prose genres. In the invention of subject matter, the writer must consider the most natural means of communicating thoughts to another mind and whether or not "the immediate object through which this ultimate end is reached may lie in the understanding, the feelings, or the will of the persons addressed" (Day, *Elements* 42). Henry N. Day's treatment of invention is representative of the approach to invention that gained popularity after midcentury. Unlike the strictly belletristic approach that treated invention under discussions of individual genres, Day's more neoclassical discussion defines invention as a major canon in composing. This stance toward invention reinscribes the classical status of this canon; however, Day's overall treatment of invention is epistemological in orientation. Day defines invention as "the art of supplying the requisite thought in kind and form for discourse"; supplying the appropriate kind of thought and form for discourse "consists in the selection of the theme and in the determination of the particular form in which it is to be discussed" (35–38). In developing a subject or theme, the writer can choose among four forms of invention: explanation, conviction, excitation, and persuasion. Each of these processes or forms of development embodies different epistemological intentions and is suited to different subjects. Associating excitation and persuasion with oratory that typically appeals to the feelings and the will, Day explains that the processes of explanation (to inform or instruct) and conviction (argumentation) are suited to the development of compositions addressed to the understanding. Day follows the example of Campbell and Whately by defining description, narration, exposition, analysis, and comparison and contrast as modes of invention appropriate to explanation and by defining argumentation as the most effective process of conviction (confirmation of a new judgment). Day's approach to invention also reflects Campbell and Whately's theoretical conflation of invention with arrangement. Regarding the proper arrangement of a discourse as part of the process of developing the theme by "stages," Day considers the logical division of the composition into "parts" to be a "subordinate and constituent part of invention" (36).

Day's treatment of invention asserts a number of assumptions reiterated as standard principles of invention in North American treatises between 1850 and 1920: (1) Invention is the process of selecting a theme and choosing the form or mode of development best suited to the subject. (2) The selection and development of a single subject or theme provide the unity and coherence of a composition. (3) Argumentation is appropriate when conviction in the form of a change in judgment is the aim of the discourse; description, narration, exposition, analysis, and comparison/ contrast are appropriate when conviction (instruction) is the aim. (4) The developmental modes are closely associated with classes of subject matter and particular genres of prose: description, narration, argumentation, and exposition designate rhetorical methods of development as well as generic categories. (5) Part of invention is the arrangement of major ideas in a discourse in a natural order.[2]

Treatments of invention in composition stressed that the writer must consider the constraints of natural logic when developing descriptive, narrative, expository, and argumentative content. Methods of invention succeed only insofar as the writer is able to present ideas in certain associative relations—through resemblance, contiguity, or causality. Accounts of the different forms of development typically emphasized the epistemological principle that the descriptive, narrative, expository, and argumentative approaches to invention draw on the associative inclinations of the reading mind. Day explains that narration "is that process of explanation which presents an object in its relations to continuous time. . . . The human mind . . . can hardly avoid, when it contemplates events transpiring in succession, conceiving of a *cause* which binds those events together. . . . This relation of cause to the succession of events in time, shows at once the philosophical propriety of regarding the relation of cause and effect as the true governing principle in narration" (*Elements* 57). John F. Genung defines the ar-lytical method of exposition (explanation) as a process that relies on "the fixing of meanings by generalization" to exhibit "qualities and resemblances" that the reading mind will associate with reality (*Working Principles* 556). Alfred H. Welsh points out that the "associated feelings and circumstances" characteristic of description present the reader with a variety of examples and details by which the object can be recognized or recalled (184). David J. Hill observes that argumentation succeeds only insofar as the premises of a proposition seem to elicit a conclusion that the reader will "draw in accordance with the laws of thought" such as cause and effect or resemblance (*Science* 107). Day, Genung, Welsh, and Hill assume that description, narration, and exposition derive their inventional force by appealing to the associative and deductive nature of thought.[3] This epistemological rationale predisposed nineteenth-century treatments of description, narration, exposition, and argumentation as inventional forms for composition in the same manner that it influenced nineteenth-century explanations of the nature and application of argumentation and persuasion to oratory (chapter 3). Although some theorists provided more extensive philosophical explanations of the dynamics of description, narration, and exposition as "natural" forms than did others (e.g., Genung, Day, and David J. Hill provide far more philosophical explanation than does A. S. Hill), nineteenth-century rhetoricians in general offered standard accounts of the inventional processes that generate prose intended to describe, define, present a succession of events, or demonstrate the probability of a proposition. Guidelines for invention in composition stressed the obligation of the writer to develop and order content in forms that appeal to the associative and deductive activities by which the reader draws on experience and commonsense.

Description was defined as a technique by which an object, scene, or mental state is recalled to the mind of the reader or defined for a particular purpose. The chief rule in description is to enumerate the parts of the object being described in a complete, unified, and brief manner. Description furnishes an idea of what class the object belongs to and what constitutes it as a whole. Descriptive technique relies on the use of words, phrases, figures, and successive images that convey some sense of the comprehensive aspect of the object. Techniques include representing the shape, size, color, and posture of the object; locating the object through spatial relations (center, left, right, etc.); likening the object to a familiar type or contrasting it with well- known opposites; and defining a physical scene through the eyes of an observer. Welsh offer as an example "Carlyle's portrayal of Cromwell's personal features":

> Massive stature; big, massive head, of somewhat leonine aspect; wart above the right eyebrow; nose of considerable, blunt aquiline proportions; strict, yet copious lips; full of all tremulous sensibilities; and also, if need be, of all fiercenesses and rigors; deep, loving eyes-call them grave, call them stern-looking. (179)

Genung provides the following description of Chartres cathedral:

> The doors are rather low, as those of the English cathedrals are apt to be, but (standing three together) are set in a deep framework of sculpture-rows of arching grooves, filled with admirable little images, standing with their heels on each other's heads. . . . Above the triple portals is a vast round-topped window, in three divisions, of the grandest dimensions and the stateliest effect. (*Working Principles* 487)

Narration is defined as a technique that presents a succession of events or an account of unfolding or changing circumstances. The chief rule in narration is to establish a clear purpose or relationship between the events and to place the events or circumstances before the reader in an order that creates a sense of events being witnessed or experienced. Unity and completeness must be established in a narrative: a narrative "must commence at the beginning and continue to the end of an action" (David J. Hill, *Elements* 167). The narrative (or plot) should have continuous movement; to convey a realistic sense of shifting and unfolding events, a scene should not be changed needlessly and transitions should be marked. There should be a clear distinction between principal and subordinate actions. Inventional techniques include establishing causal relations be-

tween events, establishing the chronology of events by assigning specific
dates or references in time to significant events, providing summaries or
precis of events as they unfold, and recreating events by beginning with a a
familiar reference. A. S. Hill gives the following example from Macaulay's
History of England:

> Mackay, accompanied by one trusty servant, spurred bravely
> through the thickest of the claymores and targets, and reached a
> point from which he had a view of the field. His whole army had
> disappeared, with the exception of some Borders whom Leven had
> kept together, and of Hastings's regiment, which had poured a
> murderous fire into the Celtic ranks, and which still kept unbroken
> order. All the men that could be collected were only a few hun-
> dreds. The general made haste to lead them across the Garry, and,
> having put that river between them and the enemy, paused for a
> moment to meditate on his situation. (*Principles* 293)

Exposition is a technique by which the sense and meaning of notions
and propositions are explained. The chief aim of exposition is to define the
essential nature of a thing by establishing its general traits. The object should
be defined with a class of objects (genus) with the particular properties of
the object identified and explained (differentia). Exposition differs from
description in its attention to general rather than unique traits and in its
objective stance. Exposition may proceed inductively, antithetically, or
analytically, but a logical division of features must be established. Exposition must provide definitions that cover all cases of the idea treated in
terms more familiar than the defined object. Expository techniques include
exemplification, antithesis, analogy, definition of terms, and etymological
or historical accounts of words. Genung quotes John Stuart Mill's definition
of the "distinction between *poetry* and *eloquence*" as an example:

> Poetry and eloquence are both alike the expression or utterance of
> a feeling; But, if we may be excused the antithesis, we should say
> that eloquence is *heard;* poetry is *overheard.* Eloquence supposes
> an audience. The peculiarity of poetry appears to us to lie in the

poet's utter unconsciousness of a listener. Poetry is feeling confessing itself to itself in moments of solitude, and embodying itself in symbols which are the nearest possible representations of the feeling in the exact shape in which it exists in the poet's mind. Eloquence is feeling pouring itself out to other minds, courting their sympathy, or endeavoring to influence their belief, or move them to passion or to action. (*Working Principles* 566)

Argumentation is a technique by which the truth of a proposition is established to the satisfaction of the understanding. The chief rule in argumentation is to establish a distinct proposition and to provide proof of the correctness of that idea through analytical or empirical evidence. Argumentation proceeds either inductively through the the step-by-step presentation of reasons and facts that lead to an irrefutable conclusion, or deductively, establishing a logical connection between a particular proposition and a general truth. Argumentative evidence must be developed along the lines of natural logic: in terms of cause to effect (arguing from antecedent probability); in terms of resemblance (arguing from example and analogy); and in terms of the association of ideas (arguing from sign). These strategies of argumentation can also be used in refutation, a process by which the truth or probability of a proposition is disproved (see chapter 3).[4] Bain, remarking that "Analogy is much resorted to as a means of Proof," offers the following example:

When we argue from one man to another man, on any common property of men, as their birth, growth, &c., we reason Inductively, they being the same kind; when we reason from men to animals far removed from them in structure, or to plants, we reason Analogically; there is a sameness, but accompanied with a vast amount of difference. It is an argument from Analogy, when we compare nations to individuals in respect of vital constitution, and infer that every nation will pass through the successive stages of maturity, old age and death. So because there is a certain resemblance between the metropolis of a country, and the heart, it has been argued that its expansion becomes at last a disease. (*English Composition* [1866] 191)

180

Arrangement in Composition

Nineteenth-century theorists maintained the view that the arrangement of prose is related intrinsically to invention; the order in which ideas are presented in a discourse must respect natural logic and the writer's epistemological purpose. When conviction through argumentation is the object, the writer plans the treatise around establishing the proposition and presenting evidence; when description of an object or scene is the central aim, the writer organizes the discourse in terms of the identification and exhibition of prominent traits or particulars; when the intention of the writer is to provide a narrative of events, the major consideration in arrangement is the dramatization of a chain of events; when the writer's aim is exposition, the discourse must be arranged in terms of an initial definition of the idea or object and the subsequent explication of unique characteristics. Nineteenth-century theorists regarded arrangement as a two-part process: the writer must establish the proper order of ideas and organize the major parts or divisions of the discourse. To establish logical divisions in the discourse, the writer adapts the six-part arrangement scheme (introduction, statement, division, narration, argument, conclusion) or the three-part scheme (introduction, discussion, conclusion) to the subject matter and aim of the composition. To arrange the major ideas (heads) according to principles of natural order, the writer uses analysis, exemplification, classification, cause and effect, or comparison and contrast to develop a plan for the whole composition and for the structure of paragraphs.[5]

Regarding the six-part and the abbreviated three-part schemes as rhetorical formats applicable to the conduct of orations and all prose forms, nineteenth-century rhetoricians characterized the conduct of composition in terms of a basic format or formula. Genung's treatment of prose arrangement under the heading "The Three Fundamental Elements of the Plan" indicates the extent to which nineteenth-century theorists presumed that all forms of prose depend on the introduction, the development, and the conclusion "in some form and proportion." Genung offers a definition of the generic function of the three-part arrangement scheme:

Nineteenth-Century Rhetoric

The Introduction: The introduction comprises whatever is necessary to make proper approach to the theme. . . . The natural place
to state the theme, therefore, when it is expressed, is at the end of
the introduction. Sometimes to the statement of the theme there is
added a brief indication of the plan, but only of its leading heads.
[As in most analyses of the three-part scheme, Genung collapses
the traditional functions of the statement and the narrative.] The
introduction is to furnish such preliminary information as is
needed to put the readers in possession of the subject, the point of
view, and the manner of treatment. . . .

The Development: When the introduction has called in from its
general surroundings and concentrated on a single point or theme,
it is now the business of the development, or body of the discourse, to separate into its component parts, and follow out into
the various aspects and stages necessary to present treatment. The
suggestions of the theme are to be examined anew and classified
in a continuous and progressive course of thought.

The Conclusion: The object of a formal conclusion at the end of
a literary work is to gather together the various threads of argument, thought, or appeal, and so to apply them as to leave on the
reader's mind a unity of impression corresponding to the aim of
the discourse. It is important that there be one comprehensive effect, one central truth, by which the work shall be remembered.
(*Practical Elements* 273–80)

Genung's definition of the three-part scheme typifies the view of
arrangement in composition outlined by a number of his contemporaries,
including Day, Bain, David J. Hill, Hart, De Mille, and Hunt, who
insisted that the format of discourse contributes to unity and comprehensibility (Day, *Elements* 45–50; David J. Hill, *Elements* 16–20). The
underlying philosophy predisposing nineteenth-century theories of prose
arrangement was that the writer should work with rhetorical equivalents
of natural order in the arrangement of the formal divisions of a
composition. "Though the divisions may greatly vary, some division is
called for. Discourse cannot be unified and symmetrical without it.
These parts [introduction, proposition, analysis, discussion, conclusion]

themselves simply state the habit of the best discoursers. . . . The art itself is nature" (Hunt 24–25).

Nineteenth-century rhetoricians recommended that the writer arrange the argumentative composition in terms of a formal introduction, statement of the subject, a plan or division, the presentation of proof, and a conclusion. This neoclassical scheme was justified in terms of the function of arrangement in appealing to the understanding. Newman offers this type of rationale for the conduct of the argumentative treatise when he explains that "in the discussion of a subject, which is of an argumentative nature, the direction is generally given, then the arguments should rise in importance. In this way the attention excited by novelty at first may continue to be held, and a full and strong conviction be left on the mind at the conclusion of the reasoning" (36). Similarly, Welsh points out that "in the natural and logical order, the proposition is announced, or the question is stated and the answer is given, then the arguments follow" (206). Being just as responsible to epistemological constraints as is the orator, the writer utilizes arrangement to facilitate the reader's acceptance of the proposition as probable or factual. Quackenbos's discussion of the conduct of the argumentative treatise deals directly with how the six-part scheme promotes this effect:

> The object of the Exordium, or Introduction, is to render the reader or hearer well-disposed, attentive, and open to persuasion. . . . To awaken attention, he should hint at the importance, novelty, or dignity of the subject. Finally, to make his readers open to conviction, he should endeavor to remove any prejudices they may have formed against the side of the question he intends to espouse. . . . The Division is that part of a discourse in which the writer makes known to his readers the method to be pursued, and the heads he intends to take, in treating his subject. . . . The third division of discourse is the Statement, in which the facts connected with the subject are laid open. . . . The writer must state his facts in such a way as to keep strictly within the bounds of truth, and yet to present them under colors that are most favorable

to his cause. . . . The fourth division is the Reasoning; and on
this every thing depends. It is here that the arguments are found
which are to induce conviction, and to prepare from which is the
object of the parts already discussed. The writer should select such
arguments only as he feels to be solid and convincing. He must
not expect to impose on the world by mere arts of language; but,
placing himself in the situation of a reader, should think how he
would be affected by the reasoning which he proposes to use for
the persuasion of others. . . . The fifth division is the Appeal to
the Feelings. This should be short and to the point. All appearance
of art should be strictly avoided. To move his readers, the writer
must be moved himself. The last division of a discourse is the
Peroration; in which the writer sums up all that has been said, and
endeavors to leave a forcible impression on the reader's mind.
(386–90)

As was the case with nineteenth-century analyses of the conduct of
oratory, Quackenbos's discussion of arrangement of the prose argument
maintains the integrity of a neoclassical scheme of arrangement but also
shows a theoretical interest in how the divisions of the written argument
appeal to the reader's understanding and emotions.[6] This type of epistemological rationalization characterized nineteenth-century discussions of how
the writer should adapt the basic formats of arrangement (the three-part
scheme or the six-part scheme) to the particular aims of argumentative,
descriptive, narrative, and expository composition.

   Argumentation. The introduction engages reader interest, an-
nounces the proposition or theme to be pursued, and the facts of the
case or issue (exordium, division, and statement); the proof or discussion
presents the evidence supporting the argument; the conclusion (peroration)
summarizes the proofs. (The conclusion may include or be preceded by
an appeal to the feelings—the pathetic division.)

   Description. The introduction identifies an object and defines a
particular theme that characterizes the nature of the object as a whole; the
development "fills in" that characterization by presenting detail after detail

that result in a complete view of the object, which is stated (or restated) in the conclusion or concluding statement.

Narrative. A descriptive passage establishing setting (time, place) and point of view serves as an introduction; the development of the narrative unfolds events in a temporal sequence; in fiction this recounting works toward a definite focus or denouement (analogous to a conclusion).

Exposition. An introduction identifies and defines the subject according to its class; the development or discussion amplifies on those characteristics that endow the subject with its distinctive nature; the summary reviews how the various features or constituents of the object contribute to its nature or use.

Theoretical affirmation of the generic function of the introduction-development-conclusion format proceeded on the epistemological assumption that any composition that strives for order and wholeness must utilize some type of beginning-middle-end structure. By outlining this structure, the writer conforms to the general dictates of natural logic and also facilitates the different types of associative links that argumentative, descriptive, narrative, and expository development promote. Nineteenth-century rhetoricians viewed the arrangement of content under heads (major premises or topics) to be another means by which a unified and complete treatment of an idea is developed; the ordering of heads (which develop the theme or proposition) was defined by a number of theorists as the process of "making the plan" of the composition and treated as part of invention.[7] Arranging content by heads preorders information according to associative connections; implementing these principles or "laws of thought-association," the writer generates a plan for the arrangement of the whole composition as well as for the structure of paragraphs. Making the plan consists of ordering ideas or heads by patterns of natural logic. These patterns or principles of arrangement consist of classification, analysis, exemplification, cause and effect, and comparison and contrast. Classification is the process of "arranging all the regular divisions (heads) according to the character that may belong to each" (De Mille 315); analysis (or division) is a plan by which the theme is divided into component parts, each of which is then amplified in the discussion (synthesis is the reverse of this process); exemplification treats the theme in terms of one example that illustrates the nature of the whole; a cause-and-effect plan treats the theme in terms of a primary cause and subsequent effects (or the reverse); a comparison-and-contrast plan explains the theme by tracing resemblances or oppositions along common lines.

Nineteenth-century rhetoricians advised writers that one or some combination of the principles of arrangement should govern the plan of the whole composition, and they stressed the dual inventional/arrangement functions served by these schemes. In description, the writer typically arranges details under headings addressing prominent physical characteristics, parts, dimensions, materials, and relations in space. For example, when describing a location, the writer could arrange the composition around the discussion of situation, general appearance, and peculiar features or surroundings, climate, populations, and civilization; when describing a person, the writer could focus on age, form, face, manners, dress, peculiarities of appearance or character, disposition, mental abilities, and education (Welsh 184; Quackenbos 351–53). In the development of these heads, the writer could apply any one or combination of the principles of arrangement. When pointing out the versatility of the principles of arrangement in descriptive invention, theorists like De Mille and Quackenbos stressed that the chosen plan (analysis, classification, etc.) serves to establish clear associative connections between details:

> [On classification as a means of grouping details around external and internal scenes in "Macaulay's essay on Warren Hastings":] The place was worthy of such a trial. It was the great hall of William Rufus—the hall which had resounded with acclamations at the inauguration of thirty kings; the hall which had witnessed the just sentence of Bacon and the just absolution of Somers; the hall where the eloquence of Strafford had for a moment awed and melted a victorious party inflamed with just resentment. (De Mille 318)

> ["A well drawn character," David Gamut, the singing-master, from Cooper, *The Last of the Mohicans:*] The person of this re-

markable individual was to the last degree ungainly, without being in any particular manner deformed. He had all the bones and joints of other men, without any of their proportions. . . . The same contrariety in his members seemed to exist throughout the whole man. His head was large; his shoulders, narrow; his arms, long and dangling; while his hands were small; if not delicate. . . . The ill-assorted and injudicious attire of the individual only served to render his awkwardness more conspicuous. A sky-blue coat, with short and broad skirts and low cape, exposed a long thin neck, and longer and thinner legs. (Quackenbos 352; this paragraph makes use of an analytical structure that treats the appearance in terms of the common heads: form, face, dress.)

In the dual role of inventional topoi and organizational rubrics, the principles of arrangement provide the writer with a repertoire of strategies for constructing the development of themes along logical lines that anticipate the reader's intellectual disposition to understand ideas in terms of experience and common sense. Newman observes that the "methodical arrangement of thoughts" according to "certain principles or laws of association" allows the writer to present "a clear and connected view of whatever subject he examines . . . before the minds of others" (*Practical System* 21). In exposition, the "methodical" arrangement of heads constructs the logical substance of the primary definition, which corresponds to the "theme" of the exposition. The writer can treat this theme by employing a variety of plans: the object or process can be analyzed in terms of its constituent parts; classified as a type with distinguishing characteristics; defined by comparing it to analogous objects or contrasting it with examples of a different kind; defined through the amplification of examples; or treated in terms of the causual relations implicit in its mechanical aspects or developmental origins. Nineteenth-century theorists stressed that these schemes of arrangement are fundamental to the expository method despite the wide range of subjects that can be approached from the expository point of view:

[On the function of particular instance and concrete example in exposition of a general principle:] Paley states the question "whether the moral Sentiment be innate" by mentioning a painful incident in Roman History, and supposing it propounded to a certain wild boy caught in the woods of Hanover. . . . Adam Smith's exposition of the principle of Division of Labour is embodied in the manufacture of a Pin. (Bain, *English Composition* [1866] 157–58)

[On definition through "contrasts" and "by stating its constituents":] Thus roundness may be explained by showing, or referring to, a number of bodies of that general figure—a wheel, a turnip, a hill, an apple, the sun, etc; straight by its opposite, bent or crooked; geometry, by its elementary conceptions, the science of position, extension, and form. (Welsh 190)

[On the use of cause and effect in Darwin, "Earth Worms and Their Function":] Worms have played a more important part in the history of the world than most persons would at first suppose. . . . In many parts of England a weight of more than ten tons . . . of dry earth annually passes through their bodies and is brought to the surface on each acre of land. . . . By these means fresh surfaces are continually exposed to the action of the carbonic acid in the soil, and of the humus—acids which appear to be still more efficient in the decomposition of rocks. (Lewis 138)

In developing a theme using the expository method, the writer concentrates on what form of arrangement is best suited to the definition of the subject. In argumentation, the major consideration is the analytical division of the proposition into heads or major premises and the ordering of proofs in a logical progression that adheres to the precedence of a priori arguments (cause to effect) over arguments from sign (testimony or induction). The writer's aim in the arrangement of the written argument is the same as that of the orator: the main proposition must be asserted, the main proposition or theme must be subdivided into the supporting premises, and the arguments supporting these subordinate premises must be arranged according to strength (chapter 3). Using this analytical process, often defined as "dividing" the argument, the writer outlines a plan for the whole composition. One of the more popular nineteenth-century recommendations regarding the arrangement of ideas in argumentation is the stipulation that the writer (or speaker) equate "dividing" the argument with making a detailed outline of the main proposition–subordinate premises structure. Newman, Genung, and De Mille were among the many theorists who insisted that conceiving of the arrangement of the argument in terms of an analytical outline ensures the logical continuity of the analysis across the entire discussion. To illustrate his point that argumentation "admits of an extended plan," Newman explains how the proposition "Children should render to their parents obedience and love" could be "divided":

1. Because they are under obligation to their parents for benefits received from them.
2. Because in this way they secure their own happiness.
3. Because God has commanded them to honor their parents.
   In this division there is a manifest reference to the object of the writer. The different heads are also distinct from each other, and taken together give a sufficiently full view of the subject.[8] (*Practical System* 35)

In Newman's example, the major proposition is subdivided into heads and the arguments are arranged according to the "progressive" method, proceeding in ascending strength toward what the reader would certainly regard as the most irrefutable proof ("God has commanded"). This plan illustrates that the writer will often combine arrangement schemes in the course of the composition: the principle of analysis is fundamental to Newman's arrangement, as is the cause-and-effect scheme that orders the series of arguments. (In an argument that makes use of arguments from sign, the principle of exemplification would be applied to the development of inductive arguments from example.)

Whereas argumentation makes the most use of the principles of analysis, cause and effect, and exemplification in arrangement, the most "natural" arrangement of narrative traces a scheme of causal relations within a succession of events. By arranging ideas according to the order of events, the writer simulates the progress from cause to effect that the reader commonsensically associates with the passage of time and the culmination of action. Nineteenth-century rhetoricians took the view that inventional attention to temporal order and causality inevitably imposes this logical arrangement on all varieties of narrative, historical and fictitious. The general stance affirmed Blair's advice that the first virtue of narration is "Clearness, Order, and Due Connection" (272). As Bain observes, "The first principle of Narrative is to follow the Order of Events. This is to place the events before us as we should have witnessed them. It is also the order of dependence, or cause and effect, a relationship commonly made prominent in narrative. . . . Chronology is the skeleton, the chart, of History" (131). Unlike description and exposition, which can employ a variety of principles of arrangement, narrative development relies primarily on connecting events in a chain of circumstances that appear to begin with a first cause and lead to a final effect. Genung offers this example of what he defines as "one of the prime essentials of story-telling," an arrangement that subordinates every event and description to the "end for which the story exists"; in this instance, the purpose of the narrative is to show how a military defeat came about:

> A detachment of troops was marching along a valley, the cliffs overhanging were crested by the enemy. A serjeant, with eleven men, chanced to become separated from the rest by taking the wrong side of a ravine, which they expected to terminate, but which suddenly deepened into an impassable chasm. The officer in command signalled to the party an order to return. They mistook the signal for a command to charge. . . . On they went, charging up one of these fearful paths, eleven against seventy. The contest could not long be doubtful with such odds. (*Working Principles* 516)

Genung's assumption that the narrative must proceed toward some end was reiterated by a number of nineteenth-century theorists who described the proper conduct of fictitious narrative as an unfolding of events moving toward a denouement through the force of circumstances. The plot of a fictitious narrative is organized around a connected series of incidents and actions leading to a significant result. While the fictitious narrative must incorporate an element of suspense or curiosity and ensure that the events and characters as depicted satisfy the reader's sense of the probable, the unity of the plot is derived from the same attention to order and causality that determines the structure of historical narrative.

Style in Composition

When discussing the application of arrangement principles to prose composition, nineteenth-century theorists were concerned primarily with the design of texts intended to present ideas in terms of natural relations. To communicate ideas effectively, the writer must appeal to the reader's sense of natural order and associative logic. Similarly, the writer's challenge in devising an effective style is to see to it that "the productions of the pen exhibit the characteristics of the mind" (Newman, *Practical System* 157). When discussing the application of general principles of style to prose composition, nineteenth-century rhetoricians affirmed the belles lettres principle that style must appeal to the understanding, the imagination, and the faculty of taste. The writer, like the speaker, must control (1) grammatical correctness in diction and sentence structure; (2) the major qualities of style (perspicuity, energy or vivacity, and elegance); and (3) the use of figurative language (chapter 3). Nineteenth-century theorists reiterated classical advice in a number of their stipulations regarding style, particularly with respect to purity, sentence arrangement, and the major figures; however, the abiding theoretical stance in such discussions was an attention to how style affects the mind. As Hope explains, the essential properties of style spring "out of the necessary laws of thought and feeling" (169).

Perspicuity, energy, elegance, correct diction, and figurative language represent those forms of expression that anticipate the associative dynamics of the mind. Newman, Hope, Day, Bain, and De Mille were among those who promoted an epistemological/belletristic rationale for style and who discussed how principles of style are to be adapted to prose composition as well as oratory (chapter 3). These theorists assumed that a grounding in the principles of style provides the writer (and speaker) with a working understanding of how to use diction, syntax, sentence arrangement, and the figures to produce desired effects on the reader. A consideration of the intellectual and aesthetic effects of various forms of expression is a consistent theme in definitions of the qualities of style and in discussions of how the writer is to apply the rules of style.[9]

Perspicuity, often defined as "clearness" or "clarity," was regarded by nineteenth-century rhetoricians as a necessary condition for "the full effective transfer of thought." In order to achieve this "transfer," the writer never presents the reader with a word or construction that requires undue scrutiny or that creates confusion regarding what meaning is intended. Nineteenth-century rhetoricians followed Blair's lead in considering perspicuity a prerequisite for an effective style. "Indeed, it may be shown that in most cases the so-called beauties of style would be unattainable unless in the first place the language be clear and intelligible" (De Mille 17–18). Affecting word choice and the construction of sentences in both prose and oratory, perspicuity is achieved (1) by purity, or the use of what nineteenth-century theorists often described as "pure English idiom" or "good English usage"; (2) by propriety, or the choice of the most appropriate or "fittest" words for the ideas or emotion being expressed; and (3) by precision, or the selection of words that convey neither more nor less than the meaning that the writer intends (occasionally defined as economy). Correct usage in diction, idiom, and syntax is the necessary foundation for perspicuity: clarity is not possible if the composition is riddled with grammatical errors that distract and confuse the reader. Perspicuity relies on the writer's command of grammar, diction, and skill in arranging clear, unambiguous phrases and sentences; only through a command of these elements of style can the writer compose the type of flawless prose that facilitates the communication of ideas. As A. S. Hill explains, "It is not enough to use language that *may* be understood; he [the writer] should use language that *must* be understood. . . . He should remember that, as far as attention is

Composition and Belles Lettres

called to the medium of communication, so far it is withdrawn from the ideas communicated. How much more serious the evil when the medium obscures or distorts an object" (*Principles* 82). To add emphasis to his point that clearness is one of the major elements in developing "rhetorical excellence" in style, Hill reviews Trollope's comments in *An Autobiography* regarding the importance of developing "the habit of writing clearly":

> "Any writer who has read even a little," says Anthony Trollope, "will know what is meant by the word 'intelligible.' It is not sufficient that there be a meaning that may be hammered out of the sentence, but that the language should be so pellucid that the meaning should be rendered without an effort of the reader; and not only some proposition of meaning, but the very sense, no more and no less, which the writer has intended to put into his words. . . . A young writer, who will acknowledge the truth of what I am saying, will often feel himself tempted by the difficulties of language to tell himself that some one little doubtful passage, some single collocation of words, which is not quite what it ought to be, will not matter. I know well what a stumbling block such a passage may be. But he should leave none such behind him as he goes on." (82)

Hill's deference to Trollope is in keeping with standard methodology: nineteenth-century rhetoricians consistently alluded to the views and techniques of well-known writers in their treatments of the general elements of style. Like Newman, Quackenbos, Hope, and Bain (among others), Hill cites the exemplary style of numerous writers and also provides literary models as illustrations. For example, in his discussion of clarity in word choice, Hill reviews contemporary opinion regarding the clarity of style characteristically achieved by Thomas Macaulay in *The History of England,* quoting first from George M. Trevelyan's *Life and Letters of Macaulay* and then from *The International Review:* "Macaulay never allowed a sentence to pass muster until it was as good as he could make it. He thought little of recasting a chapter in order to obtain a more lucid arrangement, and nothing whatever of reconstructing a paragraph for the sake of one happy stroke or apt illustration"; "Macaulay never goes on, like some writers, talking about 'the former,' and 'the latter,' 'he, she, it, they' through clause after clause while his reader has to look back to see which of several persons it is that is so darkly referred to" (*Principles* 84). Such attention to how the writer can best make use of fundamental stylistic techniques ensures that Hill's treatment of stylistic elements will be taken as general advice for the writer as well as the speaker.

Hill's treatment of clearness points out that writers and speakers alike are obliged to express their thoughts lucidly; clear expression ensures intelligibility. Consequently, perspicuity is the foundation for the more complex rhetorical dimensions of style, energy, and elegance. *Energy* (also *force* or *vivacity*) was defined by nineteenth-century theorists as that property of style which creates a vivid or powerful impression on the reader. Through the use of specific words and "graphic terms" rather than general words and abstractions, the writer creates a vivid image that engages the reader's imagination or memory (Hope 197). Energy depends (1) on the impact of simple and particular words; (2) on the absence of superfluous words and generalizations; (3) on the disposition of words according to strength; (4) on perspicuity in the use of conjunctions and prepositions when connecting parts of sentences; (5) on arranging short and longer sentences in alternating order; (6) on closure of sentences with words of semantic importance rather than with adverbs, prepositions, or unaccented words; and (7) on the use of figures of resemblance and contrast. The general effect of such devices is to express thoughts in a distinctive and arresting manner. Newman explains that distinctiveness and force in composition can be enhanced by a number of means ranging from the the simple substitution of a proper noun for a comparatively bland word to the more complex construction of figurative expressions such as synecdoche or metonymy:

> "An ambition to have a place in the registers of fame, is the Eurystheus, which imposes heroic labors on mankind." In this example, Eurystheus, the name of an individual, is put for a class of

men. The same idea would have been expressed, had the word *taskmaster* been used. But by introducing the word Eurystheus, besides the pleasure derived from the classical allusion, a more distinct idea of what is imposed by ambition on its slaves, is given to the mind. . . . "When we go out into the fields in the evening of the year, a different voice approaches us." The word *evening*, which is properly applied only to the close of the day, is here used in a more extended signification. . . . In the same manner, we speak of the evening of life. In this example, besides the increased distinctness of view, there are pleasing images and associations connected with the close of the day, which are brought before the mind. This example may be classed under either metaphor or synecdoche. (*Practical System* 169–70)

Newman's treatment of vivacity proceeds on the epistemological assumption that distinct ideas are much more easily understood and the belletristic assumption that the imagination is engaged by vivid impressions and "pleasing images." When the understanding and the imagination are so engaged, the reader inevitably finds the discourse more informative and persuasive.

Although nineteenth-century discussions of perspicuity and energy in prose style offered an epistemological rationale, these treatments reinscribed traditional wisdom regarding "pure and clear diction" and "distinction" (*Ad Herennium* 4.12; *De Oratore* 3 38–52). Treatments of elegance, however, drew primarily on belles lettres ideals of taste. Elegance, or beauty, is defined as that quality of style which satisfies the reader's taste or pleasure in the aesthetic. Pleasure intensifies the reaction of the understanding, the emotions, and the will, thus enhancing the reader's acceptance of the writer's ideas. Nineteenth-century treatments of this quality of style conflated elements of both Whately and Blair's discussions of style. Although Whately defines elegance as one of the three major qualities of style, he restricts his recommendations to the simple rule that the writer should strive for "a smooth and easy flow of words in respect of the sound of the sentences" (328–38). Blair associates ornament or grace with melody, harmony, and figurative language and treats these elements as the major qualities of beauty in writing (247–94). Although dependent on Whately's systematic approach of defining elegance as one of three major qualities of style, nineteenth-century treatments of elegance were influenced primarily by Blairian views on what constitutes beauty in writing: elegance or beauty designates those elements of style that appeal directly to the reader's taste. Most influential nineteenth-century theorists, including Day, A. S. Hill, and Genung, offered a treatment of elegance that reviewed all the elements that Whately and Blair ascribed to this quality of style: euphony, rhythm, harmony, and the use of figures to create pleasure.

Nineteenth-century theorists stressed the belletristic principle that beauty cannot be achieved through devices of style alone: the thoughts and emotions that the writer seeks to express must be of a tasteful nature in the first place. As Hope explains, "The *first* constituent *element of beauty*—available in style—resides in its *matter,* of which the main *essential quality* is ITS TRUTH" (211; Hope's italics and capitalization). To develop sentiments of this quality, a writer must study the principles of taste and acquire a "familiarity with what is beautiful in literature" (Genung, *Practical Elements* 24–25). Having developed a tasteful sensibility, the writer must select forms of expression that will affect the reader's imagination and higher sentiments. Elegance in prose style is achieved (1) through *euphony* and *rhythm* (often defined as *melody,* the use of agreeable-sounding words that are easy to pronounce and the arrangement of accented words and pauses to produce a natural rise and fall in tone; (2) through *harmony* in diction and sentence structure, the choice of words appropriate to the subject, balance and unity in sentence construction, unity in the relation of sentences to one another; and (3) through the use of *imagery* or *figures* in the service of expressing profound thoughts and the higher emotions (see Welsh 109–20). The writer, like the speaker, must consider not only what type of words will create melody and harmony in diction and sentence structure but also what harsh sounds or syntactical arrangements are to be avoided. Genung explains, "The writer needs to be on his guard against successions of sounds hard to pronounce together; against jingling recurrence of the same sound; and against harsh constructions of accented or unaccented syllables. Further, he needs to guard against hitches and abruptness in construction, and against ill balance in clauses or phrases related to one another. In a word, he is to aim at smoothness and melody of expression" (*Practical Elements* 23).

By far the most cultivated of the qualities of style, elegance depends on the writer's acquaintance with how natural beauty exhibits itself in sound, design, and image. Genung, Welsh, Hope, and Bain were among the many who provided a range of literary examples intended to illustrate how elegance is achieved in written composition. Whether the writer seeks to compose a poem, a narrative, or some form of nonfiction prose, the essential rule of elegance is the same: thoughts must be expressed in pleasing forms and call forth an imaginative and deeply felt response.[10]

Nineteenth-century rhetoricians regarded figures as a major element of style, and they explained their use primarily in terms of how the they serve perspicuity, energy, and beauty. Figures were classified primarily in terms of epistemological function. Figures of similitude or resemblance include simile, metaphor, and allegory; figures of contrast include antithesis, epigram, and irony; and figures of contiguity include metonymy and synecdoche. Interrogation, exclamation, apostrophe, hyperbole, personification, and climax were also regarded as principal figures because of their use in creating a mixture of epistemological effects (chapter 2). Nineteenth-century treatments of the principal figures analyzed how each figure appeals to the mental faculties and illustrated their use in various types of composition. Whether composing a poem or a philosophical treatise, the writer can use a variety of figures to add distinctiveness to ideas (energy): Bain explains that "some Similitudes enable us to picture an object vividly to the mind, and are called on that account, *pictureseque;* as in Chaucer's Squire, 'With lockes crull, *as they were laid in press*' "(*English Composition* [1866] 6). Writers can sharpen the force of ideas by using the figures of synecdoche and metonymy to "reduce an idea to its focus and centre, and make that do the work" (Genung, *Working Principles* 90). Climax, antithesis, exclamation, repetition, and interrogation can be used to structure sentences and sentence combinations to make a "striking" impression on the reader (Newman, *Practical System* 176–178). Newman offers an analysis of interrogation and repetition that points out the nineteenth-century view that the use of the figures in the service of energy (or any other effect) is the consequence of the writer capitalizing on a natural conjunction between thought and language:

> The Interrogation and Repetition are the language of an excited mind. Where the former is used, the writer seems so impressed with the truth of what he asserts, that he is not content to state it in the cold form of a proposition, but utters it in a manner that challenges any one to regard it with doubt. The Repetition also gives evidence of a full conviction of the truth of what is asserted, and of a deep sense of importance, and is well calculated to convey these impressions to the reader in a striking manner. (178)

A writer can also use the figures to create elegant effects by appealing to the reader's natural attraction to novelty, higher sentiments, and images of natural beauty. The reader's imagination and taste can be affected by employing figures that represent ideas in an unfamiliar or startling way (e.g., metaphor and antithesis), express powerful emotions (e.g., apostrophe and exclamation), or create harmonious sounds, rhythms, and a felt sense of temporal experience (e.g., onomatopoeia and climax).

Providing various illustrations of how the figures can be adapted to these ends in composition, theorists such as Genung, Newman, De Mille, and Bain made the point that figurative language is indispensable to the writer who wishes to call on deep feelings or stimulate the reader's imagination. In this representative discussion of the use of figures of resemblance, Bain explains how figures create intensity of feeling in various types of composition:

> For this purpose, the comparison should be to something that excites the feelings more strongly than the thing compared. Thus, Sir Philip Sydney, in endeavoring to give a lively idea of the rousing effect of the ballad of Chevy Chase, says, 'it stirs the heart *like the sound of a trumpet.*' Chaucer's description of the Squire, contains several comparisons for raising the feelings.

> Embroided was he, *as it were a mead, As full of freshe flowers white and rede* Singing he was, or fluting all the day *he was as fresh as is the month of May.*
> So, the following simile from the Odyssey is calculated to give a more lively sense of the speaker's sentiment of veneration. "I follow behind, *as in the footsteps of a god.*" Again, "Justice" (says Aristotle) "is more glorious than the Eastern Star or the Western Star." (*English Composition* [1866] 5–6; Bain's italics)

Bain assumes that the effect of the figures will be fundamentally the same no matter what species of composition (or oratory) the rhetorician produces. This theoretical assumption is characteristic of nineteenth-century treatments of style, which defined technique primarily in terms of the epistemological effects that elements of style can be expected to create in all rhetorical genres. Since the writer is always obliged to consider what form of expression best suits the response called for by the subject, the choice of stylistic techniques must always be governed by a general consideration of how language affects the faculties (taste included) and by the specific consideration of how diction, sentence structure, and the use of figures can serve the writer's intention. Rather than regarding style as an artifice of expression, nineteenth-century theorists favored Blair's view that "style is nothing else, than the sort of expression which our thoughts most readily assume" when the obligations of perspicuity, energy, and elegance have been met (202).[11]

The Species of Composition

A philosophical interest in how the principles of composition are related to the natural processes of the mind extended to nineteenth-century treatments of the prose genres. When discussing argument, description, narrative, and exposition as species of prose, nineteenth-century theorists had in mind compositions in which proof of a proposition, representation of an object, narration of a plot, or definition of an idea or object correspond to the formal subject of the discourse. These genres of prose were defined in terms of the dominant inventional process employed in the development of subject matter and the overall epistemological aim of appealing to the understanding and the imagination. Nineteenth-century rhetoricians viewed argument as both an oral and written form, but they linked description, narrative, and exposition primarily with prose composition. Although theorists in this period reiterated the New Rhetorical view that both literary and nonliterary discourse rely on the same principles, they provided a more extensive account of the various forms of nonliterary prose than did their eighteenth-century predecessors. By applying the generic categories description, narration, and exposition to a broader range of subjects and popular writing forms, nineteenth-century rhetoricians extended the formal range of prose genres.[12]

Throughout the nineteenth century, argumentation was identified as a species of discourse that can take its form in oratory or prose. Judicial oratory and deliberative oratory were regarded as types of public speaking that are often argumentative in substance (chapter 4). Newman observes that argumentative composition takes in all "the various forms of argument" that employ the argumentative method: "the statement of proofs, the assigning of causes, and generally those writings, which are addressed to the reasoning faculties" (*Practical System* 28). Comprehending all forms of writing that promote a proposition or support the affirmative or the negative view of a question, argumentation was often equated with what Quackenbos refers to as the "thesis," or any composition in which "the writer lays down a proposition" (385). Nineteenth-century theorists addressed the nature of argument under two different headings: in treatments of the methods and invention of argument and in discussions of the kinds of discourse. Most theorists provided both discussions, alluding to examples of argumentative composition in analyses of argumentative invention and providing explicit illustrations of the genre. These treatments stressed the fact that the range of argumentative composition cuts across a broad field of interests including theology, education, philosophy, social welfare, politics, and history.

In the conclusion of his analysis of the methods of argument, A. S. Hill provides an inventory of the types of prose that fall into the category

Composition and Belles Lettres

"examples of argumentative composition": "the chapter on 'Fundamental Principles Respecting Capital,' in Mill's 'Principles of Political Economy;' Sir James Fitzjames Stephen's article on the suppression of boycotting, published in 'The Nineteenth-Century,' December, 1886; Mathew Arnold's 'Last Words' at the end of his papers 'On Translating Homer,' in 'Essays in Criticism'; Huxley's 'Three Lectures on Evolution' delivered in New York, 1876" (*Principles* 399–400). Similarly, David J. Hill and Bain refer to a variety of texts in their discussions of argumentative invention: Burke on the "Sublime and the Beautiful," "Paley in his Evidences," "Locke's controversy with Stillingfleet"; and "Hobbes's defence of his theory of the Will" (Hill, *Science* 129, 132; Bain, *English Composition* [1866] 188, 196, 197). Welsh lists a variety of subjects that the student could examine in an argumentative thesis:

> (1) Under Chatham, the British nation rose suddenly to prosperity; therefore, he was the cause of the improvement. (2) States, in respect to vital constitution, are like individuals—they pass through the successive stages of infancy, youth, maturity, old age, and death. (3) The sun and the planets gravitate; therefore, the stars gravitate. (4) Designing persons are untrustworthy; Everybody forms designs; Nobody can be trusted. (5) Whatever represses the liberty of mankind ought to be resisted; Among things that do so, are governments; Governments ought to be resisted. (212–13)

Welsh, Bain, and David J. Hill confirm the range of subjects implied by A. S. Hill's list of illustrative texts. These theorists unanimously promoted the maxim that the characteristic element of argumentative composition is method; the writer's options regarding subject matter are relatively unlimited. Any composition that aims to convince the reader through logical proof falls under the heading of argument.[13] Since they assumed that the principles of argumentation apply equally to public speaking and to the composition of theses, nineteenth-century theorists made few specific recommendations regarding the preparation of the argument to be delivered or read. The methods of composing oral and written arguments are the same:

the proposition must be clearly defined; analytical or empirical proofs must be presented in support of the proposition; opposing arguments must be refuted; and the whole argument must develop progressively toward an irrefutable conclusion. Writers of theses were reminded, however, that in written argument there is a more compelling necessity to anticipate what objections any reasonable reader might make to the facts and principles cited in support of the proposition. While the orator can develop an argument in response to the views of a particular audience or adversary, the writer must develop evidence and logical connections with a more general readership in mind.

Description was defined as a genre made up of a variety of types of prose including travel literature, geographic tracts, and writing in the "natural sciences" such as anatomy, zoology, and botany (Bain, *English Composition* [1866] 120–27; A.S. Hill, *Principles* 251). These subgenres were not analyzed in and of themselves but simply cited as examples of the type of prose that creates an image or picture in the reader's mind. In the course of treating the nature of descriptive invention, nineteenth-century theorists defined the unique subject matter of descriptive composition by identifying the content of description and by referring to models that illustrate effective descriptive techniques. As with most nineteenth-century treatments of the descriptive genres, Bain's discussion of description defines a range of subjects typically associated with descriptive writing:

> We describe a field or a space of ground as triangular, square, oblong, semicircular, &c. A building is represented as long, narrow, lofty, circular, or quadrangular. A hill is conical, or dome-shaped, or truncated. A valley is straight or winding. A city is round and compact, or long and straggling. A geographical tract is given in the first instance by form. (118)

> In the orderly enumeration of the contents, it is shown how the containing whole is made up. Any well-recognized form is sufficient. . . . A thing may be heart-shaped, leaf-shaped, egg-shaped; it may resemble a boot, like Italy, a spider or familiar shapes. A star is then known as in the belt of Orion, or in the tail of the

Composition and Belles Lettres

Great Bear. Carlyle calls the map of Austria without Bavaria "a human figure with its belly belonging to somebody else." (119)

Although the theoretical emphasis in this analysis is on how fundamental descriptive principles such as enumeration of the parts and outline and size are to be realized, Bain refers directly and indirectly to the types of prose that fall under the rubric of description ("geographic tract," Carlyle's map). Bain's method is indicative of the way in which nineteenth-century theorists typically identified a range of descriptive genres in the course of defining the appropriate subject matter and unique scope of description. Taking this approach in his analysis of how descriptive writing makes "things perceptible by the senses" to "things cognizable by the mind," Welsh observes that description comprehends a range of subgenres such as

> books of travel or adventure, in writings which give an account of cities or civilized countries, as Kane's voyages to the Arctic regions, Livingstone's explorations in Africa, Prescott's histories of Mexico and Peru . . . the delineation of mental states, as in Satan's or Hamlet's soliloquy; of the moral and intellectual faculties, as in scientific treatises; of individual character, as in biographies . . . [and as] regards natural scenery and human handiwork.
> (*Complete Rhetoric* 179)

A. S. Hill also outlines a broad range for description. Drawing on a distinction between two general categories of description, "one in the service of science, the other in the service of art," Hill points out that scientific description is exemplified in treatises focusing on the analysis of an object in order to distinguish its parts. This type of discourse includes descriptions of plants, animals, and events as well as many common documents such as passports, inventories, title deeds, and advertisements (*Principles* 251–53). Like Bain and Welsh, who assume that fundamental rhetorical principles shape the form and effects of all types of discourse, Hill sees no essential rhetorical difference between the descriptive passage in a literary work and the descriptive treatise on geography: the scientific writer, novelist, and poet must attend to basic principles such as enumeration of parts, size, shape, and natural order of spatial relations. Scientific description provides useful information, while artistic description employs descriptive techniques to create an image.

Nineteenth-century theorists included literary texts among those that rely on descriptive principles and frequently cited literary models to illustrate the characteristic subject matter and techniques of description (and narration). In this summary of the "conditions of a good description," David J. Hill comments on the "masterly description of the Puritan Balfour and his surroundings, by Sir Walter Scott":

> "Upon entering the place of refuge, he found *Balfour seated* on his humble couch, with a pocket *Bible open* in his hand, which he seemed to study with intense *meditation*. His *broadsword,* which he had unsheathed in the first alarm, at the arrival of the dragoons, lay naked across his knees, and the little *taper* that stood beside him on the old *chest,* which served the purpose of a table, threw a partial light upon those stern and harsh *features,* in which ferocity was rendered more solemn and dignified by a wild cast of tragic enthusiasm. His *brow* was that of one in whom some strong o'ermastering principle has over-whelmed all other passions and feelings,—*like the swell of a high spring-tide,* when the usual cliffs and breakers vanish from the eye, and their existence is only indicated by the chafing foam of the waves that burst and wheel over them." Notice how the writer has fulfilled the conditions of a good description. First, he takes his point of view at the entrance of the place where Balfour is. He then notes the posture of the Puritan, the couch on which he is seated, the open Bible in his hand, his meditation in study, his broadsword, the taper by his side, the chest on which he stands, the light on his features, his brow so expressive of his character, and finally completes his picture with the impressive comparison which closes the passage. (*Elements* 166; Hill's italics)

Through such commentary, nineteenth-century theorists illustrated the application of descriptive principles to the composition of literary as well as nonliterary treatises. In his discussion of description as "the portrayal of concrete objects, material or spiritual," Genung identifies works embodying the range that nineteenth-century rhetoricians usually assigned to description: Ruskin, *Stones of Venice*, Henry James, *Portraits of Places*, Victor Hugo, *Les Misérables*, John Richard Green, *A Short History of the English People*, Dickens, *David Copperfield*, Tennyson's "Palace of Art," Stevenson, *Travels with a Donkey*, Shakespeare, *Antony and Cleopatra*, act 2, scene 2, and Milton, *Paradise Lost*, book 9, (*Working Principles* 481–503). Genung's view of the species of description presupposes one of the most distinctive nineteenth-century attitudes toward genres: species of rhetoric were identified according to inventional procedures and overall epistemological intention. By applying this rationale to the analysis of descriptive composition, nineteenth-century rhetoricians defined description as a broad genre comprehending fiction, drama, and poetry, travel literature, history, scientific treatises, and a host of commonplace informative documents.[14]

In treating narration as a generic classification, nineteenth-century rhetoricians identified two general categories of narrative—history (including biography) and fiction. In composing history and fiction, writers draw from a repertoire of rhetorical strategies designed to re-create a realistic sense of unfolding time and changing circumstances. In all forms of narrative, the writer aims to convince the understanding of the probability of the plot and move the imagination to associate the dramatized events with experience. "The transaction to be narrated may be real or fictitious; in either case, however, the procedures are essentially the same" (Genung, *Practical Elements* 357). The composition of narratives must respect epistemological constraints: events are related from a specific point of view with attention to a logical temporal sequence; all elements of a narrative are parts of a greater whole and are interrelated in such a way as to satisfy the demands of probability. By defining the proper subject matter and techniques of narration through references to prose types and by the citation of representative treatises, nineteenth-century rhetoricians provided an inventory of the various types of composition that rely on narrative techniques:

Nineteenth-Century Rhetoric

[On the simple succession of time as the principle of arrangement in narration:] As it is possible in discourse, thus, only to present the object at successive stages, passing over the intermediate intervals, judgment is necessary in the selection of those phases of the object which are most important. In the history of a nation, the most important changes in the direction of its exertions . . . may, thus, be selected as the points to be exhibited to view. (Day, *Elements* 58)

[On the simple and more complex forms of narration:] Narrative is easier both to compose and to comprehend than Description. The Narrative of incidents in a Fable is such as to dispense with rules of art. And, even in many large operations, as in Government, there may be no more than a single thread to follow. . . . But events of importance usually imply a mechanism and a set of arrangements more or less complicated, and occupying a definite space. . . . Such are—the movements of armies, and the occupation of new countries; the larger processes of industry; the busy life of cities; the workings of Nature on the great scale—the vicissitudes of the seasons, day and night, storms, tides, and the flow of rivers; Geological changes; the evolution of vegetable and animal life. (Bain, *Elements of Composition* [1866] 129–30)

[On shaping the narrative to convey different types of information:] We have a story to tell . . . in what order shall the incidents be narrated? If the story be a long one, there must probably be many shifts in scene. . . . How shall each be treated? To propose a concrete example, suppose we are telling a story, historical or fictitious, in which one of the incidents is the first battle of Bull Run. Shall we describe it in detail, as Carlyle describes the battles of Frederick, and Tolstoi the battles of Napoleon's wars in Russia; or shall we keep it in the background as Thackeray keeps Waterloo in "Vanity Fair"? (Wendell 163)

Nineteenth-century theorists applied the term *narrative* to various types of nonfictitious history. The historian's narrative can address a range of diverse topics: the rise of nations, cities, and industry; accounts of battles; geographical and natural developments; "the state of science"; or literary history. Biography and autobiography are forms of narrative closely related to history in subject matter and technique. Like the historian, the biographer must respect the order of time and the principle of unity; the story of the life of a prominent man or woman proceeds from birth to death and chronicles events in terms of cause and effect. Historical narratives trace successive events and effects in the service of an overall observation or characterization; the explanatory force of the narrative lies in the historian's ability to offer a story that provides a unified and complete explanation of a particular theme: "The theme may be the life or the transaction of an individual; the history of a community or nation through the whole or particular stages of its existence; it may be a cause producing its effects on a single individual . . . it may be an effect experienced over the world . . . or of a single continent, as the civilization of Europe" (Day, *Elements* 63).

Comprehending texts ranging from Trevelyan's *Life of Macaulay* and William Minto's *Manual of English Prose Literature* to Homer's *Odyssey* and George Eliot's *Silas Marner,* narrative was defined in nineteenth-century theory as any form of discourse that instructs and pleases through a chronicle of facts or experience. One of the most distinctive features of the narrative is what nineteenth-century theorists often referred to as *movement* or the flow of the plot. In fictitious narrative, movement is a consequence of the structure of the plot. A unified plot utilizes principles of natural order and completeness and is distinguished by significance, probability, suspense, and climax. Unity in fiction also depends on consistent point of view. Closely related to the principle of purpose, point of view establishes a consistent focal point from which the events are related. Without consistent point of view or shifts in point of view for which the reader is fully prepared, the reader loses sight of temporal relations between events, causal connections between primary and subordinate elements of the plot, and the general point of the story. Nineteenth-century theorists cited exemplary models and provided excerpts from well-known works to illustrate elements of narrative such as point of view and qualities of plot. For example, Genung illustrates the logic of episodic structure through an analysis of Dicken's *Barnaby Rudge:*

Nineteenth-Century Rhetoric

Transition from one kind of scene to another is frequently exemplified in Dicken's *Barnaby Rudge*. The main story of this novel is an historic episode of stormy and tragic import—the Gordon Riots of 1780. With this, however, is interwoven a story of contrasted character, illustrating no less strikingly all that is good and simple and peaceful,—the story, namely, of Barnaby and his mother. The following transition will show how the points of alternation between the stories were chosen: "While the worst passions of the worst men were thus working in the dark, and the mantle of religion, assumed to cover the ugliest deformities, threatened to become the shroud of all that was good and peaceful in society, a circumstance occurred which once more altered the positions of two persons [Barnaby Rudge and his mother] from whom this history has long been separated, and to whom it must now return." (*Working Principles* 540)

Other writers whose works were cited frequently as exemplary models of narrative method include Poe, Irving, Austen, Eliot, Hawthorne, Maupassant, Trollope, Defoe, Scott, Bret Harte, Hughes (*Tom Brown at Oxford*), and Kipling (A. S. Hill, *Principles* 281–99). These writers command the rhetorical skill on which fictitious narrative is founded—the ability to explain events so logically and imaginatively that the reader is convinced of the probability of the tale. While the challenge to the historian or the biographer is to transform facts into lifelike pictures, the novelist's challenge is to strike a balance between verisimilitude and novelty.[15]

In analyzing narrative, nineteenth-century theorists paid consistent attention to how the writer keeps the interest and the attention of the reader by appealing to the associative dynamics of the understanding. All appeals to conviction rely on providing the mind with knowledge framed along certain lines: narratives present an idea by clearly delineating sequence and synchronism of events, order of time, and retrospective references; descriptions provide systematic analyses of complex objects that allow the reader to identify and locate the object in space. Similarly, expository prose is intelligible because it frames information in terms of generalizations supported by individual facts. Exposition explains an idea as a general notion or common term that applies equally to any individual of the class. The expository writer is objective and aims to set forth the "pure truth"; such an intention can account either for the major substance of the work or a substantial portion of the discourse. Nineteenth-century theorists referred to various types of exposition within discussions of the proper subject matter of exposition and the methods of definition. Comprehending subjects ranging from the physical and natural sciences, exposition was viewed as the most inclusive of the prose genres:

> [Exposition treats either a term or a proposition:] Examples.—1. Of terms. Scientific terms and subjects, as gravitation, evolution, law, . . . biology, psychology, eschatology; multitudes of terms used in common discussion, as nature, art, literature, criticism, public opinion, reform, common-sense, culture, orthodoxy. 2. Of propositions. Many of the maxims, proverbs, and terse assertions in frequent use are subject to exposition as well as argument. For instance: "Curiosity is but vanity"; "the poet is born, not made"; "the style is the man"; "no man is a hero to his valet." Indeed, it may be said that every proposition needs to be examined as to its meaning before it is tested as to its truth; this is the first logical step. Under this head are to be reckoned the texts of sermons, which are taken as embodying some moral idea or lesson to be expounded. (Genung, *Practical Elements* 386)

The nineteenth-century formalization of exposition as a multivaried genre departed from the eighteenth-century attitude toward "instructive" prose. Blair identifies instructive prose as a "species of composition" but offers little in the way of explanation as to exactly what constitutes what he defines as "philosophical writing" (290–93). Widening the belletristic category "philosophical writing" to include all species of systematic analysis, nineteenth-century theorists outlined a range of expository subjects and stipulated a number of types of prose that aim to define or instruct. De Mille expresses this view when he characterizes exposition as addressing knowledge in "all the departments of human thought, knowledge, or inquiry" (467). Claiming any variant of prose in which the objective definition of terms and principles is the subject, exposition subsumes all forms of objective analysis: textbooks; analytical, philosophical, and theological treatises; guidebooks to moral behavior and religious practices; practical instructions regarding machinery and industrial processes; instructions regarding household skills and agricultural methods; scientific treatises on natural and mental phenomena; political analysis; newspaper reports; and critical explanations of literary and artistic principles. A. S. Hill refers to a number of these forms in his analysis of exemplary models of exposition; Hill's wide-ranging treatment of exposition gives an account of the variety of prose forms that can present objective information: "political writing" in the *London Spectator;* Asa Gray, *Botanical Text-Book;* Horace Bushnell, *Work and Play;* Phillips Brooks, *Lectures on Preaching;* J. S. Mill, *Principles of Political Economy;* H. Taine, *On Intelligence;* William James, *The Principles of Psychology;* William Kingdon Clifford, *On the Aims and Instruments of Scientific Thought;* Cardinal Newman, *The Idea of a University;* and Alfred Russel Wallace, *Darwinism, an Exposition of the Theory of Natural Selection* (*Principles* 301–26). Considered the predominant form of prose in general use, exposition enjoyed the reputation among nineteenth-century and early twentieth-century rhetoricians as the "workaday form" of composition.[16]

Nineteenth-century theorists considered exposition to be that type of composition which presents a subject "exactly as it is." The expository writer does not aim to charm the fancy or to engage the emotions through personality and feelings; the expository writer aims to simplify the complex and make the abstract clear by accounting for the nature of a thing, its scope, and its relations. In identifying the qualities of expository prose, nineteenth-century theorists stressed that exposition proceeds in one of two methodological directions: toward the definition of an object as a representative of a class or toward the definition of an object in terms of its individual features. In defining a term, a principle, or a process, the writer amplifies a logical definition through developmental strategies such as etymological and historical review, analysis, "iteration and obverse iteration," and exemplification (Genung, *Practical Elements* 384–98; Welsh,

Complete Rhetoric 190–94). To illustrate such methods, nineteenth-century theorists provided excerpts from exemplary models. Welsh identifies exemplification as "the leading method of expository writing" and notes its use in this excerpt from a popular scientific treatise (Arnott, *Elements of Physics*) explaining the principle that motion is as permanent a state as rest: "A ball rolled on level grass soon stops—if rolled on a carpet over a smooth floor, it goes longer—if on the bare floor, it goes longer still—on a smooth sheet of ice, it hardly suffers retardation from friction, and, if the air be moving with it, will reach a distant point" (*Complete Rhetoric* 192). Genung provides an excerpt from "an encyclopaedia article on the oak" to illustrate how the expository writer establishes a clear sense of class through the identification of characteristic traits: "Most of the trees belonging to the oak family are remarkable for their rugged bark and for the great abundance of tannin which it contains. They have large and strong roots, penetrating very deeply or extending very far horizontally. The trunks are distinguished for their massiveness, and for the weight, strength, and . . . the durability of the wood" (*Practical Elements* 385). Newman cites the explanatory structure of a guide to the morning prayer as an illustration of the analytical method of exposition in "didactic preceptive writing": "First . . . every morning, make your private prayer unto Almighty God, give him thanks for his protection of you the night past. . . . Secondly, a little before you go to bed, make again your private prayers to God. . . . Always be attentive to your prayers, and keep your mind upon the business you are about. . . . Let no occasion whatsoever hinder you from your private, constant devotion" (*Practical System* 225–26). Whether addressing matters of popular interest or scientific subjects, expository composition provides a systematic explanation of class, distinguishing traits, constitution, and function.

    Nineteenth-century theorists regarded the letter and the critical essay as forms of composition with close ties to exposition. In recognizing letter writing as a species of composition, nineteenth-century rhetoricians followed Blair's example of designating the epistolary form as a mode of rhetoric, but they generally took a much wider view of this genre. Early nineteenth-century theorists such as Jamieson and E. A. Ansley, who were heavily indebted to a Blairian theoretical system, reiterated Blair's categorical definition of epistolary writing as one of the leading divisions of literature (along with narratives, descriptions, expository essays, argumentation, and oratory). Several later theorists, such as Quackenbos, David J. Hill, and John G. R. McElroy, treat the letter as a minor rather than major form of composition.[17] Those who did treat epistolary composition were consistent in defining the letter as a form with several subgenres: didactic letters are designed for instruction; news letters are communications to papers and periodicals containing accounts of events, ceremonies, celebritions, and expressions of opinion; official letters are exchanged between "men in their public capacity" (David J. Hill, *Elements* 172); business letters are concise treatments of transactions and mutual interests; letters of friendship conduct "conversations" in a more dignified manner than common to verbal exchange; condolence letters are written to express sympathy to those who have experienced a loss; and letters of congratulation express joy at the achievement or personal happiness of another. In writing a letter, the writer must be aware of its essential parts (the superscription or introduction, the body or substance, the subscription or closing expression and signature, and the address) and the importance of using a correct and natural style (David J. Hill, *Elements* 171–74; Quackenbos 357–58). Because the letter was regarded as a form in which presentation is an important aspect of communicating effectively, nineteenth-century treatments of the letter also stressed neatness in handwriting and in "folding and sealing."

Criticism and Composition

Nineteenth-century theorists considered criticism a highly complex form of exposition that is analytical and evaluative in intention. Frequently requiring the definition and explanation of political, philosophical, or aesthetic principles, criticism relied on an analytic method that supports a judgment regarding "almost every variety of subject," including current events (Hart 288). Beyond an account of the quality of an intellectual or artistic work, the critic must evaluate exactly how the work has served truth and beauty. Criticism in the fields of "antiquarian, scientific, or historical investigation" typically appears in the form of the didactic treatise or the personal essay (Quackenbos 316). When writing in the didactic form, the critic centers on a definite proposition regarding the achievement of the work in question and proceeds by logical explication to substantiate that view. In the personal form of criticism, the critic sets aside the formal methods of exposition in favor of a more conversational style and a more speculative stance. This personal mode of criticism is more typical of the literary essay and criticism in the fine arts. Welsh comments on the range of subjects a critic potentially can address and names several of the writers whom nineteenth-century rhetoricians regarded as "masters" of the critical form:

> Under the auspices of a confederacy of men of wit and learning in the early part of the present century, essay writing assumed a new phase. We allude to the foundation of the Reviews and Magazines,—Edinburgh, London Quarterly, North American, Blackwood's, Westminster, all of which became the exemplaries of numerous similar publications. The primary object of most was to furnish thorough criticisms of books and careful papers on the current topics of politics and reform. As their scope enlarged, contributions were received on any subject to which the writer had devoted special attention. Hence a peculiar style—brief, pithy, trenchant, often eloquent, but always positive. The master spirits were Jeffrey Sidney Smith, Lamb, Hazlitt, De Quincey, and Macaulay. . . . Meanwhile, Irving's *Sketch Book* appeared, forming in America an epoch in this kind of literature; of the same generic character as Addison's essays. . . . With one or another modification, the chief of which are editorials, criticism, reviews, and dissertations, the essay has latterly absorbed an enormous amount of the productive energy of mind on both sides of the Atlantic. Indeed the number of essayists is almost identical with the number of writers. A few, like Emerson and Whipple, have limited their writings to essays; the most are also, like Arnold, Froude, Sted-

213

man, and Lowell, historians, biographers, poets, and so forth. (270–71)

Although nineteenth-century rhetoricians regarded the review as one of the most common venues for the critical point of view, they considered the aim and methods of critical writing to be the same no matter the mode. In citing "Macaulay's celebrated article in the Edinburgh Review, in 1825, on the occasion of the recovery of a lost work of Milton's" as a model work of criticism, Kellog expresses the popular nineteenth-century opinion that the critical method should both inform and evaluate: "The reviewer, in the first few paragraphs, gives a brief, but comprehensive and sufficiently critical judgment of the book or essay whose title is quoted, and then takes occasion to go on and give a general review of the character of Milton as an author and a man" (289). In general, the critical essay explicates a particular point of view toward the work. In the service of explaining this point of view, the critic provides a summary of the work as well as an account of whether the work should be regarded as valuable, significant, or tasteful. The critic explicates the meaning of texts (1) by identifying and analyzing the sense of the work and (2) by offering an interpretation of the artistic or intellectual achievement of the work. In stipulating how these methods apply to literary criticism, Genung describes this two-stage process as grammatical exegesis and interpretation. Grammatical exegesis of the text is a process not unlike the "historian's ascertainment of facts": the critic ascertains what is actually and literally said; what is conveyed indirectly; and what relative weight and rank are to be attributed to the various ideas expressed (*Working Principles* 579). The literary critic ultimately aspires to an explanation of how the work came to be and how the artist in question has established some claim on universal truth. In providing this interpretation of the work, the writer calls on a variety of methods that allow the reader to gain a sense of the text and its literary dimensions: abstract or précis-writing, in which the thought of the literary work is reproduced in an abbreviated form; paraphrase and metaphrase, in which the author's expressed thoughts are reproduced in other words;

and translation, in which the author's expression is reproduced in exactly equivalent expression. Reviewing these methods of criticism in slightly different terms, Quackenbos describes how the critic evaluates a literary work:

> He must look at the sentiments expressed, and judge of their correctness and consistency; he must view the performance as a whole, and see whether it clearly and properly embodies the ideas intended to be conveyed; he must examine whether there is sufficient variety in the style, must note its beauties, and show, if it is susceptible of improvement, in what that improvement should consist; he must see whether the principles of syntax or rhetoric are violated; and finally, must extend his scrutiny even to the individual words employed. (318)

Whether the critic is writing a review of a literary work, play, musical performance, or public event, the writer is obliged to analyze the prominent elements of the performance or text and provide some sense of its worth. Without an attempt at judgment, the critical essay becomes merely a description or informative exposition in the simplest sense. The most distinctive aspect of criticism as a species of composition is that it goes beyond the aims of ordinary exposition to provide the reader with edifying opinions regarding both the subject matter and the aesthetic achievements of the work.[18]

The best critical writing is free from bias; the critic must rely on objective standards such as the principles of taste and the rhetorical principles of argumentation and style in the assessment of the work. Nineteenth-century rhetoricians valued the objectivity of criticism for philosophical and pedagogical reasons. Like their eighteenth-century colleagues, nineteenth-century rhetoricians considered criticism a primary means by which standards of taste are defined and promoted. When the critic offers an evaluative account of an idea or event, the reading public receives explicit as well as implicit instruction in what constitutes intellectual and aesthetic merit. That work which is admirable conforms to the standards of taste; that work which is flawed errs in some fundamental way either in concept or execution. Although nineteenth-century rhetoricians regarded criticism as a type of writing that focuses more on "how genius surmounts difficulties" than on defects in a composition, they affirmed the belletristic view of criticism by promoting the notion that the critical method exemplifies the process of intellectual discrimination crucial to the cultivation of taste. From the nineteenth-century point of view, criticism performs two edifying functions: (1) the critic provides specific assessments that guide the reader as to whether or not an event or work is worthy of attention; and (2) the critic furthers the reader's understanding of the nature of taste by affirming certain principles of taste as the universal standard of critical judgment.

While the promotion of standards of taste among the reading public was considered the major function of critical writing, nineteenth-century rhetoricians also considered critical judgment to be beneficial to the writer's development. Nineteenth-century rhetoricians were committed to the assumption that the writer's ability to improve in the composition beyond the simple level of correct writing depends on the degree to which a critical sensibility is acquired. By developing critical abilities through the study of taste, the appreciation of the "masters of literature," and frequent exercise in critical analysis, the writer learns to identify flaws and also to develop rhetorical force in all species of composition. Nineteenth-century theorists considered this interrelationship between the critical and the constructive aspects of rhetoric as the only dynamic that allows writers to move beyond competence to true eloquence (chapter 3). Genung expresses the attitude of his age when he describes the connection of the study of rhetorical principles to the study of literary models as the complete "circuit of rhetorical training" needed to help the student "discover his own rhetoric" (*Handbook* vii).[19]

Presuming that the development of critical judgment is indispensable to the writer, many nineteenth-century theorists appended critical exercises to their discussions of compositional principles and the nature of criticism. Quackenbos, Bain, Newman, David J. Hill, Genung, and Wendell were just a few of the the influential theorists who assumed that by

Composition and Belles Lettres

evaluating texts in terms of fundamental rhetorical principles, writers learn a variety of methods for implementing these strategies and come to appreciate even more how techniques of form and style contribute to rhetorical force. Critical exercises typically focused on the application of specific rhetorical principles and covered a range of elements such as correct and appropriate diction, sentence arrangement, techniques for creating perspicuity, energy, and elegance, and the methods of description, narration, argumentation, and exposition. In these exercises, attention is directed to exemplary rhetorical practices as well as examples of faulty execution:

> Correct the Redundancies in the following.
> 1. Magnanimity and greatness of mind.—*Ferguson*
> 2. The mysteries of the arcana of alchemy.—*D'Israeli*
> 3. The vice of covetousness is what enters deeper into the soul than any other.—*Guardian* (David J. Hill, *Science* 282)

> Point out the figures that occur, stating which are faulty, and why. Explain any violations of the essential properties of style. Name the elements of sublimity or beauty that you may find in any of the selections:—
> 1. "Roll on, thou deep and dark blue ocean—roll!
>   Ten thousand fleets sweep over thee in vain;
>   Man marks the earth with ruin—his control
>   Stops with the shore". . . . *Byron.*
> 2. "Here is a letter, lady;
>   The paper as the body of my friend,
>   And every word in it is a gaping wound,
>   Issuing life-blood." *Merchant of Venice*
>   (Quackenbos 323–24)

> Literary Analysis. ["Intimations of Immortality"] Express briefly (and in general terms) the idea contained in stanza ii. . . . Literary Analysis.—160–166. The pupil will observe the grandeur of the thought imaged in these splendid lines, which should be committed to memory. (Swinton 293–99)[20]

The present Selection [John Ruskin, "Of the Pathetic Fallacy"] exemplifies the use of Exposition in literary criticism, addressed to the reader of general culture, and put in a style adapted to give pleasure as well as instruction to all. Lines 1–9. What is the exact subject of exposition laid down in this paragraph? By what antithetical adjectives are the two sides of the subject set over against each other? (Genung, *Handbook* 233)

Exercises such as these are had two purposes: to aid the student of rhetoric in the development of a critical habit of thought and to train the writer to criticize and improve his own work. Nineteenth-century theorists presumed that a complete understanding of the laws of discourse and the principles of composition could not be obtained without protracted exercise in "criticism and production" (David J. Hill, *Science* 264).

The nineteenth-century view that the development of critical judgment is fundamental to the development of eloquent writing abilities ensured that the study of composition was linked inextricably to the study of literature. This relationship between poetics and the study of rhetorical abilities was encouraged by the neoclassical commitment to imitation, a deep-seated aspect of nineteenth-century theory; however, the primary influence that fused poetics and rhetoric was the powerful control belletristic philosophy exerted on nineteenth-century attitudes toward rhetorical expertise. The alignment of poetics and rhetoric was so fundamental a tenet in nineteenth-century composition theory that throughout the century critical judgment was equated with the most educated insight into the nature of rhetorical composition. Channing comments on the interrelationship between critical judgment and an understanding of compositional principles in his lecture "Forms of Criticism":

Ask the man of taste, the true critic, how he accounts for the great, the whole impression which he has received from a poem, and he will refer you, in no small measure, to words used with such force and appropriateness, that the slightest change would be as hurtful as throwing a false light on a landscape. True vigor of composition depends as much upon a pervading exactness in what some deem little things, as upon the reverent observance of great

principles of style. Hence, the importance of verbal criticism;—
not that it can mechanically give us an insight into the life and
beauty of words . . . but it draws attention to their importance and
helps us to discriminate their significance. (172)

The long-range impact of the nineteenth-century commitment to
the rhetoric-poetics relationship is observable in the theoretical stance of
rhetoric treatises appearing at the turn of the century and during the early
decades of the twentieth century. Those rhetoricians whose treatises exerted
the greatest theoretical influence over composition theory between 1880
and 1910 were Bain, A. S. Hill, Genung, and Barrett Wendell.[21] These
theorists all recommended critical study as a major means of improving in
the art of composition, prescribing critical exercises as a means of mastering
elements of form and style and providing critical analyses of literary works.
Bain's approach in *English Composition and Rhetoric: Emotional Qualities
of Style* (1908) is to explain the nature and form of the major qualities of style
through a method he describes as "the line-by-line method of examining
[literary] passages with a view to assigning merits and defects. This,
however, is not a new thing in literary criticism. It is occasionally practised
by all rhetorical teachers" (xi). Bain's method is reminiscent of Newman
and Quackenbos's (and certainly Blair's) attention to the critical analysis
of literary selections and indicates how persistent and enduring a pedagogical issue literary criticism was for nineteenth-century theorists. Bain assumes, as did all nineteenth-century rhetoricians, that a course of study in
literary criticism can "vanquish the difficulties of the highest composition"
(x): rhetorical excellence or literary effects are achievable by any writer
who can come to understand the nature and forms of tasteful discourse.
While the works of the great authors provide the best material for the study
of composition, the purpose of critical study is to identify those rhetorical
techniques that are imitable.

Wendell did not construct his treatise on rhetorical style as an
instructional guide to the art of literary criticism; however, he affirms
the theoretical and pragmatic link between criticism and composition by

providing a number of occasions for the practice of literary analysis. His analytical discussions model the methods of criticism while explicating the nature of rhetorical effects, and his discussion of elegance represents how this dual focus on criticism and composition was promoted in nineteenth-century theory. While discussing elegance as the "exquisite" adaptation of language to the expression of thought and emotion, Wendell comments on how this style is achieved in the verse of Shelley, Wordsworth, and Shakespeare:

> [On Wordsworth's "Skylark" and Shelley's "Ode to a Skylark:"]
> In the long words and slow measure of Wordsworth's first line
> "Ethereal minstrel! pilgrim of the sky!" there is something that
> keeps the mind where the contemplative poet would have it,—
> down on earth. In the short, ecstatic words of Shelley's first
> line—"Hail to thee, blithe spirit!"—there is something that lifts
> the mind straight away from all things earthly. Change a word in
> either of these, change even a syllable or a letter, and something
> is lost. Again, take, almost at random, one of Shakespeare's de-
> scriptions: the beginning of the speech that tells how Ophelia died:
> "There is a *willow* grows *aslant* a *brook* / That shows his *hoar*
> leaves in the *glassy* stream." . . . Read the passage through; and
> when you have finished, see for yourselves how this simple pic-
> ture that begins it sets the whole in a background of just such gen-
> tle, homely nature as should best make us feel the loveliness of
> the dying girl, and the mournfulness of her end. (285–86; Wen-
> dell's italics)

Representing more than the typical habit of nineteenth-century rhet-oricians of illustrating rhetorical principles with literary models, Wendell's analysis of these verse samples directs attention to the nature of literary effects and instructs the student of composition in the methods of criticism by focusing on questions such as how diction and syntax contribute to the general sense and emotional effects of verse. Because he assumes that criticism is the most effective means of coming to know "what good use is in a living language," Wendell considers instruction in critical analysis a fundamental component of learning to compose (20).

Composition and Belles Lettres

Sharing with Wendell and Bain the belletristic conviction that the rhetorical elements that confer excellence on literature and composition are one and the same, A. S. Hill provides analyses of literary texts intended to account both for the nature of literary genres and the structure of composition. For example, in his analysis of narration as a species of composition Hill discusses movement, point of view, and straightforward narrative as elements of fiction and also as rhetorical elements all writers should master. Here he explains the importance of consistent movement in narrative:

> In a long narrative, whether of real or of fictitious events, pages of reflection, of analysis, of comment, may properly be introduced if they clear the way for the story, intensify interest in it, or assist in its development; but if they obstruct the story or divert from its natural course, they cannot but injure it as a narrative. . . . Compare "Henry Esmond" with "Les Trois Mousquetaires." In "Les Trois Mousquetaires," Dumas never drops the thread of his story. In "Henry Esmond," Thackeray drops his thread very often; but he does so in order to make observations on life. (*Principles* 288–89)

Hill's equation of critical criteria with compositional principles represents a standard commitment of nineteenth-century theory; however, treatises appearing after 1880 became increasingly preoccupied with theoretical explanations of both rhetorical principles and the methods of literary criticism.[22]

From the nineteenth-century point of view, the critical and constructive aspects of rhetorical study collaborate to provide the writer with a self-conscious sense of the useful and the beautiful. No writer can hope to achieve success without an understanding of the rules of rhetoric, and no writer can aspire to eminence who has not internalized a standard of excellence through the appreciation of literature. The study of critical rhetoric was supported not only by the attention given to the development of this aptitude by rhetorical theorists but also by the popularity that literary anthologies enjoyed throughout the century. Literary anthologies, often titled "rhetoric readers," were collections designed to provide the writer with the opportunity to practice critical abilities. These collections were promoted as aids in the development of compositional skills and were often recommended as complements to the study of theoretical treatises in rhetoric. For example, Genung's collection *Handbook of Rhetorical Analysis* (1888) was "Designed to Accompany the Author's Practical Elements of Rhetoric." Throughout the nineteenth-century and and the early decades of the twentieth century, editors of rhetoric anthologies offered the same belletristic/neoclassical rationale for formal attention to critical analysis and the study of literary models:

> The language of the pieces chosen for this collection has been carefully regarded. Purity, propriety, perspicuity, and, in many instances, elegance of diction, distinguish them. They are extracted from the works of the most correct and elegant writers. . . . The frequent perusal of such composition naturally tends to infuse a taste for this species of excellence; and to produce a habit of thinking, and of composing, with judgement and accuracy. (Murray iii)

> The selections that make up this Handbook . . . are simply, as the title indicates, extracts to be analyzed, in style and structure, for the purpose of forming, from actual examples, some intelligent conception of what the making of good literature involves; . . . testimony as . . . to the value of the study of literary models is universal. Biographies of authors are full of it; reports, gleaned from every available source, of "books which have influenced me," and accounts of the great literary works which have been at eminent writers' elbows, constant companions and inspirers, are eagerly read and treasured for their helpfulness to workers who aspire to like eminence. (Genung, *Handbook* v)

> The study of models has its purpose to-day, as truly as when Raphael plucked out the heart of Perugino's secrets, and proceeding to other masters bettered the instruction of each. The purpose is perhaps three-fold: to help the student to underlying principles of invention; to familiarize him with certain living organisms as informed by these principles, lest in forgetful haste he apply the

principles mechanically; and finally to reveal his powers to himself by experiment and self-comparison.[23] (Lewis iii–iv)

These comments stress more than the value of imitating exemplary models; compilers of rhetoric anthologies explicitly assumed that the critical "perusal" of literary masterpieces develops habits that shape a writer's own skills.[24] The format and contents of rhetoric anthologies reflect this same assumption: selections are organized according to rhetorical elements rather than by subject matter, author, or period. In general, anthologies were organized by one of two theoretical rubrics: selections were grouped under canonical headings (such as invention and style) or, more typically, arranged according to species of discourse. Anthologies arranged by canons normally introduced selections by defining what rhetorical process was illustrated in the excerpt and appended questions defining topics for critical analysis. For example, in *Handbook of Rhetorical Analysis,* a model for early twentieth-century composition anthologies, Genung prefaces each major division of selections, "Studies in Style" and "Studies in Invention," with a checklist of rhetorical elements that constitute the major elements of each canon. These lists review the fundamental elements of style and processes of invention that received extensive explanation in the rhetorical treatises of this period: under style, choice of words, kinds of diction, figures of speech, sentence structure, and paragraph development; under invention, selection and ordering of material, argumentation and persuasion, and techniques of description, narration, and exposition (xii, 133). In introducing subsequent selections, Genung refers to this list of elements and also focuses on these same issues in critical exercises. For example, he devotes an entire set of exercises to the study of figures; these exercises are designed to sharpen the student's perception of which figures are the most striking and which accomplish "the most for the writer's purpose." In reference to an excerpt from Bunyan's "Christian's Fight with Apollyon," Genung asks a series of questions intended to educate the reader in a critical understanding of allegory: "How do these names of places connect the allegory with what it illustrates? How does the quotation from Romans vi.

preserve the allegory? How does Bunyan use Isa. xxxv. to explain the meaning of the road in which Christian is traveling?" (64).[25]

Genung's method of keying critical exercises to explicit rhetorical principles is representative of how critical exercises were outlined in all types of rhetoric readers: commentary identifying key rhetorical elements in each selection rationalizes the direction of critical exercises. Anthologies organized by species also outlined critical exercises focusing on the analysis of explicit rhetorical principles. The major difference between the two genres of rhetoric readers is that anthologies organized by species typically relied on a Blairian scheme for designating the forms of rhetoric and offered selections from all major belletristic categories: "Descriptive Pieces," "Narrative Pieces," "Didactic [expository] Pieces," "Pathetic [persuasive] Pieces," and "Public Speeches." The Blairian scheme was more typical of readers appearing between 1800 and midcentury. Readers appearing in the latter half of the century and in the early decades of the twentieth century tended to offer selections under the epistemological categories, the description-narration-argument-exposition scheme that dominated theoretical treatments of the modes of rhetoric after 1850. Although rhetoric anthologies did not represent a primary pedagogical enterprise in the nineteenth-century tradition, these collections appeared with some consistency throughout the 1800s and enjoyed increasing popularity toward the end the century. At that point, the use of anthologies in conjunction with rhetorical treatises had become standard practice in North American colleges and universities. Often performing a second function as elocutionary readers, rhetoric readers offered excerpts from those authors whose works figured as exemplary illustrations in treatments of rhetorical principles. By 1900 the "canon" of authors anthologized in rhetoric readers was fairly standardized and represented English and American authors who were considered significant literary figures: Joseph Addison, Matthew Arnold, Edmund Burke, Thomas De Quincey, George Eliot, Thomas Huxley, William James, Charles Lamb, Thomas Macaulay, George Meredith, John Stuart Mill, John Henry Newman, Walter Pater, Edgar Allan Poe, John Ruskin, Sir Walter Scott, Henry David Thoreau, and William Makepeace Thackeray. Whereas the contents of rhetoric anthologies consisted mainly of selections from these "masters" of prose, it was not unusual for compilers to add "occasional" pieces representing journalists and essayists who had achieved popular recognition. Although the list of "masters" offered in rhetoric anthologies remained virtually unchanged throughout the nineteenth century and into the twentieth century, the "occasional" pieces varied a good deal from decade to decade.[26] The stability of this canon is consistent with the general nineteenth-century view that critical analysis is best practiced on those works of literature that have satisfied the test of time and taste, proving to be universally appealing in substance and exemplary in rhetorical technique.

In the nineteenth-century tradition, the edifying function of the study of criticism and belles lettres was regarded as both an education in intellectual and moral taste and a means by which practical rhetorical skills could be acquired. Like the orator who must be educated in the critical appreciation of the works of the great orators, the writer's acquaintance with the canon of English literature was a necessary part of the study of rhetorical principles and their application. Nineteenth-century rhetoricians were convinced that there was no fundamental distinction between the rhetorical structures and devices of literary texts and the rhetorical disposition of the various types of prose that the writer might want to produce. The difference between the models studied and the prose the student of rhetoric composed was only a matter of excellence yet to be achieved. Although nineteenth-century rhetoricians did not deny that some writers (and orators) have natural talent, they consistently downplayed the role of genius or special gifts in favor of an idealistic view of the consequences of rhetorical study: the intellectual and rhetorical achievements exemplified by the great authors can be attained by any writer who masters the principles of rhetoric, cultivates the powers of taste, and practices the techniques of composing.

The art of speaking and writing with purity, propriety, and elegance, is of the highest importance to the mere English, as well as to the classical and general scholar. It invests the talents and knowledge of its possessor with more than a double value. . . . The power which an eloquent orator exerts over an assembly, an able writer exerts over a country. . . . The noble prize and the enviable power of elegant and forcible writing are within the grasp of ordinary minds, and may, in general be viewed as the certain reward of patient industry. The value of such an acquirement cannot be estimated, as its resources of enjoyment and influence are unmeasured.

Egerton Ryerson, *address at the opening of Victoria College, Toronto, 1842*

Whatever then may be your employment in future life, though you may never be called to the pulpit or to the bar, it is a sacred duty which you owe to yourselves and your friends, to cultivate those graces and accomplishments of our nature—those elegances of taste and imagination; of language and of address, which, in every profession, give the crowning ornament to intellectual superiority.

Chauncey Allen Goodrich, *"Lectures on Rhetoric and Public Speaking"*

The work in rhetoric assumes considerable study and practice in the art of composition, devotes itself largely to a consideration of the science of effective discourse, embracing the laws of mind, the laws of language. Opportunities for original work in the writing of essays and in the preparation and delivery of orations are afforded in the literary societies, in class, and before the faculty and body of students.

DePauw College Catalogue, 1887

6

Conclusion: Habits of Eloquence

The nineteenth-century theoretical tradition exceeded the accomplishments of the New Rhetoric by synthesizing the epistemological, belles lettres, and classical rationales to justify a broader range of rhetorical practice. The articulation of this broader range of practice can be traced to two characteristics of nineteenth-century theory: (1) the fundamental presumption that rhetorical principles are applicable to all types of oral and written communication; and (2) a wider interpretation of the function of rhetoric in social and cultural exchange. Nineteenth-century rhetoricians presumed the philosophical verifiability of rhetorical principles and the inherent relationship between the structure and techniques of rhetorical discourse and the laws of the mind; they equated the study of rhetorical principles with an understanding of communication in a general sense. As the century progressed, the nineteenth-century tradition promoted an ever more encompassing definition of the relevance of rhetorical principles. The abiding assumption that every communicative occasion represents an instance in which rhetorical principles must be applied in a strategic manner was the dominant attitude of influential theorists such as Henry N. Day, Alexander Bain, A. S. Hill, and John F. Genung, who shaped the theoretical stance of the tradition after 1850.

The pervasive influence of the epistemological rationale of the New Rhetoric was primarily responsible for the marked tendency of the nineteenth-century tradition to regard practice as a matter of coordinating the natural principles of rhetoric with the demands of particular occasions.

227

Nineteenth-Century Rhetoric

Theorists promoted the notion that the effective writer and speaker must convey ideas with the clarity and liveliness required to engage the associative dynamics of mind (processing ideas in terms of logical links to experience and common sense). In this view, the challenge for the rhetorician is to select ideas, order content, and apply the principles of style in the manner best suited to a given instance. The belletristic views incorporated into nineteenth-century theory also reinforced the notion that rhetorical practice involves the application of natural laws of the mind. Incorporating a rational philosophy of taste within a general epistemological account of rhetorical practice, nineteenth-century theorists added the aesthetic imagination to the list of the mental faculties that rhetorical technique must engage. Although especially useful in speeches and prose intended to move the will, appeals to the imagination must be satisfied in all discourses through harmony in arrangement and the principles of style—perspicuity, force, and ornament. Whether foregrounded in the nature of the subject, the structure of the discourse, or the devices of style, the principles of harmony, elegance, and the sublime provide the writer and speaker with the means of intensifying the response of the imagination and the higher passions and elevating the reader or listener's apprehension of the beautiful. Just as the rhetorician must always consider what content and structure will best facilitate the associational responses of the faculties, the writer and speaker must also evaluate how to appeal to the taste of the audience through subject matter and technique.

By asserting epistemological and belletristic rationales for practice, nineteenth-century rhetoricians reconfirmed the classical principle that the content and technique of rhetorical discourse must be relevant to those addressed and the particular circumstances of the rhetorical event. The theoretical weight given in nineteenth-century theory to the consideration of human nature in the devising of subject matter and technique had the effect of reinscribing the classical precept that the rhetorician must adapt to subject, audience, and occasion. In nineteenth-century rhetoric, rhetorical occasion was not defined strictly in contextual terms but in terms of what effect the writer or speaker would characteristically be seeking in that setting. For example, when a congregation gathers to hear a sermon, the preacher provides Bible lessons (appeals to the understanding) and also exhorts the assembly to change their behavior and live a good life (persuasion by moving the will). To devise the appropriate content and techniques of the sermon, the preacher combines a scientific knowledge of human nature with an insight into what people typically expect a sermon to provide. The rhetorician must evaluate the epistemological conditions of the occasion as well as the the ways in which the formal nature of the occasion may have imposed on the listener's frame of mind. Claiming the authority of the classical maxim that the essence of rhetoric lies in adaptation as further support of the natural relationship between the dynamics of communication and the science of rhetoric, nineteenth-century theorists consistently asserted that an understanding of fundamental rhetorical principles (canons) can be applied to any type of public speaking or writing.

The presupposition that natural laws authorize the applicability of rhetorical principles to all forms of discourse supported significant innovations: (1) the definition of description, narration, exposition, argumentation, and persuasion as types of rhetoric constrained primarily by epistemological intention and method and (2) the formalization of "popular oratory" as a distinct type of oratory appropriate to occasions at which the public is addressed on a topic of collective interest. The formalization of description, narration, argumentation, and persuasion as generic categories (Campbell and Whately simply treat these as inventional techniques) allowed nineteenth-century theorists to define genres extending across an unprecedented range of venues. For example, the writer whose intention is to appeal to the understanding through exposition could do so in a scientific article, a travel lecture, or a treatise on botany. Exposition is intended to have a particular effect on the mind; it is this intention (to define the term or concept) that characterizes the rhetorical strategies employed in this type of discourse. Epistemological intention presumes a consideration of audience since an evaluation of how best to inform the understanding, move the will, or please the imagination and the passions focuses explicitly on the mental nature of the reader or listener. The formal designation of popular oratory

229

as a major form of public speaking (which adds a fourth category to the New Rhetoric's list of judicial, deliberative, and sacred oratory) was rationalized theoretically by the assumption that popular oratory, like sacred and deliberative oratory, represents another instance of persuasion, or an attempt move the will. This view of popular oratory is typical of the nineteenth-century tendency to define generic varieties in terms of epistemological intention. While the powerful influence of the New Rhetoric predisposed this tendency in great measure, the nineteenth-century tradition itself was responsible for incorporating a greater range of oral and written forms under epistemological and belletristic rubrics for practice.

One of the consequences of this innovative outline of the range of rhetoric was that nineteenth-century theorists accounted for a greater number of modes through which rhetoric can function as an agency of social well-being and cultural education. By the late nineteenth century, rhetoricians perceived the domain of rhetoric as including public speaking, all forms of argumentative, expository, descriptive, and narrative composition, and the critical study of literature. Whether engaged in the delivery of a lecture from the platform or in the composition of a critical review, the rhetorician is involved in airing matters of the public interest or in dispensing needed information; whether providing a historical account of past wars or urging the legislature to take action, the rhetorician is taking active responsibility for the education or the welfare of the public. The nineteenth-century tradition never represented the obligations of the rhetorician in strictly pragmatic terms. Throughout the century, rhetoricians promoted the notion that rhetorical skill enables the individual to participate in and contribute to society and to engage in that communication which ensures an informed populace. Whenever the speaker or writer informs others, moves them to needed action, or provides them with insight into the literary experience, the rhetorician affects the intellectual and moral constitution of the community. Because nineteenth-century theorists conflated the acquisition of rhetorical skills with the development of taste, they assumed that the orator and the writer influence the community through the subject matter conveyed as well as through the aesthetic appeal of rhetorical form.

Habits of Eloquence

The special status of the rhetorician was ensured by the nineteenth-century assumption that the study of rhetorical principles is a type of scientific study that confers a philosophical understanding of human nature and deep appreciation of the beauty and art of language. This view of the study of rhetoric and of the culturally significant function of its practice was supported by the pedagogies of rhetoricians who argued that the study of rhetoric cultivates higher intellectual and moral sensibilities. Under the influence of such views, nineteenth-century educators came to view rhetoric as an important subject in the liberal arts. Three important documents— Samuel P. Newman's *Lecture on a Practical Method of Teaching Rhetoric* (delivered to the American Institute of Instruction in 1830), Bain's article series "The Teaching of English" (*Journal of Education,* 1869), and Genung's *Study of Rhetoric in the College Course* (1887)—reveal the theoretical and ideological presumptions governing attitudes toward rhetorical education. Despite the span of decades between the date of Newman's lecture and the publication of Bain and Genung's guidelines for rhetorical instruction, these three discussions review similar issues: (1) the salutary intellectual effects of the study of rhetoric; (2) the irrefutable usefulness of rhetorical skills to every individual; (3) the pedagogical centrality of the study and practice of rhetorical principles; (4) the importance of criticism in the development of rhetorical skills; and (5) the qualifications of the effective instructor of rhetoric.

Newman and Bain explicitly defend the value of rhetorical education on the grounds that the study of rhetoric contributes to intellectual discipline and the cultivation of taste, and they share the same conception of what makes up a sound course in rhetoric. Newman points out that the student must be taught something of "the science of intellectual philosophy" and the nature of "literary taste" as preparation for the study of rhetorical principles. These studies acquaint students with the operations of the mind and with what constitutes tasteful achievement in discourse. The student who has been educated in the philosophy of rhetoric is better able to understand the "the nature of the rules and directions" of rhetoric and its "intricate principles" (*Lecture* 5). Arguing that a philosophical understanding of rhetoric must precede the study of technique, Newman outlines what a "practical method of studying rhetoric" should provide: "1. Some acquaintance with the philosophy of rhetoric. 2. The cultivation of the taste, and in connexion, the exercise of the imagination. 3. Skill in the use of language. 4. Skill in literary criticism. 5. The formation of a good style" (3–4). This course of study disciplines the powers of reason, improves the imagination, and allows the individual to develop the powers of expression. Newman recommends a number of pedagogical methods including the study of literary models; instruction in the rules of diction, sentence construction, and arrangement; and correction of student's work. The objective of the study of rhetoric, Newman advises, should be for each student to "acquire a manner of writing, to some extent, peculiarly his own, and which is to be the index of his modes of thinking—the development of his intellectual traits and feelings. It is the office of the instructor to facilitate the accomplishment of this important end, both by wisely directing the efforts of his pupil, and by removing every obstacle in his way" (14).

In his analysis of "instruction in English," Bain defines the nature and scope of instruction in "Composition and Rhetoric," along with two other subjects, grammar and English literature. Bain regards rhetoric and composition to be the most advanced of these subjects and claims "training in prose composition" as the ultimate end of all the work done in "the English classroom" ("On Teaching English" 201). Like Newman, who acknowledges the relationship between philosophical training and the study of rhetoric, Bain observes that the cultivation of taste is "ministerial to composition" and that "intellectual discipline" in the art of expression is the end of rhetorical instruction. Bain defines rhetoric as the science that lays down the rules for effective composition. By the term *composition* Bain means the general art of expression: "A wide scope is to be allowed to the meaning of composition. It is not confined to mere business composition, nor even to that coupled with the expository art for the purposes of science; it takes in the graces and amenities of style, as an art refining social intercourse, and for aiding in oratory" (201). A course in rhetoric should provide instruction in sentence construction, arrangement (what Bain calls "the rhetoric of the paragraph"), the different kinds of composition (description, narration, exposition, persuasion), and the principles of style. Like Newman, Bain affirms the usefulness of studying exemplary models of style and of correcting student exercises. Bain particularly recommends engaging students in various types of practice exercises such as rendering poetic passages in prose, developing essays from outlines, and asking students to write about familiar subjects (2). He insists that rhetoric is largely a matter of the study and practice of fundamental principles and rules that are generally applicable in compositions "by the pen, or by mouth" (2).

Bain and Newman argue that the study of rhetoric presumes on and affirms the intellectual powers. Because the principles of rhetoric are drawn from scientific principles and embody the qualities of taste, the study of rhetoric is an ongoing education in intellectual discipline and taste. Bain and Newman point out that instruction in rhetoric ensures the development of intellectual discipline by focusing on the principles and rules that control rhetorical practice as a rational art; likewise, involving students in the study of an exemplary canon facilitates the development of critical judgment. These views are confirmed by Bain and Newman's shared expectation that the instructor of rhetoric be an individual of exemplary intellect and taste. Newman equates the qualifications of the competent instructor with the abilities that the practicing rhetorician must possess:

1. He should possess some knowledge of intellectual philosophy. The art of rhetoric, like the other arts, is founded on science of mind. It is from a knowledge of what is in man, of the constitution of the human mind, its susceptibilities of emotion, and the various influences it feels, that the skilful writer is enabled to address himself with success to his readers and subject them to this power. And further, many of the rules of rhetoric, based as they are on principles unfolded in the science of mind, are but aids for effecting of this purpose. How absolutely necessary, then, that he who attempts to explain and illustrate these rules, and to assist in cultivating the taste and forming the style, should possess some knowledge of that science whose principles are thus applied.

2. An instructor in rhetoric should possess some acquaintance
with the prominent writings in his native language. Familiarity
with good writers will evidently prove highly serviceable in illustrating the rules and principles, which he has occasion to bring to
the notice of his pupils. With this familiarity, also, will most
probably be associated some skill in literary criticism, and some
refinement of the taste, both of which are highly conducive to the
success of an instructor. (*Lecture* 19)

Like the rhetorician, the instructor of rhetoric must understand the
philosophical foundations of rhetorical practice and must possess critical
skills and a knowledge and appreciation of an exemplary canon—exactly
the same attributes that the rhetorician must develop. Bain agrees with this
assessment, observing that the instructor must know the rules of composition and have a "mind practised, up to the rapidity of an instinct, in
discriminating good and evil in composition, in showing how the good
may become better, and the better, best" ("On Teaching English" 1). An
internalized instinct for critical analysis presupposes a highly developed
sense of taste and a scientific understanding of the relationship between
rhetorical form and intellectual and emotional response. Only this kind
of background can prepare the instructor of rhetoric and composition to
"engender a habit of excellence in style" (1).

In his analysis of "the direction and scope" of the college course in
rhetoric, Genung reiterates many of Newman and Bain's views on rhetorical
education. Genung considers the study of rhetoric to be philosophical in
nature because "it draws from every department of nature and life" (*Study*
10). He defines the study of rhetoric as a process by which an individual
learns how to apply "the facts and principles" of rhetoric to "the tasks of
life" (4–5). Like Bain and Newman, Genung assumes that mental discipline
is acquired when one engages in the systematic study of natural principles
of language and art. Genung argues that the mental discipline acquired
through the study of rhetoric is a unique resource to every individual who
hopes to make an intellectual contribution: "The study of rhetoric in college
aims to forstall that coming time of need. . . . It is preparing in secret for

the future when the student shall begin to think for himself. And most of all, it seeks to induce that attitude of watchfulness, carefulness, contrivance, creativeness, which must be his when he has done with merely taking in knowledge, and addresses himself to giving it out again, newly minted and stamped with his individuality" (*Study* 5–6). Sharing Bain's view that the rhetoric course should provide general instruction in the art of composition, Genung points out that the student of rhetoric should learn to compose for a variety of purposes. He insists that rhetoric courses must address the increase in popular and periodical literature, which has "multiplied the forms of literary production," by teaching students how to apply the principles of style and invention to "prevailing literary forms" (11). Conceiving of "prevailing forms" quite broadly, Genung stresses that rhetorical study should take in all possible forms of "reading matter": political essays, scientific and descriptive treatises, short stories, editorials, and reporter's columns as well as the the traditional forms of the sermon and the lyceum address (12).

Genung's overall pedagogical view confirms what both Newman and Blair recommend: the most effective way to teach rhetoric is to provide instruction in principles. The theoretical phase of study should be complemented with a variety of exercises that allow the writer (or speaker) to practice applying rhetorical techniques to various types of composition. Genung suggests two terms of theoretical study: the first term would provide a review of the grammatical and mechanical features of composition including diction, figures of speech, sentence structure and paragraphs; the second term would provide instruction in invention, arrangement, and style and applications to description, narration, exposition, argument, and persuasion. Sharing with Newman and Bain the conviction that the development of critical judgment reinforces an understanding of rhetorical principles, Genung considers the study of exemplary models a necessary aid to the study of rhetorical theory, and he also recommends extending critical exercises to include class members exchanging comments on each other's work. He refers to this entire sequence of study as "a systematically ordered, progressive series" that allows students of rhetoric to "gain freedom with

Nineteenth-Century Rhetoric

the pen and confidence in [their] own powers of portrayal" (*Study* 26).[1] Although nineteenth-century theorists stressed the importance of theoretical and critical study in this "series," Genung, Bain, and Newman insist that the ultimate aim of theoretical study and critical exercises is to instruct students in how to express their own thoughts on subjects of personal significance or community interest. As Genung points out, the aim of every rhetorician is to "impart a clear and moving idea of common things, common events, common thoughts" (27). The aim of rhetorical education is to provide instruction in the nature and application of those principles that allow the writer or speaker to compose this type of discourse. In the course of developing the art of expression, the student comes to an understanding of human nature and the qualities of taste that in turn enhance the powers of thought.

The fact that Newman, Bain, and Genung promote a similar pedagogical program and share the conviction that the study of rhetoric has long-lasting salutary effects indicates the homogeneous nature of philosophies of rhetorical education during the nineteenth-century, a period during which the goals of both liberal education and rhetorical education were highly compatible. The hegemony of the pedagogical program of the nineteenth-century tradition is obvious in the make-up of rhetoric courses given at colleges and universities in the United States and Canada throughout the century. The typical nineteenth-century college rhetoric course was organized according to the structure that rhetoricians such as Newman, Bain, and Genung explicitly defined: the systematic study of the nature and application of fundamental rhetorical principles in combination with the study of rhetorical modes and exercises in critical analysis. This system of study was promoted in the prefaces and introductions of the rhetoric treatises adopted as course texts and confirmed by the attitudes of nineteenth-century educators, who assumed without question the claim that the study of rhetoric confers mental discipline as well as the powers of eloquent expression.

The nineteenth-century rhetoric course integrated the study of epistemological, belletristic, and classical theory in a course that focused on the application of rhetorical principles to both oratory and writing. The

popularity of the theory–practice–study of models sequence as an organizing pedagogical structure for the nineteenth-century rhetoric course is revealed by the consistency with which college and university calendar descriptions of rhetoric courses outlined this sequence. These calendar entries
from Amherst College (1839) and Delaware College (1883) indicate the
ways in which rhetoric courses typically combined the study of theoretical
treatises on rhetoric and criticism with practice exercises in oratory and
prose composition:

> [Amherst College, 1839–40:] Freshman Year . . . Porter, *Analysis
> of Rhetorical Delivery* . . . During the Year. A Weekly exercise
> in Declamation and Composition. Sophomore Year . . . New-
> man's *Rhetoric* . . . Cicero *de Oratore*. During the Year. Two
> Weekly Rhetorical Exercises, Declamations, Debates or English
> Composition. . . . Junior Year . . . Whately's *Rhetoric* with refer-
> ences to Campbell's *Philosophy of Rhetoric* . . . During the Year.
> Two Weekly Rhetorical Exercises, Composition, Declamation,
> Debates, or English Composition. . . . Senior Year . . . Kames's
> *Elements of Criticism*. . . . On every Wednesday afternoon is an
> exercise in Declamation, in which all the classes take part. Seniors
> and Juniors deliver original essays. (18–22)

> [Delaware College, 1883] English Language and Literature. . . .
> The Freshman, Sophomore, and Junior Classes are regularly re-
> quired to write essays, which are carefully criticised; and there are
> weekly exercises in declamation and reading. The Senior class
> prepare essays and original orations to be read or spoken in the or-
> atory in the presence of the assembled students; questions of inter-
> est and importance are selected for discussion by members of the
> Class. The Freshman Class during the first and second terms have
> weekly recitations in Rhetoric, using Hart's work on the subject,
> and their knowledge is tested by examples on the blackboard.
> Books of Reference—Hill's *Science of Rhetoric*. (19)

Frequently joined with the study of elocution, logic, or English
literature, the study of rhetorical theory was complemented by exercises in
declamation, essay writing, and the study of literary models. This pedagogi-

cal program changed very little over the decades. Although college and university courses offered before midcentury focused on the treatises of Campbell and Blair (or Kames), whereas later courses tended to require the study of more contemporary rhetoricians such as Whately, G. P. Quackenbos, A. S. Hill, David. J. Hill, John S. Hart, and Genung, the theory–practice–study of models sequence remained intact (appendix A). Critical exercises and the study of an exemplary canon continued as mandatory components of rhetoric courses throughout the century, as did instruction in oratory and the forms of prose composition.[2]

Calendars published in the latter decades of the century tended to be more detailed than earlier publications and often provided descriptions of rhetoric courses that reiterated dominant pedagogical rationales for rhetorical study. For example, these descriptions of courses offered at the Andover Theological Seminary, the University of Wyoming, and the University of Georgia between 1870 and 1900 corroborate the standard pedagogical format and also confirm a number of assumptions fundamental to the theoretical stance of the nineteenth-century tradition:

Lectures.—General Rhetoric: Province of Rhetoric; History of the Science—Alliance with other Sciences; Relation to Preaching; The Rhetorical and Scientific forms of Truth. Sources of Rhetorical Science.—Study of Men . . . Study of Models in Literature, Its Objects, Its Subjects, Its Methods . . . Methods of Study of English Literature . . . Study of Rhetorical Treatises . . . Exercises in Criticism. Sermons and Plans of Sermons by the Class, criticized in private. (Andover Theological Seminary, 1870, 19)

Rhetoric, English Literature, and oratory receive attention throughout the University course. The student's work in literature is made to furnish the occasion as well as the material for the preparation of essays. These essays are subject to criticism both in the class and with the individual writers. The formal study of rhetoric begins with the junior year and is designed to ground the student in the principles of English composition and to cultivate his literary sense by analytical study. The work in oratory is of a practical character. An effort is made to secure readings that shall be intelligent, natural, and forcible, and to develop spontaneous expression from the mental side. The student meets the instructor personally for rehearsal and criticism. (University of Wyoming, 1887)

Rhetoric—. In this course the subject is pursued by Sophomores who meet the professor twice a week throughout the year. Frequent practical exercises in all forms of composition are required. In illustration of the subject, selections from standard authors are used. This has the double advantage of acquainting the student with the principles of Rhetoric and of creating and forming a taste for classic English literature. (University of Georgia, 1898, 33)

All three of these course descriptions stress the pedagogical relationship between practice and the study of "principles." The detail of the Andover entry illustrates how the theory–practice–study of models sequence served rhetoric courses organized primarily for instruction in the rhetoric of the sermon. Even in this narrowly focused course, the study of the principles or "science" of rhetoric, "exercises in criticism," and practice in composition comprised the basic program of study. The attention awarded to the study of literature in the Andover course, and in the Wyoming and Georgia courses, indicates the normative status of critical study in the nineteenth-century rhetoric course. In addition to validating the theory–practice–study of models sequence, these course descriptions confirm a number of key assumptions of nineteenth-century rhetorical theory: (1) the governing assumption that principles of rhetoric are "scientific" in foundation ("The Rhetorical and Scientific forms of Truth"); (2) the governing definition of rhetoric as the study of both oral and written discourse ("all forms of composition"); (3) the assumption that the study of rhetorical principles, the practice of criticism, and the study of the literary canon are theoretically and practically interrelated ("Study of Rhetoric Treatises . . . Exercises in Criticism "); (4) the assumption that the acquisition of eloquence depends on the development of control over the natural mental faculties ("develop spontaneous expression from the mental side"); and (5) the assumption that the study and practice of rhetoric improves intelligence and taste ("analytical study," "forming a taste").

By incorporating the theoretical assumptions of the nineteenth-century tradition in the curricular design of rhetoric courses in such obvious ways, nineteenth-century educators contributed to the authority that these assumptions exerted over definitions of the nature and aims of rhetorical education. The powerful parallel between the curricular substance of nineteenth-century rhetoric courses and the philosophical and pedagogical stances of the tradition as a whole was further encouraged by the prominent attention given in popular textbooks to defining the nature of rhetoric and the correct system for studying it. The treatises of Newman, Quackenbos, Day, Bain, David J. Hill, A. S. Hill, and Genung, all texts that enjoyed wide adoption in nineteenth-century colleges and universities, explicitly define rhetoric as a science and as the general art of communication, prescribe the importance of taste, stress the importance of the canons and critical study, and confirm the importance of the neoclassical pedagogical scheme theory–practice–study of models (appendix B). These tenets were reinscribed in treatise after treatise, course after course, standardizing a theoretical context that dominated nineteenth-century rhetorical education from the early decades of the century through the 1890s (see chapter 3).

In addition to institutionalizing the mandate of nineteenth-century theory in the design of rhetoric courses, nineteenth-century educators confirmed the status of rhetorical study by regarding rhetoric as an essential subject in the liberal arts curriculum. Nineteenth-century educators perceived the goal of higher education to be the cultivation of the mental powers. By midcentury this psychological conception of the goal of education had displaced the classical model favored by eighteenth-century educators, which stressed the command of subject matter. Nineteenth-century educators assumed that the most important consequence of higher education is not the acquisition of special knowledge but the development of the powers of perception and reason. The study of particular subjects such as classical and modern languages, logic, history, natural philosophy, literature, and rhetoric all contribute to the development of mental discipline by presenting the student with opportunities to sharpen intellectual habits: the abilities to observe, to compare, to reason, to concentrate on a single object or problem, and to evaluate an issue with an open mind. In the view of nonsecular educators, a significant force in the first part of the nineteenth century when many colleges had religious affiliations, the development of mental discipline also extended to the improvement of Christian morality. Although a dominant theme in the early decades of the century, an emphasis on the moral aspect of mental discipline was a less insistent theme in educational philosophy after 1860. By that time a number of new public institutions had reinterpreted the moral mission of education in secular terms as the development of taste and a sensibility to truth. Despite various interpretations of what "moral" education entailed, secular and nonsecular educators alike persistently held to the philosophy that the mission of higher education was "the development of intellectual and moral faculties and correct habits of thought and study" (Indiana University, 1854).[3]

The opinion that the development of mental discipline is the most significant aim of higher education was so widely affirmed in nineteenth-century commentaries on the nature of college education that it achieved the status of ideology. The laudable mission of the college and university was a frequent theme of addresses at baccalaureate ceremonies and university celebrations; in such speeches prominent educators promoted the idea that only higher education can confer the mental and moral habits necessary for the advancement of the individual and society. In his account of the nature of college education, Horace Mann expresses this view:

A College is a place where character is developed with fearful rapidity. Seeds which might never, or not for years, have germinated at home spring into sudden vitality and shoot with amazing luxuriance. . . . A young man of fair intelligence and an uncorrupted heart cannot have been in a College class for a single year without perceiving that he has crossed a boundary and entered a new realm; the realm of thoughts instead of the realm of the senses. The reflecting student cannot have been in College for a single year, without discovering that there is *periodicity* in his nature. Under the force of habit, the most difficult things become easy. . . . So of the intellectual faculties. Every cultivated mind which has arrived at mature age knows that what, at first, cost great efforts, is now performed without consciousness. Ideas which once seemed heavy as the hills to lift, are now handled like toys. . . . It is in this way that the intellectual and moral character of man grows up . . . into sturdiness and loftiness.[4] ("Antioch College: Baccalaureate Address of 1857")

Mann believes that the training of the mind to think accurately and systematically fulfills a natural phase of mental development that subsequently liberates original thinking and the finer sensibilities. The conflation that Mann makes between higher education and the development of "loftiness" of mind and heart is typical of how nineteenth-century educators rationalized the social and cultural value of college education. When the intellectual faculties are developed to a higher level, a moral disposition and sense of social responsibility are cultivated as well. The university experience sponsors the development of the whole individual by educating the powers of reason and taste and by cultivating special abilities; in turn, the individual with these traits contributes to the maintenance of a high standard of culture and a harmonious society.

Daniel Coit Gilman, first president of Johns Hopkins University (1875–1901) and founder of the graduate school model of the American university, reiterates this belief in his definition of "the idea of the university": " It may include a college; or several colleges; but it is more than a college, more than a group of colleges. It is the highest expression which any community can give to its intellectual aspirations; the most complex, diversified, and fruit-bearing organism which any community can devise for the intellectual and moral welfare of its people" ("Address").[5] Although Gilman's comment marks the view of educators at the end of the century, his characterization of the university as the site at which the highest intellectual and moral aspirations of a community can be instilled simply affirms rather than redefines the mandate of higher education formulated in earlier decades. Gilman's claim for the interrelationship between intellectual training, moral welfare, and the good of the community was reiterated by nineteenth-century educators as a guiding philosophy for college and university education.[6] In this general philosophical context, the study of rhetoric was rationalized as a pursuit that contributes directly to the development of mental discipline and that provides the individual with the means to express his ideas and thus make a contribution to society.

Because of the systematic nature of rhetorical study, its foundation in philosophically sound principles, and its practical value to the individual and literate culture in general, nineteenth-century educators considered the development of "the powers of expression" one of the components of a liberal education. In *College Education for Men of Business* John A. Broadus, author of the popular textbook *A Treatise on the Preparation and Delivery of Sermons* (1870), expresses the widely held opinion that "development and strengthening and discipline of [the student's] principal faculties" must be complemented by the development of communication skills (8). In his description of the well-educated man, Broadus reviews those traits that nineteenth-century educators equated with mental discipline:

1. An educated man is one whose mind is *widened out,* so that he can take broad views, instead of being narrow-minded; so that he can see the different sides of a question, or at least can know that all questions have different sides. 2. An educated man is one who has the power of *patient thinking;* who can fasten his mind on a subject, and hold it there while he pleases; who can keep looking at a subject till he sees into it and sees through it. . . . 3. Again, an educated man is one who has sound judgment, who knows how to *reason* to right conclusions, and so to *argue* as to convince others that he is right. 4. And finally,—not to speak now of imagination and taste, important as they are—an educated man is one who can *express* his thoughts clearly and forcibly.[7] (7; Broadus's italics)

Nineteenth-Century Rhetoric

Broadus's definition of the well-educated man links rhetorical study to the development of the mental powers. Through the study of rhetoric, the individual learns to argue and communicate in a rational and principled fashion; this activity trains the mind while it confers practical skills.

So common was this view of the function of rhetorical study in a college education that nineteenth-century commentaries on the nature of college education typically defined rhetorical training as a mandatory component of the bachelor of arts curriculum. F. A. P. Barnard, president of Columbia College during its rise to the status of a major university (1864–89), defines the importance of rhetorical training in his analysis of higher education in nineteenth-century America, "On Improvements Practicable in American Colleges": "Nothing can possess a higher practical value, to any man, than that which . . . gives him habits of clear, systematic, and independent thought, which . . . invigorates his powers of reasoning, teaches him to analyze, chastens and refines his taste . . . and confers upon him the priceless gift of lucid and forcible utterance" (181). Barnard shares Broadus's view that the development of rhetorical skills facilitates mental development by providing the student with the means to apply the powers of reason to the communication of ideas. Like Daniel Gilman, Barnard was a highly regarded spokesman for college education in the decades after midcentury, and his innovative restructuring of Columbia provided a model for others; thus, his regard for rhetorical instruction was not only typical but authoritative.[8]

The same legislative authority can be assigned to the views of Egerton Ryerson, the most influential nineteenth-century educator in Anglo-Canada and first president of Victoria College (Toronto). Ryerson confirms Barnard's high opinion of rhetorical instruction in his discussion of the function of rhetoric studies in the college curriculum:

> *Rhetoric* may be considered as relating to *discourse; Belles Lettres,* to *writing*. Both are founded in nature; the principles of good taste are common to both; and both are eminently subservient to individual and public interests. . . . Not to be able to communicate our knowledge is but little better than to be without knowl-

244

edge. To be useful to others, and to be in the fullest sense advan-
tageous to ourselves, our knowledge must be communicated; how
to communicate it to the best advantage, it is the province of
Rhetoric to teach. . . . Cultivation is essential to the fruitfulness
of both the intellectual and natural soil. . . . The noble prize and
the enviable power of elegant and forcible writing are within the
grasp of ordinary minds, and may, in general, be viewed as the
certain reward of patient industry.[9] (18–19)

In this inaugural address at the opening of Victoria College (1842),
Ryerson articulates an attitude toward rhetorical education held by Canadian
and American educators throughout the century: the study of rhetoric cultivates the habits of mental discipline and furthers the general health of
society by teaching the speaker and writer how to communicate knowledge
to the "best advantage" of all concerned. Strikingly similar to the rationale
advocated by nineteenth-century rhetoricians who defended the study of
rhetoric as an intellectually elevating and culturally significant discipline,
Ryerson's remarks indicate how closely entwined the aspirations of education and the rhetorical tradition were in this era. Educators and rhetoricians
alike assumed that the systematic study of principles trains the mind to
higher powers; the attainment of elevated mental abilities inclines the
individual to rational thinking, service, and an appreciation of nature, truth,
and art, which culminates in the development of taste and moral character.
The marked ideological reciprocity between the professed goals of the
nineteenth-century discipline of rhetoric and the mandate of higher education served to assure the conventional status of rhetoric as an academic
subject and preserve the authority of rhetoricians' claims that the study and
practice of rhetoric liberalized the mind.

From the nineteenth-century point of view, the advance of culture
and the stability of society relied on the attainment of mental and moral
development by each individual, a level of development that represents the
fulfillment of individuality *and* an enlightened commitment to the common
good. Nineteenth-century rhetoricians argued that the orator and writer
advances to this level through the systematic study of natural principles and

standards of taste. As a consequence, the rhetorician becomes an agent of edification, a delegate of culture. Rhetorical practice provides the individual with an expressive voice and society with the means to dispense justice, debate policy, and exalt the beauties of truth and nature. By justifying the study and practice of rhetoric in these terms, the nineteenth-century rhetorical tradition corroborated one of the most earnest beliefs of nineteenth-century North American society: that the productive exchange of ideas between rational minds furthers the progress of democratic society and protects the fortunes of all.

Nineteenth-century rhetoricians claimed for rhetoric the status of science, practical art, and civil servant. In laying this claim, they addressed and confirmed the dominant intellectual and cultural values of their era. The highly self-conscious idealism of this tradition remained essentially unchanged as the century closed, as did the theoretical disposition of nineteenth-century theory with its debt to New Rhetorical and classical precedents. By perceiving the study and practice of rhetoric as a means by which the mind and heart are trained to the service of the individual intellect and the social good, the nineteenth-century tradition supported a discipline that maintained a neoclassical regard for the social significance of rhetoric while relying on an extremely contemporary set of epistemological and aesthetic principles to explain the nature and effects of rhetorical practice. Throughout the century, rhetoricians persisted in urging educators and those who would be educated to believe that the mastery of eloquent speech and writing represented an inevitable challenge and opportunity that no one hoping to fulfill his natural gifts or take part in society could afford to decline. (Nineteenth-century rhetoricians unfailingly characterized the practitioner of rhetoric as male.) The nineteenth-century tradition was able to sustain a theoretical and pedagogical authority over institutional and public standards of higher literacy because it formulated a mandate for the discipline of rhetoric that inevitably evoked the ambitions and ideals of the dominant culture it was designed to serve. Consistently validating the interests of social progress, democracy, individuality, and cultural literacy (the knowledge of what is best in art and literature), the nineteenth-century tradition reinvented a role for the orator and the writer in the grand scheme of things. After the turn of the century, William Jennings Bryan offered a particularly American view of this grand scheme in an explanation of the function of oratory that recalls both the practical and idealistic commitments of the nineteenth-century tradition:

> The age of oratory has not passed; nor will it pass. The press, instead of displacing the orator, has given him a larger audience and enabled him to do more extended work. As long as there are human rights to be defended; as long as there are great interests to be guarded; as long as the welfare of nations is a matter for discussion, so long will public speaking have its place. (x)

Appendixes

Notes

Bibliography

Index

Appendix A

Sample College and University Calendar Descriptions of Rhetoric Courses, 1824–1900

Brown University, 1824

Freshman Class. . . . Sheridan's *Lectures on Elocution* . . . Cicero *De Oratore* begun. Sophomore Class. Cicero *De Oratore* finished. Blair's *Lectures on Rhetoric and Belles Lettres.* Kame's *Elements of Criticism.* . . . Junior Class. Campbell's *Philosophy of Rhetoric.* . . . Senior Class. Cicero's *Oration.* Campbell's *Philosophy of Rhetoric,* Kaim's *Elements of Criticism.* . . . Weekly declamations are attended by all classes. The Senior, Junior, and Sophomore Classes have weekly exercises in English composition. (10–11)

Dartmouth College, 1856–57

Freshman Year. . . . Spring Term . . . Rhetoric. Themes and Declamations once a week. Summer Term . . . Rhetoric. Themes and Declamations. Sophomore Year. Fall Term. Rhetoric. Campbell's *Rhetoric;* Themes and Declamations . . . Spring Term . . . Rhetoric. Themes and Declamations; Russell's *American Elocutionist* . . . Summer Term . . . Rhetoric. Themes and Declamations. Junior Year . . . Rhetoric. Themes and Declamations . . . Spring Term Whately's *Rhetoric;* Themes and Declamations. Summer Term . . . Rhetoric. Themes and Declamations; Lectures on Rhetoric and Criticism. Original Declamations before the College during the year. Senior Year . . . Rhetoric . . . Themes and Declamations; Lectures on the English Language and Literature

251

Appendix A

. . . Summer Term . . . Rhetoric. Themes and Forensic Discussions. Original Declamations before the College during the year. (xxviii–xxx)

University of Virginia, 1868–69

School of History, General Literature and Rhetoric. . . . In the Class of Literature and Rhetoric, the English Language, English Composition, Rhetoric and the English Classics with the History of English Literature are studied. . . . the general principles of Rhetoric and Criticism will be taught; the lives of the most eminent authors in the language will be studied in their historical order and connection; and the critical examination and appreciation of their chief productions will occupy much of the time of the student. The class will also be required to practice Literary Composition. . . . Jamieson's *Grammar of Rhetoric*. (26–27)

Dalhousie College and University, 1875–76

Rhetoric.—Text Books: Quintilian's *Institutes of Oratory*. Whately's *Elements of Rhetoric*. Campbell's *Philosophy of Rhetoric*. Essays and exercises on the principles of Rhetoric, weekly. Elocution. Exercises every week after the Christmas holidays. Books recommended: Porter's *Analysis of the Principles of Rhetorical Delivery*. Russell's *Elocution*. Sargent's *Standard Speaker*. *Dominion Elocutionist*. *Nova Scotia Readers No. 6 and No. 7*. (17)

Harvard University, 1889–90

English. A. [Freshman]. Rhetoric and English Composition.—A. S. Hill's *Rhetoric*.—Lectures on Rhetoric and on English Literature.—Written exercises and oral discussion. . . . B. [Sophomore]. Twelve Themes. Lectures and discussions of themes. . . . C. [Juniors]. Forensics.—Lectures on Argumentative Composition.—Four forensics, preceded by briefs.—Discussions of briefs and forensics. D. [Seniors]. Forensics. (110–11)

University of Wyoming, 1897–98

English. . . . Principles of Rhetoric. Elementary rhetoric as illustrated in Shakespeare's *Macbeth;* Milton's *Paradise Lost* Books I and II; Burke's "Speech on

Descriptions of Rhetoric Courses

Conciliation with America"; Carlyle's "Essay on Burns." Exercises in writing and recitation based on these works. . . . Rhetoric. Genung's *Rhetoric* and *Rhetorical Anlaysis*. Practice in Composition. . . . Oratory. Study of selections from great English and American orators. Principles of oratory exemplified in practice. (83–84)

Appendix B

Nineteenth-Century Rhetoric Treatises Adopted as Textbooks

1800–1825	1825–50	1850–75	1875–90	1890–1900
Blair	Jamieson	Bain, *English*	A. S. Hill, *Principles Composition*	Bascom
Campbell	Porter, *Analyses*	Day, *Elements*	D. J. Hill, *Science*	Genung, *Practical Elements*
Kames	Newman, *Practical System*	Hart	Hunt	Hart
	Whately	Quackenbos	Welsh, *Complete Rhetoric*	A. S. Hill, *Principles*
	Blair	Russell, *American Elocutionist*	De Mille[a]	Welsh
	Campbell	Whately	Bain	
	Kames	Blair	Day	
		Campbell	Hart	
		Kames	Whately	
			Blair	
			Campbell	

[a]Adoption limited.

254

Appendix C

Theoretical Authorities Most Frequently Cited by Nineteenth-Century Rhetoricians

The following authors are those cited most often as major influences in prefaces or introductions and in the text by those rhetoricians whose treatises were most widely used in the academy (see appendix B).

1800–1850	1850–75	1875–1900
Blair	Whately	Bain
Cicero	Blair	Bascom
Campbell	Cicero	Day
Kames	Kames	De Mille
Quintilian	Quintilian	J. S. Hart
		A. S. Hill
		Theremin
		Whately
		Blair
		Campbell
		Cicero
		Quintilian

Notes

1. Introduction: A Profile of Nineteenth-Century Rhetoric

1. Berlin makes a related observation in *Writing Instruction in Nineteenth-Century American Colleges,* where he points to the sociopolitical conditions that encourage certain rhetorical systems to power: "Rhetorics arise, fall, or alter in accordance with the conditions that make for change in society as a whole. . . . they are also a useful index of larger social developments" (3). In this work Berlin is particularly interested in charting the theoretical relationship between competing epistemolological systems and developments in nineteenth-century composition teaching (1–2).

2. See also *Gorgias:* "The good orator, being also a man of expert knowledge, will have these ends in view in any speech or action by which he seeks to influence the souls of men. . . . his attention will be wholly concentrated on bringing righteousness and moderation and every other virtue to birth in the souls of his fellow citizens" (112–13).

3. Aristotle explains in the *Nicomachean Ethics* (1–29) that complete virtue is achieved when the individual has both moral (liberality and temperance) and intellectual virtues (practical wisdom). Intellectual virtue is the result of acting rationally or practicing logic, and moral virtue is the ability to choose conduct in accordance with moral custom. In Aristotle's view, morality is not an absolute; the "right thing" to do

or to argue is defined in terms of a "mean" or intermediate between excess and deficiency, limits that are themselves set by *endoxa* or custom. Aristotle assumes that the rhetorician identifies the good by analyzing the particular situation and goes to great length in the *Rhetoric* to provide the student of oratory with information about the protocol of different speech situations, human emotions, and audience types.

4. See David Hume, *Treatise on Human Nature,* and Thomas Reid, *An Inquiry into the Human Mind and On the Principles of Common Sense.* Following the lead of Locke, Hume and Reid assert that mental activity is the consequence of three types of "association": resemblance, contiguity in time or place, and cause and effect. The belief that such associations strengthened the liveliness of ideas influenced eighteenth-century rhetoricians to stress these processes as rhetorical considerations in composition, style, and delivery. In *Observations on Man, His Frame, His Duty, and His Expectations,* David E. Hartley extended this same line of thinking but added the sensory element of "vibrations": powerful impressions on the mind aided by the sensations that the body experiences in response to pain and pleasure. This latter notion was a powerful theoretical affirmation of the important epistemological function of delivery, a "physical" form of persuasion that accentuated the impression of ideas upon listeners.

5. See Murphy for a discussion of unique developments in praxis in this period: "medieval theorists did indeed make pragmatic adaptions of ancient materials to shape special genres for their own purposes" (362). In particular, see chap. 5, "Ars dictaminis: The Art of Letter-Writing" (194–268).

6. For information on these developments in English rhetoric see Howell, *Logic and Rhetoric in England:* "The English Ramists" (146–247) and "Counterreform: Systematics and Neo-Ciceronians" (282–318).

7. Howell, *Eighteenth-Century British Logic and Rhetoric:* "The British Elocutionary Movement (1702–1806)," 145–244.

8. I paraphrase rather freely here from an unlikely source: Stanley Fish, *Is There a Text in This Class?* Fish argues that there is always

an interpretation of what any given text means; it is just never the same one because the contextual factors influencing interpretation are constantly shifting.

9. Noteworthy dissertations on nineteenth-century rhetoric include Rahe and Kitzhaber. See also Roach; Brigance and Hochmuth (the latter represents a re-edition of the original collection published in 1943). For a recent bibliography of early and recent research see Stewart, "The Nineteenth Century."

10. See Kimball, Rosner, and Reid. My review of the literature here does not refer to the many critical articles treating the rhetorical styles of various nineteenth-century orators and platform lecturers that form a large portion of first-wave nineteenth-century scholarship. For examples of this type of commentary, see Brigance and Hochmuth 1: 213–483, vols. 2 and 3. The landmark essay by Hochmuth, "The Criticism of Rhetoric," is extremely helpful in articulating the assumptions of this early body of work (3: 1–23). A long-honored tradition in speech-communications scholarship, rhetorical criticism of such subjects has continued throughout the last several decades. For a current example of this approach see Oravec.

11. Kitzhaber's dissertation, a primary scholarly source for a number of recent works on nineteenth-century rhetoric, proceeds on the assumption that the integrity of oral rhetoric and written rhetoric was compromised by a stylistic obsession in mid- to late nineteenth-century theory.

12. For examples of scholarship that express this view see Berlin, *Writing Instruction;* Connors, Ede, and Lunsford; Halloran; and Stewart, "Some History Lessons."

13. J. O. Ward has drawn attention to the problematic implications of viewing the Middle Ages as a period during which classical rhetoric "atrophied" and "suffered fragmentation and disjunction," arguing that such a view "privileges one particular formulation of preceptive rhetorical theory—the classical formulation, as the only proper, complete and respectable system of persuasive language and behavior"

and takes little account of the "range" and cultural place of medieval rhetorical systems (3–30). Very recently, historians of rhetoric have begun to explore counterhistories, or accounts of the history of rhetorical theory and language philosophy that focus on "marginalized" schools of thought and misreadings of the classical tradition. Such a revisionist project is Covino's *Art of Wonder*.

14. For a representative example of research that posits a narrow view of what is acceptable as proper rhetorical practice, see my early article "Three Nineteenth-Century Rhetoricians." This article opens on the premise that "a humanist perspective on rhetoric and education" that stresses arts of "communication" has been "opposed in every historical period by educators who insist that rhetorical education should focus on the teaching of specialized skills." I go on to say that the nineteenth-century tradition's emphasis on "the belles-lettres curriculum" amounted to this unfortunate "skills" emphasis (105–6). Demonstrating both a classicist and a praxis bias, my early work is more useful for pointing out recommendations for current pedagogy than it is as an overview of the nineteenth-century tradition.

15. One of first exponents of this view was Kitzhaber, whose survey of popular treatises and practices of the last half of the century is predisposed by his conclusion that "after 1880, American rhetorical theory splintered into many separate emphases, each having its day of popularity and its enthusiastic supporters, but none being enough to furnish the basis for a significant new tradition" (346). In his article "Where Do English Departments Come From?" William Riley Parker asserts that the "ancient subject of rhetoric . . . lost both integrity and independent vitality by dispersing itself to academic thinness" (349), a sentiment echoed by Brian Vickers, who marks the "marginalization of rhetoric" in the nineteenth century and its "ever smaller and more specialized share" of the liberal arts curriculum (24).

16. After midcentury, the popular trio of Campbell, Blair, and Whately began to be replaced by other combinations: for instance, Bain, *English Composition* (1881), and Hart at Vermont College in the 1870s;

Bain and David J. Hill, *Science of Rhetoric* (1877), at Georgia, in the
1880s; Day and Quackenbos at Acadia, Wolfville, from 1870 through
the 1880s; and Hunt and Genung, *Practical Elements,* at Wabash College in the 1890s.

    17. In these words, Samuel P. Newman, Professor of Rhetoric
and Oratory at Bowdoin College from 1822 to 1839 and author of the
widely used text *A Practical System of Rhetoric* (which went through
sixty editions), defined the consequences of the study of rhetoric before
the American Institute of Instruction, 19 August 1830. This lecture,
later published as *A Lecture on a Practical Method of Teaching Rhetoric,* outlines the aims that would remain the goals of rhetorical education throughout the century.

2. Foundations of Nineteenth-Century Theory: The New Rhetoric

    1. Howell's term "New Rhetoric" refers to developments in the
last half of the eighteenth-century that "are perhaps best interpreted as
responses to the emergence of the new science. . . . rhetoric began to
see itself as the rightful claimant to the methods of learned communication and as the still unrivaled master of the arts of popular discourse;
and by making these two activities its new concern, it came ultimately
to think of itself as the art which governed all forms of verbal expression, whether popular or learned, persuasive or didactic, utilitarian or
aesthetic" (5–6). Howell treats the nature of the New Rhetoric extensively in *Eighteenth-Century British Logic and Rhetoric.*

    2. For other perspectives on the nature of the New Rhetoric see
Howell, *Eighteenth-Century* 441–613; Golden and Corbett; Ehninger,
"Introduction"; Harding; and Bitzer.

    3. Bitzer has identified major influences on Campbell as the gen-
eral intellectual climate of the Philosophical Society of Aberdeen
(founded 1758) and the specific impact of the work of Hume, Reid, and

Alexander Gerard. Bormann points out that Campbell's inaugural lecture to the Society in 1758 demonstrates that "Campbell's enlarged definition of rhetoric was publicly proclaimed almost twenty years before the publication of his *Philosophy*" (43). For other perspectives on the origins and influence of Campbell's epistemological view of rhetoric see Bevilacqua; Hagarman; and McDermott.

4. Bitzer points out that views of perception strongly influenced Campbell's notion of what rhetorical appeals were effective: "It seems to be Campbell's view (it undoubtedly was Hume's) that not only do laws of association govern or describe the behavior of ideas, but they also provide routes for the transfer of energy. Resemblance, contiguity, causation, and other relations among ideas can become circuits through which vivacity transfers from an already lively idea to a languid one. . . . the rhetor's success largely depends upon discovering and employing methods which enliven his ideas through their relationship with other lively perceptions" (xxvi).

5. Campbell holds that the processes of logic have already been engaged before the rhetorical process begins. He presupposes that the rhetorician is also a master of logic. From this source, the rhetor draws the materials of rhetorical proof: "Logical truth consisteth in the conformity of our conceptions to their archetypes in the nature of things"; "The sole and ultimate end of logic is the eviction of truth; one important end of eloquence . . . is the conviction of the hearers. Pure logic regards only the subject. . . . Eloquence considers the subject, but also the speaker and the hearers" (33–35).

6. See Aristotle, *Rhetoric* 3.2.3–4.

7. See, for example, *Ad Herennium* 4.12.17: "Clarity renders language plain and intelligible. It is achieved by two means, the use of current terms, and of proper terms. Current terms are such as are habitually used in everyday speech" (271).

8. Campbell's treatment of sentence structure, a standard topic in nineteenth-century treatments of style, shows the same epistemological interests (220–25).

9. See also Aristotle on "current and ordinary" usage (*Rhetoric* 3.1); and *Ad Herennium* 4.11.16–18.

10. Campbell treats the following figures: antonomasia, irony, synecdoche, metonymy, metaphor, circumlocution, periphrasis, asyndeton, polysyndeton, antithesis, alliteration, paronomasia, and pun (294–379).

11. "The design of the present undertaking, which aspires not to morality, is to examine the sensitive branch of human nature, to trace the objects that are naturally agreeable, as well as those that are naturally disagreeable; and by these means to discover, if we can, what are the genuine principles of the fine arts. . . . The science of rational criticism tends to improve the heart no less than the understanding" (Kames 11–13).

12. Howell observes that Blair secured a far wider readership in Britain than did his contemporaries such as "Priestley, Lawson, Adam Smith, Sheridan, Ward, and even Campbell" (*Eighteenth Century* 649). Guthrie observes that "wide public circulation is indicated as well, not only by the publication of many American editions, but by the presence of the work in almost all booksellers' catalogues published after 1800" (15: 61). See also Golden and Ehninger; and Ehninger, "Intrinsic Sources."

13. I rely here on Howell's treatment of Smith in "The New Rhetoric Comes of Age: Adam Smith's Lectures at Edinburgh and Glasgow" (*Eighteenth Century* 537).

14. Howell points out that Blair's theory of taste and criticism is synthetic, drawing on "the views of such distinguished authorities as Gerard, D'Alembert, Du Bos, Kames, Hume, and Burke" (*Eighteenth Century* 651); Harding points to Blair's classical sources (Quintilian, Cicero, Aristotle) and observes that Blair also depends on "Rollin, Batteaux, Crevier, Gilbert . . . but Fenelon deserves special merit for his *Dialogues sur l'Eloquence*" (xxi). Blair also cites Addison: "Mr. Addison was the first who attempted a regular enquiry, in his Essay on the Pleasures of the Imagination, published in the sixth volume of the Spec-

tator" (43–44). References to Addison would be common in nineteenth-century treatments of taste.

15. "Taste consists in the power of judging" these qualities; thus the critical faculty is crucial to the development of a perfect state of taste. See Blair 41.

16. Exemplary models of style cited by Blair include Locke, Lord Shaftesbury, Swift, Dryden, Addison, Jonson, Milton, and Pope. Interestingly, Blair does not consider Shakespeare to have had a tasteful style.

17. Blair depends heavily on Quintilian's advice regarding style, the use of figures, the nature of judicial pleading, the structure of the discourse, and address to the passions; Cicero's teachings on style, taste, harmony, figurative language, and introductions to orations; and Aristotle's rules for dramatic and epic composition and application of metaphor, as well as his theory of drama and comedy.

18. In his treatment of the divisions, Blair is far more overtly dependent on classical models and assumptions about the characteristically different appeals needed in varied situations than is Campbell, whose treatment of the types of rhetoric lacks formal distinctiveness.

19. Blair treats the establishment of an appealing ethos as part of the function of the introduction, reiterating classical advice on the need to establish goodwill with the audience (162–66).

20. Blair, like Campbell, presumes that the process of logic precedes the rhetorical process, and he does not treat the logical process.

21. Blair's stance on grammatical purity and the importance of perspicuity parallels Campbell's. Treating a similar list of figures, Blair develops the argument for the ornament-beauty relation whereas Campbell stresses the use of figures in the service of vivacity.

22. Blair quotes this excerpt from Cicero's general rationale for using the figures as an indication that his own "account" is a "full and fair one": "The figurative usage of words is very extensive; an usage to which necessity first gave rise, on account of the paucity of words and barrenness of Language, but which the pleasure that was found in it af-

terwards rendered frequent" (283). Blair also cites Kames's *Elements of Criticism* and Marsais's *Traité des tropes pour servir d'introduction a la rhetorique, et á la logique* as "sensible and instructive" works on the figures (273).

23. As we can see from examinations of classical theories of delivery (*Ad Herennium* 3.11.20), Blair reiterates classical advice regarding delivery; however, his views reveal the general tendencies of elocutionary theory of this period. For background, see Guthrie; and Haberman.

24. Guthrie observes that "Whately's strong emphasis on logical proof undoubtedly exerted great influence on American rhetoric" (65). For other views of the influence of Whately's work see Ehninger, "Intrinsic Sources"; Berlin, *Writing Instruction;* and Parrish.

25. Whately provides a good deal of pedagogical advice regarding instruction in the teaching of composition, including the directive that assigning obscure subjects is counterproductive. See Whately's discussion of composition exercises and selection of subjects, 22–26.

26. "I propose . . . to adopt a middle course between these two extreme points ['Composition in Prose' and 'Persuasive Speaking'] and to treat of 'Argumentative Composition,' generally and exclusively; considering Rhetoric (in conformity with the very just and philosophical view of Aristotle) as an off-shoot from Logic" (4).

27. For a discussion of Whately's theory of logic, see Pence.

28. Whately's treatment of the function of "Fable and Illustration" as a device of argument from example illustrates his persistent epistemological focus: "The word 'Fable' is at present generally limited to those fictions in which the resemblance to the matter in question is not direct but analogical; the other class being Novels, Tales, &c. Those resemblances are . . . the most striking, in which the things compared are of the most dissimilar nature; as is the case in what we call Fables" (107).

29. "It will be advisable however (and by this means you may secure this last advantage) when the strongest arguments naturally oc-

cupy the foremost place; to recapitulate in a reverse order; which will destroy the appearance of anti-climax" (168).

30. Guthrie observes that the "first American edition of Whately was published in Cambridge in 1832, and within the next few years, college catalogues show wide use of the work. . . . The following are the known college adoptions" before 1850: Alabama, Amherst, Andover, Brown, Colby Colgate, Dartmouth, George Washington, Hamilton, Harvard, Hobart, Kenyon, Marietta, Middlebury, Mount Holyoke, Oberlin, Pennsylvania, and Yale (15: 64).

31. The following texts include treatments of arrangement modeled on Whately and represent the general tendency of nineteenth-century treatises to adopt Whately's approach to introductions: Day, *Elements;* Hope, *Princeton Text Book;* and Broadus, *Treatise*.

32. The following nineteenth-century theorists (not an inclusive list) adopted Whately's scheme of perspicuity, energy, and elegance in their treatments of style: Hope, Day, Bain, Broadus, and Bascom. A. S. Hill renames these three qualities in terminology popular in late nineteenth-century treatises—"Clearness, Force, and Ease" (*Principles* ix).

3. Nineteenth-Century Rhetorical Theory: Legacy and Synthesis

1. Some nineteenth-century theorists presented their treatises as correctives to aspects of the New Rhetoric. Day, for example, does not believe that the study of belles lettres is a proper part of rhetoric. However, his critique is less severe in fact than it might seem, as Day incorporates a number of belletristic features in his work (*Elements*).

2. Guthrie has documented the use and circulation of Campbell, Blair, and Whately's texts between 1800 and 1850 (15: 63–65). In fact, Campbell was in use into the 1870s, Blair and Whately as late as the 1890s. Beyond the continued popularity of these texts in North American colleges, it is important to note that all three were cited as authori-

tative sources in rhetoric treatises published between 1850 and 1900. See, for example, Quackenbos, A.S. Hill, De Mille, Hunt, Jamieson, Hope, Hart, and Welsh (appendix B).

3. In this chapter, the following rhetoricians will be treated as influential in the nineteenth-century tradition: Newman, Jamieson, Day, Bain, D. J. Hill, Quackenbos, A. S. Hill, Genung, Hart, Wendell, and Broadus. Of lesser stature were Channing, Hunt, De Mille, Welsh, and Bascom. "Influence" is defined by two criteria: usage in the academy and citation as a theoretical influence or source. Some treatises are referred to merely as representatives of general theoretical and pedagogical trends in American and Anglo-Canadian colleges (e.g., Hope).

4. Bain, for example, does not provide a review of philosophical principles of the mind but presumes them in his treatment of all rhetorical elements and features in terms of appeals to the faculties; see *English Composition* (1866). For more detail on Bain's "psychology," see Mulderig. A major theoretical influence on theorists publishing after 1879, Bain's text enjoyed its greatest popularity in the academy between 1870 and 1890 (e.g., Vermont, 1875; Brown, 1870–90; Georgia, 1880s; Wabash, 1879–84; Dalhousie, 1880–85). It was reprinted twenty-three times between 1866 and 1910.

5. Bascom's *Philosophy of Rhetoric,* modestly popular in the 1880s and '90s, was considered by some to be a "modern" restatement of the philosophy of rhetoric that superseded Campbell's treatment. David J. Hill, Welsh, and Hunt cite Bascom as a theoretical authority.

6. Newman's *Practical System of Rhetoric* was published in 1834 and went through sixty editions. One of the most popular texts in the period between 1820 and 1860, it was required at a number of colleges, including Amherst, Delaware, Wabash, and Michigan (Guthrie 16: 102).

7. Between 1885 and 1915, Genung's texts—*Practical Elements of Rhetoric* (1886), *Handbook of Rhetorical Analysis* (1888), and *Outlines of Rhetoric* (1893)—were the most widely used texts in North American colleges and universities. Among the colleges and universities

using Genung's texts beween 1880 and 1900 were Alabama, Amherst,
Brown, Indiana, Purdue, Wabash, Columbia, Vermont, Virginia,
McGill, Ottawa, Toronto. Genung's *Practical Elements* was reprinted
fifteen times between 1885 and 1914; *Handbook of Rhetorical Analysis,*
nine editions between 1888 and 1900; and *Outlines of Rhetoric,* ten editions between 1893 and 1907.

8. Because Channing's lectures reflect the course of study at
Harvard over a thirty-year period, the principles and philosophy that he
expresses can be taken as fairly representative of the state of rhetorical
theory before 1850. For detail on Channing see the Introduction by Dor-
othy I. Anderson and Waldo W. Braden in Channing, *Lectures.* Channing's authority as a rhetorician might be assessed by the fact that the
Dictionary of the English Language cites Channing's definition of *rhetoric:* "When attempting a formal definition of the word, I am inclined to
consider rhetoric, when reduced to a system in books, as a body of
rules derived from experience and observation, extending to all communication by language and designed to make it efficient."

9. Although Day's treatise was not as widely circulated as other
post-1850 texts such as Bain's or A. S. Hill's, it was frequently cited
by later nineteenth-century theorists (e.g., A. S. Hill, Broadus, McElroy) as an authority, indicating that his theoretical influence was perhaps
greater than his direct curricular impact. Day's *Elements of the Art of
Rhetoric* was reprinted five times between 1850 and 1876.

10. See also Hill's *Science of Rhetoric,* in which Hill presents a
sophisticated synthesis of the epistemological view of rhetoric. Hill's
Science of Rhetoric seems to have enjoyed its greatest popularity in the
1880s, when it was adopted at Georgia, Alabama, and Franklin College
(Indiana).

11. Kitzhaber refers to A. S. Hill as one of "The Big Four"
(Hill, Genung, Wendell, and Fred Newton Scott), a status he awards
because Hill's text was widely used and imitated (97–98). Kitzhaber
chronicles Hill's career at Harvard (where he was succeeded by Wendell), pointing out that it was Hill who inaugurated the freshman En-

glish course at Harvard in 1885. "For the remaining years of the nine-teenth-century it [the course] was regarded as a model course in rhetoric and widely imitated throughout the United States" (101). Crowley ("Evolution" 152–53), Berlin (*Writing Instruction* 6), and Connors ("Textbooks" 186–87) have corroborated this opinion of Hill's influence on the curriculum. Hill's text, *Principles of Rhetoric* (1878, revised 1895), was rivaled in popularity in the academy between 1880 and 1900 only by Genung's *Practical Elements;* Hill's text was used at Virginia, Alabama, Brown, Indiana, Dartmouth, Harvard, and Yale during these years. Hill was frequently cited as a theoretical influence by rhetoricians publishing around 1900 (e.g., Wendell, Carpenter); Hill's *Principles of Rhetoric* went through fourteen editions between 1878 and 1893.

12. Bain draws not only on what would be by the 1860s stan-dard views of the workings of the mind but also on his own theories on "the meanings of Consciousness"; see Bain, *The Emotions and the Will.* The parallels between Bain's treatment of issues such as "Emotional Characters of Feeling," "Intellectual Characters of Feeling," and "The Emotions and Their Classification" in this work and the principles he treats in his rhetoric text are obvious.

13. Although British, Jamieson's text, like Newman's, was widely used in colleges and academies between 1810 and 1840—Ver-mont, Amherst, Yale, Hamilton, Trinity, and Wesleyan (Guthrie 15: 66). It went through fifty-three editions between 1800 and 1880 and ap-peared in college catalogues as late as 1879 (University of Virginia). For discussions of Jamieson see Crowley, "Evolution"; and Guthrie 15: 66.

14. See, for example, T. W. Hunt, *The Principles of Written Discourse*. Never achieving the popularity of texts by A. S Hill or even John S. Hart, Hunt's treatise enjoyed modest use in the 1880s and 1890s (e.g., Georgia, Wabash).

15. De Mille was Professor of Rhetoric at Dalhousie University between 1864 and 1880. His text, used at Dalhousie between 1878 and 1880, never established a wide influence in North American colleges but

was noted occasionally by theorists in the last decades of the century
(e.g., Welsh). De Mille's text is significant for being the only major
nineteenth-century Anglo-Canadian treatise to offer a comprehensive
theory of rhetoric.

16. Newman's approach here imitates Blair's frequent use of
classic British exemplars. This means of illustrating rhetorical principles
is also typical of Jamieson, Bain, Hill, and Genung.

17. Quackenbos's text was one of the most widely used and circulated of all nineteenth-century treatises between 1850 and 1890, going
through thirty editions between 1854 and 1888. Popular between 1860
and 1880, it was adopted at numbers of academies and colleges during
those years, including Columbia, Indiana, Alabama, and Hanover (Indiana).

18. In American theory, Webster was influential not only as an
authority on rhetorical principles but also as an orator whose skills exemplified all that was technically expert and intellectually and morally
admirable. Characterizations of Webster in late nineteenth-century textbooks (e.g., Hill, De Mille, Genung) indicate how common it was to
regard Webster as Quintilian's perfect orator.

19. De Mille, Day, and Newman also adopt the scheme of regarding literary forms and rhetorical genres as forms of "literature."

20. Hart's text enjoyed popularity in the American academy between 1870 and the turn of the century, with twenty-six editions between 1870 and 1903. A few of the colleges using Hart's text during
this period were Alabama, Vermont, and Earlham (Indiana).

21. Turn-of-the-century treatments of style tended to define the
qualities of style under other rubrics, which, despite changes in terms,
still retain the emphasis on elegance (beauty), force, and perspicuity.
See A. S. Hill *Principles,* book 2; and Wendell. In addition to Genung
and A. S. Hill, Wendell was the most frequently cited theoretical authority between 1900 and 1920.

22. Originally published in 1884, Welsh's text was used in the
academy between 1880 and the turn of the century (e.g., Earlham,

Georgia, King's College, Toronto, Wyoming). It was not nearly so widely used during this period as were texts by Hart, A. S. Hill, and Genung.

23. Broadus's *Treatise on the Preparation and Delivery of Sermons* was extremely influential in the last decades of the century not only in homiletics but also in popularizing the theoretical principles of the New Rhetoric in that dimension of rhetoric studies. The text went through forty editions between 1870 and 1898.

24. For example, see Broadus's review of works on rhetoric that are "believed worthy of the student's attention" in which the more comprehensive range of modern rhetorical theory is acknowledged (31–32); Day's discussion of rhetoric as a "developing art" (*Elements* 10–15); and Welsh on what rhetoric "asks" in "these days of paper and print" (*Complete* 1).

4. The Art of Oratory

1. Nineteenth-century homiletic treatises covered a standard set of topics: the moral aims of preaching; the necessity of moral character in the preacher; the materials of the sermon; the structure of the sermon; the nature of persuasion and its application to preaching; the nature of argument and its application to the sermon; the major qualities of style; and the techniques of delivery. For an overview of the development of homiletic theory in the United States see Hosher, who names Broadus among several other notable American homileticians, including Ebenezer Porter, William Russell, Daniel Kidder, Austin Phelps, and William G. T. Shedd.

2. Rhetoricians who treat these standard elements of argument include Day, *Elements* 94–126; Hope 8–73; David J. Hill, *Science* 107–38; Hunt 237–52; and A. S. Hill, *Principles* 327–85. George Pierce Baker relies on similar elements in *The Principles of Argumentation,* a text used in American colleges and universities well into the 1920s.

3. A. S. Hill's stance toward argument illustrates the general tendency of nineteenth-century rhetoricians to define the principles of argument as rules governing all genres of argumentative discourse. For example, in stressing the importance of formulating a clear proposition, Hill applies this principle to oratory and composition: "Nothing can free a writer or a speaker from the obligation of having the proposition directly fixed in his own mind before he begins his argument; for he cannot safely take the first step toward proving a proposition until he knows exactly what proposition is to be proved" (328–29).

4. See also Kidder, "Homiletical Praxis on the Argument," in *A Treatise on Homiletics* 195–221. Kidder's treatise circulated in the United States, London, and Hamilton, Ontario, between 1864 and 1894.

5. Other rhetoricians who treated these topics include Bain (*English Composition* [1866] 174–86) and Genung (*Working Principles* 654–56).

6. Hunt's analysis covers topics standardized in treatments of the conditions of persuasion: "Theory of Emotions," "Classification of Emotions," "Methods of Awakening Feeling," "Motives," "Classification of Motives," "Relations of Motives," "Conditions of Persuasion" (262–89).

7. Genung applies the principle of adaptation to oratory in "The Handling of Human Nature": "An accomplished orator has by a native endowment, and heightens by determinate culture, a power to read his audience, and to adapt himself instinctively to them." Genung observes that "Shakespeare illustrates this knowledge of human nature, and the lack of it, in the way the speeches of Brutus and Antony, respectively, are received by the hearers. Brutus has eloquence but neither knowledge of men nor sympathy with his mob audience. He presents to them high considerations of patriotism and honor, and all the response he gets is a vague admiration for his person. . . . Antony, who knows what chords to strike in a mob, dwells on Caesar's kindness and regard for them, rouses pity for his wounds, which he points out and describes. . . . For response, he raises in them a fury that only desperate deeds can quell" (*Working Principles* 648–49).

8. Late in the century, rhetoricians began relying on less complex rubrics for defining the sentiments and motives that move the will.
Genung summarizes the motives as self-interest, duty, and benevolence
(*Working Principles* 659). Late ninetenth-century rhetorics and treatises
on argumentation combined the major sentiments and motives under single headings such as "desire" or "motives." See Ketcham's discussion
of the forms of "desire" (necessity; interest; jealousy; vanity; hatred;
ambition; generosity; love of right and justice; love of country, home
and kindred [121–25]); and G. P. Baker's discussion of the variety and
grades of motives (*Principles* 315–28).

9. Hill's formalization of three "usual" components of discourse
imitates Whately's method of dealing with arrangement in terms of basic principles applicable to the conduct of both oral and written discourse.

10. Theremin offers a rationale for combining the functions of
the introduction and the division: "At the end of the Introduction, the
orator may announce the two or three parts which contain the development proper; for why should he not carefully employ this, as well as every opportunity, to aid the hearer's attention, and to facilitate his com-
prehension of the whole" (113).

11. Late in the century and throughout the early twentieth century, the three-part scheme (introduction-proof-conclusion) was promoted as the basic scheme for the structure of argumentation and the
debate. See, e.g., Edith M. Phelps 50–60; and Baker, "The Three Divisions of a Brief" (*Principles* 212–13).

12. Discussions of the proper placement of the argumentative
and persuasive portions of a speech or composition typically appear under headings similar to Whately's: "Of the Arrangement of Arguments"
and "Arrangement in Persuasion." See Theremin 113; Day, *Elements*
161; A. S. Hill, *Principles* 383.

13. See *Ad Herennium* 3.8.9.

14. Quackenbos expresses this attitude as he introduces his discussion of the conduct of discourse: "A Thesis, or Argumentative Dis-

course, is a composition in which the writer lays down a proposition, and endeavors to persuade others that it is true. The statements of reasons used for this purpose are called Arguments. When intended for delivery, or written in a suitable style for that purpose, a thesis becomes an Oration. In the conduct of orations and argumentative discourses, six formal divisions were adopted by the ancients" (386).

15. Many popular homiletic treatises in this period also treated perspicuity, energy, elegance, and force as basic principles of style. See Broadus, *Treatise* 329–435; Kidder, "The Style of Sermons" (292–305); and Phelps, lectures 16–35 in *The Theory of Preaching*. Phelps was Professor of Sacred Rhetoric and Homiletics at Andover Theological Seminary from 1848 to 1879. He was also president of that institution from 1869 to 1879. His treatise was a standard seminary textbook, as was his more general treatment of oratorical method of style, *English Style in Public Discourse*. This text is cited frequently by Genung in his analysis of oratory.

16. American rhetoricians like Genung and A. S. Hill were far more apt to cite American orators as exemplary speakers. English and Anglo-Canadian rhetoricians like Bain and De Mille tended to point to the virtues of British orators such as Chatham and Cromwell. All these rhetoricians shared a regard for classical speakers and rely particularly on citations to the speeches of Cicero.

17. See Day, *Elements* 26–27; Genung, *Working Principles* 642–45; Hart 301–4; Bascom; Welsh 295–307.

18. Newman cites "Webster's Address on Bunker's Hill" as an instance of the successful use of the eloquent style, the style that excites the "emotions of taste" (*Practical* 112). In her article "The Legacy of Nineteenth Century Style Theory," Marie J. Secor outlines De Quincey's contribution to popularizing this view of the tasteful style, one that "reinforces the rhetorical and associationist principles of early theorists, especially Campbell and Whately, and anticipates the work of Herbert Spencer, whose *Philosophy of Style* attempts to define the principles by which it affects the mind of the reader" (81).

19. See Channing, "Elocution, A Study" (46–59). Day observes that rhetoric cannot "in strictness be regarded as having accomplished its end until the mental states to be communicated are actually conveyed to the mind addressed. It, therefore, may properly comprehend Delivery" (*Elements* 6). Bain's acknowledgment of elocution is included in his definition of "persuasive address": "when called Eloquence, [it] usually supposes a certain energetic delivery, and elevation of manner which distinguishes oratory from common speech. . . . In this impassioned mode of address, the language becomes strongly rhythmical, approaching poetry; and is accompanied by the music of the voice and the arts of Elocution" (*English Composition* 212).

20. Porter held the Bartlett Professorship of Sacred Rhetoric at Andover Academy between 1813 and 1831. Frequently cited by other elocutionists and homileticians, Porter's text on elocution was widely used in both American and Canadian colleges (Dartmouth, Harvard, Amherst, Wabash, Dalhousie) during these decades and was reprinted twelve times between 1827 and 1881. Russell's *American Elocutionist* was popular in the academy at midcentury but never enjoyed the massive circulation of his treatise on the voice, *Orthophony: The Cultivation of the Voice in Elocution,* first published in 1846. This text, modeled on James Rush's *Philosophy of the Human Voice* (1827), went through eighty-one editions between 1846 and 1900. Alexander Melville Bell was one of the most widely known elocutionists in North America and Britain between 1850 and the turn of the century. Bell lectured at the University of Edinburgh between 1843 and 1865; at the University of London, 1865–70; at the Lowell Institute in Boston in 1868 and 1870–71; and at Queen's College, Kingston, Ontario, in 1870. Bell was also one of the major innovators in education for the deaf. His work on this subject, *Visible Speech: The Science of Universal Alphabetics* (1867), was one of the first treatises of its kind.

21. Kidder's examination of "systematic training of the voice and other physical powers" and how to avoid creating unfortunate impressions such as "awkwardness . . . haughtiness and harshness . . .

monotony and dullness" parallels the advice offered by rhetoricians and elocutionists (329–37). See also Broadus for an example of a systematic treatment of voice and gesture (*Treatise* 406–75). Phelps's *Theory of Preaching* was a popular homiletic manual from its initial publication well into the twentieth century. The last edition of this text was published in 1947. Phelps treats delivery less formally than Kidder does but offers similar advice regarding the impressions made on an audience by delivery. See Phelps's discussion of aids to "natural elocution" in "The Conclusion: Appeals" (560–75).

22. Caldwell's *Practical Manual of Elocution* was designed for the use of "Schools, Academies and Colleges, as well as for Private Learners" and represents the type of multiaudience orientation that elocutionary manuals had in the nineteenth century. Caldwell cites Rush's *Philosophy of the Human Voice* and Austin's *Chironomia* as sources and observes that a discussion of elocution properly addresses both the voice and gesture. Fulton and Trueblood's *Practical Elements of Elocution,* popular at the turn of the century (e.g., at Notre Dame and Earlham College), is theoretical rather than technical in its focus. An earlier example of a theoretically oriented elocution treatise is McIlvaine's *Elocution: The Sources and Elements of Its Power*.

23. Elocution manuals of both types often included selected readings for practice and performance. These excerpts were either included as practice exercises for specific techniques or were intended to be appreciated as models. See Porter's readings for study and practice under the categories "Familiar Pieces" and "Secular Eloquence" (*Rhetorical Reader* 267–402). Toward the end of the century elocutionary readings and oratorical performances had become such popular forms of social entertainment and civic celebration that "Speakers" or collections of readings for elocutionary training and performance began to circulate in vast numbers. See George M. Baker, *The Handy Speaker: Comprising Fresh Selections in Poetry and Prose, Humorous, Pathetic, Patriotic, for Reading Clubs, School Declamation, Home and Public Entertain-*

ments, and the multivolume series *One Hundred Choice Selections for Readings and Recitations.*

24. American editions of Sheridan's *General Dictionary of the English Language, Lectures on Elocution,* and *Rhetorical Grammar* were published between 1783 and 1834. Guthrie observes that Sheridan's works circulated widely in America in the late eighteenth and early nineteenth centuries. Sheridan's texts were used at Brown (1783–1823) and the University of South Carolina (1806). Walker's other works included *Hints for Improvement in the Art of Reading, Rhetorical Grammar* and *The Academic Speaker.* Walker's various works were used at Dartmouth, Vermont, and Williams between 1822 and 1860. Guthrie observes that although Austin's *Chironomia* was not in popular use in America, "its indirect influence was tremendous. The system of notation [marking pauses, inflections, etc.] developed was used by most of the later writers on elocution in England and America. . . . From 1806 through 1860, *Chironomia* remained the definitive work on gesture" (18: 24, 30). For a definitive discussion of Austin and his influence, see Robb and Thonssen's introduction to Austin's *Chironomia.*

25. For an overview of major developments in nineteenth-century elocutionary theory in the United States see Robb, "The Elocutionary Movement." Robb details the theoretical influence of Rush on Barber, William Rush Russell, and James E. Murdoch and the subsequent influence of these figures on those "pioneers" such as Fulton and Trueblood who founded present-day speech departments. She observes that "many of the theories, methods, and exercises which were advanced by the early elocutionists are to be found in modern textbooks" (200).

26. For a typical example of a divisions scheme in which sacred oratory is designated as a major mode in and of itself (in keeping with Blair's categories of oral discourse), see Quackenbos's definition of the three-fold divisions: "I. Speeches to be delivered in deliberative public

asssemblies . . . II. Speeches at the bar; III. Speeches, or discourses to be delivered from the pulpit" (393).

27. Surveys of American literature appearing between 1880 and 1920 corroborated the generic status of platform speaking and public oratory by treating distinguished orators of the nineteenth century as literary figures. See Newcomer's discussion of the political oratory of Webster, Henry Clay, and Rufus Choate and the platform performances of Wendell Phillips (180–86).

28. Homiletic treatises offered similar treatments of the use of argumentative devices in the sermon. See Broadus, "Special Materials—Explanation" and "Illustration" (*Treatise* 144–57, 213–29); Kidder, "Different modes of discussion distinguished" (174–80); and A. Phelps, "The Explanation: Definition, Objects, Materials" (*Theory* 138–52). In his outline of the theoretical content of the Lyman Beecher Lectures on Preaching at the Divinity School of Yale University (initiated in 1871), Baxter notes that attention to the methods of illustration comprised one of the most consistent elements in discussions of preaching method (148–58).

29. Bain, Welsh, David J. Hill, Genung, and De Mille offered treatments of these qualifications, agreeing that the development of these qualities depends on the acquisition of taste, the study of exemplary works, and frequent practice in public speaking. Homileticians also treated this issue as a prominent topic. In his discussion of how the Yale lecturers treated qualifications of the preacher, Baxter notes that the following qualifications were stressed: character, sincerity, enthusiasm, mentality, knowledge, courage, imagination, and originality (17–92).

30. The view that demonstrative and popular oratory plays a necessary part in the building of a flourishing and moral nation was affirmed in surveys of American literature, which noted the contribution of renowned orators to shaping the political conscious and patriotic identify of the nation in the "The Era of National Expansion" or "The

First National Period" (Newcomer). See Henry A. Beers's discussion of Choate, Webster, and Channing (109–19).

5. The Arts of Composition and Belles Lettres

1. Woods argues that nineteenth-century composition theory was also influenced by European "romantic" psychological theory, including the work of Wilhelm Wundt and the works of Rousseau, Pestalozzi, and Froebel. Berlin offers a different analysis of the theoretical influences on nineteenth-century composition theory: he argues that there were three distinct rhetorics—classical, epistemological, and romantic. Rather than viewing classical rhetoric as an enduring influence on the nineteenth-century tradition, Berlin argues that it was "overthrown" by a "scientistic" philosophy of rhetoric; this scientistic philosophy formed the basis for "current-traditional rhetoric," which had triumphed over nineteenth-century composition theory by the last decades of the century (*Writing Instruction* 1–18, 58–76). For a similar view of the demise of classical views of theory and practice see Halloran.

2. Crowley offers this model of the inventional process as defined by Newman, Genung, and David J. Hill: "1) utilization of prior knowledge and natural ability; 2) disciplined exercise of the mental faculties; and 3) method, called 'planning' by most writers" ("Invention" 52); see also Crowley and Carter's analysis of the epistemological orientation of belles lettres theory.

3. For other analyses of Day's theory of invention see Crowley "Evolution" 147–49, and Guthrie 16: 108–9.

4. Berlin argues that Day's treatment of these inventional techniques was actually a treatment of arrangement; *Writing Instruction* 39.

5. For an analysis of how arrangement theory influenced nineteenth-century views on paragraph arrangement, see Berlin, *Writing Instruction* 67–70; Rodgers; and Shearer.

6. For a similar analysis of the conduct of the argumentative composition see Newman, "On the plan or divisions" and "Arrangement" (*Practical System* 33–39); and Day (*Elements* 119–32). Day intends his analysis to address both written and oral arguments.

7. So integral was the arrangement-invention relationship that several theorists, including Quackenbos and Day, treated the arrangement of ideas under the canon of invention. See Quackenbos 325; and Day, *Elements* 35.

8. The plan or outline approach to arrangement is given a good deal of authority by Whately, who discusses the "drawing up of outlines or skeletons" as a method which writers can employ to "give coherence to the Composition, a due proportion of its several parts, and a clear and easy arrangement of them" (25). The outline approach is treated both as an organizational tool and an inventional aid by several theorists, including Quackenbos, Genung, and George Pierce Baker, whose treatment of the outline or "brief" set a standard for the treatments of argumentation found in early twentieth century texts. See Baker, "Brief Drawing" (*Principles* 205–85.) For early twentieth-century treatments of the brief see Greenough and Hersey 92–100; and Grose 184–92.

9. Berlin suggests that the "theoretical apparatus" for style was dropped in American textbooks after 1870 and cites A. S. Hill and Genung as among those who cite "abstract" principles (*Writing Instruction* 71). Berlin may be influenced in this opinion by Kitzhaber, whose review of nineteenth-century theories of style proceeds from the opinion that stylistic theory in this period was overly "abstract": "[In] no area of rhetorical theory did Blair cast a longer shadow than in that of style" (266). True, A. S. Hill is far less elaborate in his theoretical observations than earlier writers such as Day, Hope, and Quackenbos. However, Hill consistently explains what epistemological effect stylistic elements are intended to have. See, for instance, his treatment of "Choice of Words" (74–144). Genung too offers theoretical rationales for stylistic elements, explaining the relationship between technique and effect in some detail. See, for instance, Genung's explanation of the "Qualities

of Style" (*Working Principles* 19–24). Genung's theoretical interests in this discussion are epistemological and belletristic, as his analysis of "beauty" illustrates: "Beauty . . . is the quality of style which answers to the endeavor to please. It can easily be seen how real is the occasion for beauty. An idea may be stated with perfect clearness, may make also a strong impression on the reader's mind; and yet many of the details may be an offense to this taste, or crude expression and harsh combinations of sound may impair the desired effect by compelling attention to defective form" (23). Genung's definition of elegance essentially reiterates Campbell's notion that beauty consists of "the perceived fitness of means to their end" (215).

10. Welsh offers this excerpt from Poe as an example of "euphonic beauty": "And neither the angels in heaven above / Nor the demons down under the sea / Can ever dissever my soul from the soul / Of the beautiful Annabel Lee" (*Complete Rhetoric* 110).

11. For an overview of the various classification schemes for the figures used by Quackenbos, De Mille, David J. Hill, Genung, Wendell, and A. S Hill, see Kitzhaber 274–91.

12. A hybrid system of classification that reassigned the belletristic categories under the headings of the epistemological modes was evident as early as the 1820s. Connors argues that classification of the species of composition by "modes"—narration, description, exposition, and argument—had replaced the belletristic system of classification by the late nineteenth century. "During the late nineties, nonmodal texts almost completely disappeared; of twenty-eight books dating between 1893 and 1906 surveyed by Kitzhaber, only four made no mention of the modes" ("Rise and Fall" 448).

13. Early twentieth-century texts designed for the first-year writing course promoted the notion that argumentative composition can address a wide range of subject matter. Canby and Opdycke offer a familiar definition of argumentation in their text *Elements of Composition:* "we may define Argument as that [any] form of composition which aims to win others over to a realization of the truth or falsity of a given prop-

osition" (256). Canby and Opdycke's text was widely used in Canadian universities between 1915 and 1925.

14. Twentieth-century composition texts continued the nineteenth-century practice of defining description as a wide-ranging genre. In *College Composition* (1926), for example, Grose comments on the the power of description to appeal to the "world of eye and ear": "Those of us who have followed the sea with Dana and Bullen and Conrad, who have caught glimpses of India with Kipling, of Japan from Lafcadio Hearn, of the South Sea Islands from Stevenson, of France from Henry James, of Spain from Washington Irving, and John Hay, of California in the mining days from Bret Harte, of the Mississippi from Mark Twain, of old Salem from Hawthorne, of New England woods and fields from Thoreau would feel poorer if the memories of these things did not mingle with the memories of things we have actually seen" (231). Grose's text was widely used as a freshman writing text in the 1920s.

15. The nineteenth-century theoretical habit of defining narrative as a mode that includes both fiction and nonfiction continued into the early twentieth century. Composition texts appearing between 1900 and 1920 cited a variety of forms of narrative including the novel, the historical narrative, biographical narrative, and the narrative poem. Although favorite sources for examples of narrative continued to be great masters of nineteenth-century literature (e.g., Dickens, Victor Hugo, Matthew Arnold, Scott, and Cooper), early twentieth-century composition texts also provided examples of personal narrative and "newspaper narration" (Canby and Opdycke 389).

16. For an overview of the history of exposition as a species of rhetoric see Connors, "The Rhetoric of Explanation: Explanatory Rhetoric from Aristotle to 1850" and "The Rhetoric of Explanation: Explanatory Rhetoric from 1850 to the Present." Connors argues that the influence of Bain caused exposition to be defined with a "pure science stigma" (56). The "scientific" or technical scope of exposition is stressed by Bain and subsequently by A. S. Hill and Genung, but Hill

and Genung also recognize a variety of informative treatises on subjects of general interest as examples of exposition. See Hill (*Principles* 326) and Genung's discussion of "Popular Exposition" (*Practical Elements* 405).

17. Quackenbos and Ansley's treatments of epistolary writing preserve Blair's belletristic interest in the arrangment and style of the letter (Quackenbos 355–67; Ansley 86–87). McElroy's text, *The Structure of English Prose* (1885), defines the letter as a type of "representative discourse" (39–40). As the century advanced, fewer and fewer theorists treated the letter in texts addressed to the college- and university-level student or the adult learner. Letter writing was considered in treatises addressed to the high school or academy level—e.g., David J. Hill's *Elements of Rhetoric and Composition*. Hill defines letters as a species of composition and treats "The Purposes of Letters," "The Kinds of Letters," "Parts of a Letter," and "General Rules for Writing Letters" (170–86).

18. Hart's discussion of the "review" and the "essay" indicates that both of these types of composition were perceived as forms of criticism. Hart's distinction between them is based on the fact that reviews appear as a regular feature in magazines, whereas the critical essays, often making first appearances in a magazine, are often "collected and published in separate volumes"; in both forms, the writer expresses an opinion or judgment on a work, event, or issue (289–91).

19. Both Genung's *Handbook of Rhetorical Analysis* (1888) and *Outlines of Rhetoric* (1893) contained critical exercises. Both texts were widely used at American colleges between 1890 and 1915; e.g., Genung's *Handbook* was used at the University of Virginia and the University of Alabama between 1890 and 1910.

20. Swinton is quite self-conscious of criticism as a rhetorical art: "on the side of rhetoric, it supplies a working outfit of definitions and principles, thus teaching the pupil to 'name his tools'; and further and more important, it applies the canons of the literary art to the analysis of the texts here presented" (iv). Swinton appears to be appropriating

rhetoric under literary study, and in fact, he is. However, his viewpoint simply represents the pedagogical fusion that literary studies and rhetoric studies underwent under the influence of the belles lettres rationale.

21. Influence here is defined by two criteria: usage in the American and Anglo-Canadian academy and citation as theoretical influences by theorists writing after 1880.

22. At the turn of the century, courses in rhetoric often addressed both rhetorical principles and their application to speaking and writing as well as the methods of literary criticism. In the early decades of the twentieth century, courses offered under the title *rhetoric* were often introductory courses in criticism. The constructive aspect of rhetoric was taught under the heading of "Composition." After 1930 courses in rhetorical analysis began appearing more and more frequently under the title "Criticism"; by this time the term "Rhetoric" had started to disappear from the curricular vocabulary. Although nineteenth-century rhetoricians considered the critical and practical aspects of rhetoric to be equally important, their differentiation between critical rhetoric and constructive rhetoric in pedagogical terms set up a distinction that eventually allowed the split between these two components of the curriculum.

23. Lewis's anthology was published in 1900, a time when the study of models had become a manadatory component of the rhetoric course. An early precursor of the anthologies used today in composition classes, Lewis's collection is organized according to mode and includes "Notes" defining the rhetorical principles that each selection exemplifies. Here Lewis comments on the use of contrast in Walter Pater's "The First Period of Greek Art" (included as an example of historical exposition): "In this passage of historical exposition, early Greek art is contrasted with early Eastern art. Just as we found descriptive imagery heightened by juxtaposition with descriptive imagery, now we find principles heightened by contrast with principles. Here likewise we find the contrast strengthened by chosen detail" (184). For an example of an early twentieth-century rhetoric anthology see Loomis.

24. Murray's *English Reader* is directed to "Young Persons,"

but it was widely used in early academies in colleges. Murray intends for the selections to be read aloud for the improvement of elocution and to be studied as examples of good prose. He assumes that such study will improve "the language and the sentiments" (title page).

25. While questions like these may sound quite "literary," they merely represent the kind of analysis that most nineteenth-century rhetoricians considered part of the art of rhetoric. Not simply a development of the late nineteenth century, the promotion of critical awareness was a consistent feature in treatises on rhetoric from the early decades of the century. For instance, both Newman and Quackenbos encourage critical awareness, Quackenbos by outlining practice exercises in criticism and Newman by providing extensive analysis of exemplary passages. See Newman, "Exercises" and "Historical Dissertation on Style" (*Practical System* 225–311), and the series of analytical questions that Quackenbos consistently incorporates in the footnotes accompanying his discussion of rhetorical principles; see, for example, Quackenbos's series of critical questions regarding the nature and function of the sublime (200–202).

26. Occasional pieces were drawn from various genres—drama, fiction, essays, poetry, etc.—and represented the work of writers enjoying extreme popularity at a given time, works speaking to a timely issue, or pieces included for their entertainment value or appropriateness to a special occasion. Similar selections also appeared under headings such as "Promiscuous Pieces"; see Murray 219–49. Elocution anthologies directed to the general public consisted nearly exclusively of these types of selections.

6. Conclusion: Habits of Eloquence

1. For another defense of this same pedagogical method see Russell, "Articulation": "Rhetoric, to become a useful branch of modern education, should embrace a gradually progressive course of exercises, embodying successively the facts of language, in the use of words and

the construction of sentences: it should include the practice of daily writing; frequent exercises in the logical arrangement of thought for the purposes of expression, and the adapting of the forms and character of expression to thought; and it should be accompanied by the close study and critical analysis of the works of distinguished writers with a view to acquire a perfect mastery over every form of style" (332).

2. Essay topics for composition exercises were often assigned. Topics assigned to the sophomore class of the College of New Jersey during the term 1873–74 (when John S. Hart was the instructor of rhetoric and composition) indicate that composition exercises typically ranged across the major genres: "The Influence of Prejudice"; "Iron"; "The Aristocracy of Wealth"; "Indulgence in Slang"; "Topic Selected by the Writer"; "My Favorite English Author"; "My Favorite American Author"; and "The Approaching Centennial." John S. Hart, *Essays of the Sophomore Class for 1873–74,* Department of English, College of New Jersey (University of Virginia Archives).

3. For expressions of this philosophy of education by renowned nineteenth-century figures, see Ralph Waldo Emerson, "Modern Education," and the views of Henry Barnard, founder of the *American Journal of Education,* first U.S. Commissioner of Education, and organizer of the U.S. Bureau of Education. Barnard expresses this creed: "The education of a people bears a constant and most pre-eminently influential relation to its attainments and excellences—physical, mental, and moral. . . . [T]he history of education affords the only ready and perfect key to the history of the human race, and of each nation in it—an unfailing standard for estimating its advance or retreat upon the line of human progress" (qtd. by Downs 123).

4. Mann was one of the foremost educators in the first half of the century and one of the chief architects of the modern system of education in the United States. He created the Massachusetts Board of Education and was first secretary for several years. His annual reports to the board are now regarded as landmark documents in the history of education. Mann believed that public education for all was essential to a

healthy democracy. Applebee confirms that Mann approved of rhetoric because it "offered a 'scientific' rigor and discipline" (39)

5. Gilman was president of the University of Calfornia, 1872–75, before accepting the position at Johns Hopkins. Gilman was one of the leading figures during the expansionist period beween 1870 and 1890, during which offerings at universities became far more diversified. For other works by Gilman on higher education see his *University Problems in the United States*.

6. Other educators who promoted this view included Charles W. Eliot, president of Harvard from 1869 to 1909, and John Bascom, president of the University of Wisconsin from 1874 to 1887 and author of the highly regarded *Philosophy of Rhetoric* (1888). Like Gilman, Eliot was one of the leading philosophers of higher education in the latter decades of the century. Although a less well known figure, Bascom wrote extensively on the aims of higher education. Bascom perceived the college to be a place at which the individual could develop mental abilities that contribute to the social good. See James, *Charles W. Eliot,* and "The Mind of John Bascom," in Curti and Carstensen, *The University of Wisconsin.*

7. The mental abilities that Broadus defines here were associated with the study of rhetoric, belles lettres, and literature. For an analysis of nineteenth-century educators' views of the general relevance of instruction in English and literature to the development of mental discipline, see Graff. For an analysis of the influence of the mental discipline philosophy on Canadian higher education in particular, see Johnson, "Rhetoric and Belles Lettres."

8. Frederick Augustus Porter Barnard was president of the University of Mississippi between 1850 and 1858 and chancellor from 1858 to 1861. He assumed the presidency of Columbia College in 1864 and was the guiding force in the development of Columbia into a major university and research institution. Barnard College for women is named after him. Like Eliot of Harvard and Bascom of Wisconsin, Barnard was a champion of women's education.

9. Like his contemporary Horace Mann in the United States, Egerton Ryerson promoted the common school movement in Canada; he also pressed for the development of institutions of higher learning in Canada. Committed to the notion that education develops the mind and the Christian virtues, Ryerson defined higher education as that level of education which cultivates the mind to the highest extent: "Man is made for physical, mental, and moral action; and the grand object of education is to develop, improve, and perfect, as far as possible, his physcial, mental and moral faculties. . . . education signifies the cultivation of the mind by means of Schools and Colleges" (9). For background on Ryerson see McDonald and Chaiton; for an analysis of Ryerson's contribution to the development of English studies and the discipline of rhetoric in Canada, see Hubert.

Bibliography

Primary Sources

Ad Herennium. Trans. Harry Caplan. Cambridge: Harvard UP, 1954.

Ansley, E. A. *Elements of Literature; or, An Introduction to the Study of Rhetoric and Belles Lettres*. Philadelphia: Lippincott, 1849.

Aristotle. *Nicomachean Ethics*. Trans. David Ross. Oxford: Oxford UP, 1980.

———. *Rhetoric and Poetics*. Trans. Rhys Roberts and Ingram Bywater. New York: Modern Library, 1954.

Austin, Gilbert. *Chironomia; or, a Treastise on Rhetorical Delivery*. 1806. Ed. Mary Margaret Robb and Lester Thonssen. Carbondale: Southern Illinois UP, 1966.

Bain, Alexander. *The Emotions and the Will*. London: Longmans, Green, 1875.

———. *English Composition and Rhetoric: A Manual*. London: Longmans, Green, 1866.

———. *English Composition and Rhetoric: Part Second. Emotional Qualities of Style*. London and New York: Longmans, Green, 1908.

———. "On Teaching English." *The Journal of Education, Devoted to Education, Literature, Science, and the Arts* 13.12 (December 1869): 201–3; 14.1 (January 1870): 1–5.

Baker, George M. *The Handy Speaker: Comprising Fresh Selections in Poetry and Prose, Humorous, Pathetic, Patriotic, for Reading*

Bibliography

Clubs, School Declamation, Home and Public Entertainments.
Boston: Lee and Shepard, 1876.

———. *One Hundred Choice Selections for Readings and Recitations.*
Philadelphia: Garrett, 1886.

Baker, George Pierce. *The Forms of Public Address.* New York: Holt,
1904.

———. *The Principles of Argumentation.* Boston: Ginn, 1895.

———. *Specimens of Argumentation: Modern.* New York: Holt,
1893.

Barnard, F. A. P. "On Improvements Practicable in American Colleges." *American Journal of Education* 1 (1856): 174–85.

Bascom, John. *Philosophy of Rhetoric.* New York: Putnam, 1866.

Beers, Henry A. *An Outline Sketch of American Literature.* New York:
Chautauqua, 1887.

Bell, Alexander Melville. *The Principles of Elocution with Exercises
and Notations for Pronunciation, Intonation, Emphasis, Gesture
and Emotional Expression.* Salem, MA: Burbank, 1878.

Blair, Hugh. *Lectures on Rhetoric and Belles Lettres.* 1783. Ed. Harold
F. Harding. Carbondale: Southern Illinois UP, 1965.

Broadus, John Albert. *College Education for Men of Business: A Familiar Essay, Written at the Request of the Trustees of Richmond
College.* Richmond: Ryland, 1875.

———. *A Treatise on the Preparation and Delivery of Sermons.* New
York: Armstrong, 1889.

Bryan, William Jennings, ed. *The World's Famous Orations.* Vol 1.
New York and London: Funk and Wagnalls, 1906.

Caldwell, Merritt. *A Practical Manual of Elocution: Embracing Voice
and Gesture.* Philadelphia: Sorin and Ball, 1845.

Campbell, George. *The Philosophy of Rhetoric.* 1776. Ed. Lloyd F.
Bitzer. Carbondale: Southern Illinois UP, 1963.

Canby, Henry Siedel, and John Baker Opdycke. *Elements of Composition.* New York: Macmillan, 1913.

Bibliography

Carpenter, George R. *Exercises in Rhetoric and English Composition Advanced Course*. Boston: Willard Small, 1893.

Channing, Edward T. *Lectures Read to the Seniors in Harvard College*. 1856. Carbondale: Southern Illinois UP, 1968.

Cicero. *De Oratore*. Trans. E. W. Sutton. Cambridge: Harvard UP, 1942.

Day, Henry N. *Elements of the Art of Rhetoric*. New York: Barnes and Burr, 1866.

———. *An Introduction to the Study of English Literature*. New York: Scribner, 1869.

De Mille, James. *The Elements of Rhetoric*. New York: Harper, 1878.

Emerson, Ralph Waldo. "Modern Education." *Three Thousand Years of Educational Wisdom*. Ed. Robert Ulich. Cambridge: Harvard UP, 1947. 577–614.

Fulton, Robert I., and Thomas C. Trueblood. *Practical Elements of Elocution. Designed as a Textbook for the Guidance of Teachers and Students of Expression*. Boston: Ginn, 1893.

Genung, John Franklin. *Handbook of Rhetorical Analysis: Studies in Style and Invention*. Boston: Ginn, 1888.

———. *Outlines of Rhetoric Embodied in Rules, Illustrative Examples, and a Progressive Course of Prose Composition*. Boston: Ginn, 1893.

———. *The Practical Elements of Rhetoric*. Boston: Ginn, 1886.

———. *The Study of Rhetoric in the College Course*. Monographs on Education. Boston: Heath, 1888.

———. *The Working Principles of Rhetoric: Examined in Their Literary Relations and Illustrated with Examples*. Boston: Ginn, 1900.

Gilman, Daniel Coit. "An Address Delivered in Berkeley, October 25, 1990, at the Inauguration of President Wheeler." *The Launching of a University and Other Papers: A Sheaf of Remembrances*. New York: Dodd, Mead, 1906. 223–33.

———. *University Problems in the United States*. New York: Century, 1898.

Bibliography

Greenough, Chester Noyes, and Frank Wilson Cheney Hersey. *English Composition*. New York: Macmillan, 1917.

Grose, Howard B., Jr. *College Composition*. Chicago: Scott, Foresman, 1926.

Hart, John S. *A Manual of Composition and Rhetoric*. Philadelphia: Eldredge and Brother, 1870.

Hartley, David E.. *Observations on Man, His Frame, His Duty, and His Expectations*. N.p., 1749.

Hill, Adams Sherman. *The Foundations of Rhetoric*. New York: American Book, 1892.

―――. *The Principles of Rhetoric*. New York: American Book, 1895.

Hill, David J. *The Elements of Rhetoric*. New York: Sheldon, 1878.

―――. *The Science of Rhetoric: An Introduction to the Laws of Effective Discourse*. New York: Sheldon, 1877.

Hope, Matthew B. *The Princeton Text Book in Rhetoric*. Princeton: John T. Robinson, 1859.

Hume, David. *Treastise on Human Nature*. London, 1739.

Hunt, T. W. *The Principles of Written Discourse*. New York: Armstrong, 1884.

Jamieson, Alexander. *A Grammar of Rhetoric and Polite Literature: Comprehending the Principles of Language and Style, the Elements of Taste and Criticism; With Rules for the Study of Composition and Eloquence: Illustrated by Appropriate Examples Selected Chiefly from the British Classics, for the Use of Schools, or Private Instruction*. New Haven: A. H. Maltby, 1844.

Kames, Henry Home, Lord. *Elements of Criticism*. London: G. Cowie and Poultry, 1824.

Kellog, Brainerd. *A Textbook on Rhetoric, Supplementary. The Development of the Science with Exhaustive Practice in Composition*. New York: Maynard, Merrill, 1888.

Ketcham, Victor Alvin. *The Theory and Practice of Argumentation and Debate*. New York: Macmillan, 1914.

Bibliography

Kidder, Daniel P. *A Treatise on Homiletics*. New York: Carlton and Lanahan, 1864.

Lewis, E. H. *Specimens of the Forms of Discourse*. New York: Holt, 1900.

Loomis, Roger Sherman. *Freshman Readings*. Boston: Houghton Mifflin, 1925.

McElroy, John G. R. *The Structure of English Prose: A Manual of Composition and Rhetoric*. N.p., 1885.

McIlvaine, Joshua Hall. *Elocution: The Sources and Elements of Its Power*. New York: Scribner's, 1870.

Murray, Lindley. *The English Reader; or Pieces in Prose and Poetry, Selected from the Best Writers*. Hamilton, NY: Williams, Orton, 1823.

Newcomer, Alphonso G. *American Literature*. Chicago: Scott, Foresman, 1908.

Newman, Samuel P. *A Lecture on a Practical Method of Teaching Rhetoric. Delivered in the Representatives Hall, Boston, August 19, 1830, before the American Institute of Instruction*. Boston: Hilliard, Gray, Little, and Wilkins, 1830.

———. *A Practical System of Rhetoric*. New York: Dayton and Newman, 1834.

Phelps, Austin. *English Style in Public Discourse with Special References to the Usages of the Pulpit*. New York: Scribner's, 1883.

———. *The Theory of Preaching: Lectures on Homiletics*. New York: Scribner's, 1882.

Phelps, Edith M. *Debater's Manual*. New York: Wilson, 1915.

Plato. *Gorgias*. Trans. Walter Hamilton. Middlesex, Eng.: Penguin, 1975.

———. *Phaedrus*. Trans. W. C. Helmbold and W. G. Rabinowitz. Indianapolis: Bobbs-Merrill, 1978.

Porter, Ebenezer. *Analyses of the Principle of Rhetorical Delivery*. Andover, MA: Mark Newman, 1827.

Bibliography

————. *The Rhetorical Reader; Consisting of Instructions for Regulating the Voice, with a Rhetorical Notation, Illustrating Inflection, Emphasis, and Modulation and a Course of Rhetorical Exercises*. Andover, MA: Gould and Newman, 1838.

Priestley, Joseph. *A Course of Lectures on Oratory and Criticism*. 1777. Ed. Vincent M. Bevilacqua and Richard Murphy. Carbondale: Southern Illinois UP, 1965.

Quackenbos, G. P. *Advanced Course of Composition and Rhetoric: A Series of Practical Lessons on the Origin, History, and Peculiarities of the English Language*. New York: American Book, 1884.

Reid, Thomas. *An Inquiry into the Human Mind and On the Principles of Common Sense*. 1764. Ed. Timothy Duggan. Chicago: U of Chicago P, 1970

Rush, James. *The Philosophy of the Human Voice*. Philadelphia: Grigg and Elliott, 1827.

Russell, William. *American Elocutionist; Comprising Lessons in Enunciation, Exercises in Elocution, and Rudiments of Gesture. With a Selection of New Pieces for Practice in Reading and Declamation and Engraved Illustrations in Attitude and Action*. Boston: Jenks and Palmer, 1844.

————. "Articulation of the Expressive Faculties." *American Journal of Education* 3 (1858): 321–45.

————. *Orthophony: The Cultivation of the Voice in Elocution*. Boston and New York: Houghton Mifflin, 1892.

————. *Pulpit Elocution*. New York: Wiley, 1861.

Ryerson, Egerton. *Inaugural Address on the Nature and Advantages of an English and Liberal Education: Delivered by The Rev. Egerton Ryerson, at the Opening of Victoria College, June 21, 1842: With an Account of the Opening Services, Course of Studies, Terms, Etc., in the College*. Toronto: Board of Trustees and Visitors, 1842.

294

Bibliography

Sheridan, Thomas. *A General Dictionary of the English Language*.
1780. Ed. R. G. Alston. Menston, Eng. Scolar, 1967.
————. *Lectures on Elocution*. London: W. Strahan for A. Millar,
1762.
————. *A Rhetorical Grammar*. Philadelphia: Robert Bell, 1783.
Swinton, William. *Studies in English Literature*. New York: Harper,
1887.
Theremin, Franz. *Eloquence a Virtue*. Trans. William G. T. Shedd.
Philadelphia: Smith, English, 1859.
Walker, John. *The Academic Speaker*. New York: Smith and Forman,
1808.
————. *Hints for Improvement in the Art of Reading*. London: Cadell,
1783.
————. *The Melody of Speaking*. Ed. R. C. Alston. Menston, Eng.:
Scolar, 1970.
————. *Rhetorical Grammar*. Boston: Buckingham, 1814.
Welsh, Alfred H. *Complete Rhetoric*. New York: Silver, Burdett, 1885.
————. *Development of English Literature and Language*. Chicago:
Griggs, 1886.
Wendell, Barrett. *English Composition*. 1891. New York: Frederick Un-
gar, 1963.
Whately, Richard. *Elements of Logic*. London: Fellowes, 1826.
————. *Elements of Rhetoric*. 1828. Ed. Douglas Ehninger. Carbon-
dale: Southern Illinois UP, 1963.
Worchester, Joseph E. *Dictionary of the English Language*. Boston:
Brewer and Tileston, 1868.

Secondary Sources

Applebee, Arthur N. *Tradition and Reform in the Teaching of English:
A History*. Urbana, IL: NCTE, 1974.

Bibliography

Baron, Dennis E. *Grammar and Good Taste: Reforming the American Language*. New Haven: Yale UP, 1982.

Baxter, Batsell Barrett. *The Heart of the Yale Lectures*. New York: Macmillan, 1954.

Berlin, James A. *Rhetoric and Reality: Writing Instruction in American Colleges, 1900–1985*. Carbondale: Southern Illinois UP, 1987.

———. *Writing Instruction in Nineteenth-Century American Colleges*. Carbondale: Southern Illinois UP, 1984.

Bevilacqua, Vincent M. "Philosophical Origins of George Campbell's *Philosophy of Rhetoric*." *Speech Monographs* 32 (1965): 1–12.

Bitzer, Lloyd F. Introduction. *The Philosophy of Rhetoric*. By George Campbell. Carbondale: Southern Illinois UP, 1963. ix–xxxvii.

Bormann, Dennis R. "George Campbell's Cura Prima on Eloquence—1758." *Quarterly Journal of Speech* 74 (1988): 35–51.

Brigance, William Norwood, and Marie Hochmuth, eds. *A History and Criticism of American Public Address*. 3 vols. New York: Russell and Russell, 1960.

Carter, Michael. "The Role of Invention in Belletristic Rhetoric: A Study of the Lectures of Adam Smith." *Rhetoric Society Quarterly* 18 (1988): 3–14.

Connors, Robert J. "Mechanical Correctness as a Focus in Composition Instruction." *CCC* 36 (1985): 61–72.

———. "The Rhetoric of Explanation: Explanatory Rhetoric from Aristotle to 1850." *Written Communication* 1 (1984): 189–210.

———. "The Rhetoric of Explanation: Explanatory Rhetoric from 1850 to the Present." *Written Communication* 2 (1985): 49–72.

———. "The Rise and Fall of the Modes of Discourse." *CCC* 32 (1981): 444–56.

———. "Textbooks and the Evolution of the Discipline." *CCC* 37 (1986): 178–94.

Connors, Robert J., Lisa S. Ede, and Andrea A. Lunsford. "The Revival of Rhetoric in America." *Essays on Classical Rhetoric and*

Bibliography

Modern Discourse. Ed. Connors, Ede, and Lunsford. Carbondale: Southern Illinois UP, 1984.

Covino, William Anthony. *The Art of Wonder: A Revisionist Return to the History of Rhetoric*. Portsmouth, NH: Boynton/Cook, 1988.

Crowley, Sharon. "The Evolution of Invention in Current-Traditional Rhetoric: 1850–1970." *Rhetoric Review* 3 (1985): 146–63.

———. "Invention in Nineteenth-Century Rhetoric." *CCC* 36 (1985): 51–60.

Curti, Merle, and Vernon Carstensen. *The University of Wisconsin: A History*. Madison: U of Wisconsin P, 1949.

Downs, Robert B. *Henry Barnard*. New York: Twayne, 1977.

Ehninger, Douglas Jr. Introduction. *Elements of Rhetoric*. By Richard Whately. Carbondale: Southern Illinois UP, 1963. ix–xxx.

Fish, Stanley. *Is There a Text in This Class? The Authority of Interpretive Communities*. Cambridge: Harvard UP, 1980.

Golden, James L., and Douglas Ehninger. "The Extrinsic Sources of Blair's Popularity." *Southern Speech Journal* 22 (1956): 16–32.

Golden, James L., and Edward P.J. Corbett. *The Rhetoric of Blair, Campbell, and Whately*. New York: Holt, 1968.

Guthrie, Warren. "The Development of Rhetorical Theory in America, 1635–1850." *Speech Monographs* 13 (1946): 14–22; 14 (1947): 38–54; 15 (1948): 61–71; 16 (1949): 98–113; 18 (1951): 17–30.

Haberman, Frederick W. "English Sources of American Elocution." Wallace 105–28.

Hagarman, John. "On Campbell's *Philosophy of Rhetoric* and Its Relevance to Contemporary Invention." *Rhetoric Society Quarterly* 21 (1981): 145–55.

Halloran, Michael. "Rhetoric in the American College Curriculum: The Decline of Public Discourse." *Pre/Text* 3 (1982): 245–70.

Harding, Harold F. Introduction. *Lectures on Rhetoric and Belles Lettres*. By Hugh Blair. Carbondale: Southern Illinois UP, 1965.

Horner, Winifred Bryan. "Nineteenth-Century Rhetoric at the University

Bibliography

of Edinburgh with an Annotated Bibliography of Archival Materials." *Rhetoric Society Quarterly* 19 (1989): 365–75.

———, ed. *The Present State of Scholarship in Historical and Contemporary Rhetoric*. Columbia: U of Missouri P, 1983.

Hosher, John P. "American Contributions to Rhetorical Theory and Homiletics." Wallace 129–52.

Howell, Wilbur Samuel. *Eighteenth-Century British Logic and Rhetoric*. Princeton: Princeton UP, 1971.

———. *Logic and Rhetoric in England, 1500–1700*. New York: Russell and Russell, 1961.

Hubert, Henry Allan. "The Development of English Studies in Nineteenth-Century Anglo-Canadian Colleges." Diss. U of British Columbia, 1989.

James, Henry. *Charles W. Eliot, President of Harvard University, 1869–1909*. Vol. 2. London: Constable, 1930.

Johnson, Nan. "English Composition, Rhetoric, and English Studies at Nineteenth-Century Canadian Colleges and Universities." *English Quarterly* 20 (1987): 296–304.

———. "Rhetoric and Belles Lettres in the Canadian Academy: An Historical Analysis." *College English* 50 (1988): 861–73.

———. "Three Nineteenth-Century Rhetoricians: The Humanist Alternative to Rhetoric as Skills Management." *The Rhetorical Tradition and Modern Writing*. Ed. James J. Murphy. New York: MLA, 1982. 105–17.

Kimball, Bruce A. *Orators and Philosophers: A History of the Idea of Liberal Education*. New York: Teachers' College Press, Columbia U, 1986.

Kitzhaber, Albert Raymond. *Rhetoric in American Colleges 1850–1900*. Diss. U of Washington, 1953.

Lunsford, Andrea A. "Essay Writing and Teachers' Responses in Nineteenth-Century Scottish Universities." *CCC* 32 (1981): 434–43.

Bibliography

McDermott, Douglas. "George Campbell and the Classical Tradition." *Quarterly Journal of Speech* 49 (1963): 403–9.

McDonald, Neil, and Alf Chaiton, eds. *Egerton Ryerson and His Times*. Toronto: Macmillan, 1972.

Mann, Horace. "Antioch College: Baclaureate Address of 1857." *Horace Mann on the Crisis in Education*. Ed. Louis Filler. Yellow Springs, OH: Antioch P, 1965. 197–223.

Mott, Frank Luther. *A History of American Magazines: 1850–1865*. Cambridge: Harvard UP, 1938.

———. *A History of American Magazines: 1865–1885*. Cambridge: Harvard UP, 1938.

Mulderig, Gerald P. "Nineteenth-Century Psychology and the Shaping of Alexander Bain's English Composition and Rhetoric." *The Rhetorical Tradition and Modern Writing*. Ed. James J. Murphy. New York: MLA, 1982. 95–104.

Murphy, James J. *Rhetoric in the Middle Ages: A History of Rhetorical Theory from St. Augustine to the Renaissance*. Berkeley and Los Angeles: U of California P, 1974.

Oravec, Christine. "The Democratic Critics: An Alternative American Rhetorical Tradition of the Nineteenth Century." *Rhetorica* 4 (1986): 395–422.

Parker, William Riley. "Where Do English Departments Come From?" *College English* 28 (1967): 339–51.

Parrish, Wayland Maxfield. "Whately and His Rhetoric." *Quarterly Journal of Speech* 15 (1929): 58–79.

Pence, Orville. "The Concept and Function of Logical Proof in the Rhetorical System of Richard Whately." *Speech Monographs* 20 (1953): 23–39.

Rahe, Herbert Edgar. *The History of Speech Education in Ten Indiana Colleges: 1820–1938*. Diss. U of Wisconsin, 1939.

Reid, Paul E. "The First and Fifth Boylston Professors: A View of Two Worlds." *Quarterly Journal of Speech* 74 (1988): 229–40.

Bibliography

Roach, Helen P. *History of Speech Education at Columbia College: 1754–1940*. New York: Teachers' College Bureau of Publications, Columbia U, 1950.

Robb, Mary Margaret. "The Elocutionary Movement and Its Chief Figures." Wallace 178–201.

Robb, Mary Margaret, and Lester Thonssen. Introduction. *Chironomia; or, A Treatise on Rhetorical Delivery*. By Gilbert Austin. Carbondale: Southern Illinois UP, 1966.

Rodgers, Paul C. "Alexander Bain and the Rise of the Organic Paragraph." *Quarterly Journal of Speech* 51 (1965): 399–408.

Rosner, Mary. "Reflections on Cicero in Nineteenth-Century England and America." *Rhetorica* 4 (1989): 153–82.

Secor, Marie J. "The Legacy of Nineteenth Century Style Theory." *Rhetoric Society Quarterly* 12 (1981): 76–94.

Shearer, Ned. "Alexander Bain and the Genesis of Paragraph Theory." *Quarterly Journal of Speech* 58 (1921): 408–17.

Stewart, Donald. "The Nineteenth Century." Horner 134–58.

———. "Rediscovering Fred Newton Scott." *College English* 40 (1979): 539–47.

———. "Some History Lessons for Composition Teachers." *Rhetoric Review* 3 (1985): 134–45.

———. "Two Model Teachers and the Harvardization of English Departments." *The Rhetorical Tradition and Modern Writing*. Ed. James J. Murphy. New York: MLA, 1982. 118–29.

Ulich, Robert, ed. *Three Thousand Years of Educational Wisdom*. Cambridge: Harvard UP, 1947.

Ulman, H. Lewis. "Discerning Readers: British Reviewers' Responses to Campbell's *Rhetoric* and Related Works." *Rhetorica* 8 (1990): 65–90.

Vickers, Brian. "The Atrophy of Modern Rhetoric, Vico to De Man." *Rhetorica* 6 (1988): 21–56.

Wallace, Karl R. *History of Speech Education in America: Background Studies*. New York: Appleton-Century-Crofts, 1954

Bibliography

Ward, J. O. "The Relevance of the Academic Curriculum in Rhetoric to
the Life and Literature of the Middle Ages and the Renaissance."
International Society for the History of Rhetoric. Oxford, 28
Aug. 1985.
Woods, William F. "Nineteenth-Century Psychology and the Teaching
of Writing." *CCC* 36 (1985): 20–41.

University Catalogues

Acadia College, University of. *Calendar and Catalogue of the University of Acadia College:* 1854; 1863–64; 1869–79.
Alabama, University of. *Catalogue of the University of Alabama:* 1821–
70; 1872–74; 1876–77; 1885–86; 1910–11; 1920–22; 1923–24.
Alberta, University of. *Calendar of the University of Alberta:* 1909–11;
1920–21; 1929–30; 1939–40; 1949–50; 1959–60.
Allegheny College. *Allegheny College Catalogue:* 1866–67; 1877–78;
1895–96; 1903–4.
Amherst College. *Catalogue of Amherst College:* 1827–28; 1830–31;
1839–40; 1842–43; 1850–51; 1860–61; 1879–80; 1885–86;
1890–91.
Andover Theological Seminary. *Catalogue of Andover Theological Seminary:* 1841–42; 1850–51; 1861–62; 1870–71; 1886–87; 1893–
94.
Arizona, University of. *University of Arizona. Annual Register:* 1892–
94.
Bishop's College. *The Calendar of the University of Bishop's College:*
1896–97; 1899–1900; 1905–6; 1920–21; 1928–29.
British Columbia, University of. *Calendar of the University of British Columbia:* 1915–16; 1918–19; 1920–22; 1923–30.
Brown University. *Catalogue of the Officers and Students of Brown University:* 1824–25; 1873–74; 1880–81; 1891–92; 1900–1901.
Chicago, University of. *University of Chicago: Annual Register:* 1912–
13.

Bibliography

Columbia College. *Catalogue of the Officers and Students of Columbia College:* 1860–61; 1869–71; 1889–1890; 1899–1900; 1910–11; 1919–20.

Dalhousie College and University. *Calendar of Dalhousie College and University:* 1865–66; 1871–72; 1881–84.

Dartmouth College. *Catalogue of Dartmouth College:* 1856–57; 1859–60; 1870–71; 1880–81; 1890–91; 1900–1901; 1910–11.

Delaware College. *Catalogue of Delaware College:* 1883–84; 1902–3; 1913–14.

Delaware, University of. *Bulletin of the University of Delaware. Annual Catalogue:* 1890–91; 1923–24; 1929–30.

Depauw College. *Depauw College Catalogue:* 1887–88.

Georgia, University of. *Catalogue of the Officers and Students of the University of Georgia:* 1857–58; 1873–74; 1898–99; 1909–10.

Harvard University. *Catalogue of the Officers and Students of Harvard:* 1818–20; 1825–27; 1831–32; 1832–33; 1840–41; 1848–49; 1850–51; 1860–61; 1880–81; 1889–90; 1911–12.

King's College, University of. *Calendar of the University of King's College, Halifax, Nova Scotia:* 1845–46; 1855–56; 1860–61; 1870–71; 1880–81; 1890–91; 1900–1901; 1910–11; 1920–21; 1930–31; 1940–41; 1950–51; 1959–60; 1970–71; 1980–81.

Laval, University of. *Annuaire de L'Université Laval pour L'année Académique:* 1867–68; 1870–71; 1880–81; 1890–91; 1899–1900; 1910–11; 1919–21; 1929–30.

McGill College and University. *Annual Calendar of McGill College and University, Montreal:* 1854–59; 1860–62; 1869–70; 1889–90; 1898–1901; 1910–11; 1920–21; 1930–31.

McMaster University. *McMaster University Calendar:* 1888–89; 1895–96; 1910–11; 1920–21; 1930–31; 1940–41; 1950–51; 1960–61.

Manitoba, University of. *Calendar of the University of Manitoba:* 1899–1901; 1904–5; 1909–10; 1917–18; 1920–21; 1950–51; 1970–71; 1980–1981.

Bibliography

Mount Saint Vincent College. *Mount Saint Vincent College. Halifax,
Nova Scotia:* 1897–98; 1954–55; 1961–62; 1980–81.

New Brunswick, University of. *Calendar of the University of New
Brunswick:* 1918–19.

Ottowa, College of. *Annual Catalogue of the Officers, Faculty and Students of the College of Ottawa:*1874–75; 1879–80; 1883–84;
1890–91; 1900–1901; 1909–10; 1919–20; 1930–31.

Queen's University and College. *Calendar of Queen's University and
College, Kingston:* 1864–65.

St. Francis Xavier's College, University of. *The Calendar of the University of St. Francis Xavier's College:* 1911–1912.

St. Mary's College. *Calendar of St. Mary's College:* 1897–98; 1920–
21; 1929–30.

Saskatchewan, University of. *Calendar of University of Saskatchewan,
Saskatoon:* 1910–12; 1920–21; 1924–25.

Toronto, University of. *Calendar of the University of Toronto:* 1891–
92; 1896–97; 1910–11; 1920–21; 1925–26.

Trinity College. *Calendar of Trinity College:* 1847–48; 1866–68; 1870–
71; 1873–74; 1879–80; 1885–86; 1892–93.

Trinity College, University of. *Calendar of the University of Trinity
College:* 1885–86; 1896–97; 1902–3.

Vermont, University of. *Catalogue of the University of Vermont:* 1875–
76; 1897–98; 1900–1901; 1901–2.

Victoria University. *Calendar of Victoria University:* 1891–92; 1965–
66; 1969–70; 1982–83.

Virginia, University of. *Catalogue of the University of Virginia:* 1868–
69; 1878–79; 1886–87; 1893–94; 1903–4.

Woodstock College. *Announcement of Woodstock College:* 1909–10.

Wyoming, University of. *University of Wyoming Catalogue:* 1887–88;
1890–92; 1893–94; 1896–97; 1898–99.

Yale University. *Catalogue of Yale University:* 1887–88; 1895–96;
1903–4; 1914–15; 1924–25; 1929–30.

Index

Adaptation, principle of, 27–28, 96–
101, 227–30; and oratory, 144–
46, 164–65, 272n.7
Ad Herennium, 30, 271n.7
Amherst College, 237
Andover Theological Seminary, 238,
239
Ansley, E. A., 238n.17
Argumentation, 272n.3, 273–
74n.14; and arrangement, 54–
58, 132–34, 265–66n.29; in
composition, 180, 184, 187–89,
200–202, 280n.6, 281–82n.13;
and the epistemological rationale, 51–59, 72–75, 116–22,
127–28, 135–39, 265n.28; and
invention, 119, 121–22, 176; in
the New Rhetoric, 47–49, 51–
59; in oratory, 98–99, 116–22,
158–61, 278n.28. *See also* Arrangement; Conviction; Invention; Persuasion
Aristotle, 4, 26, 41, 257–58n.3,
264n.17
Arrangement, 127–39; abbreviated
models of, 129–32, 273nn. 9–
11; and argumentation, 54–58,

121–22, 131–32, 273n.12; in
composition, 181–91, 279nn.
4–5; and the epistemological rationale, 22–25, 39–40, 75,
127–28, 135–39, 181–91; fundamental principles of, 132–34,
137–38; and introductions, 57–
58, 273n.10; and invention, 57,
175–76, 181, 185–91, 280nn.
7–8; six-part model of, 129,
130, 181, 183–84; three-part
model of, 181–82, 273nn. 9,
11. *See also* Argumentation; Invention
Ars dictaminis, 5
Ars poetica, 5
Ars praedicandi, 5
Austin, Gilbert, 55, 277n.24
Autobiography, 207

Bain, Alexander, 78–79, 99–100,
159, 267n.3, 269n.12; on argumentation, 119–20, 180; on
composition, 180, 190, 201,
202–3, 282n.16; on figures,
73–74, 197, 198–99; on peda-

Index

gogy, 219, 232–33; on persuasion, 125, 275n.19

Baker, George Pierce, 271n.2

Barnard, F. A. P., 244, 286n.3, 287n.8

Bascom, John, 67–68, 86, 115–16, 167, 267n.5; on pedagogy, 104–5, 287n.6

Bell, Alexander Melville, 149, 150, 151, 275n.20

Belles lettres. *See* Belletristic rationale, the; Composition; Criticism; Poetics

Belletristic rationale, the, 11, 12, 31–46, 167; and classical rhetoric, 32, 38–39, 41, 42–43, 44–46, 94–95; and criticism, 79–87, 174, 216, 218, 283–84n.20; and delivery, 40, 43–45; and the divisions, 31–34, 37–39, 87–91; and the doctrine of taste, 34–37, 45–46, 79–87, 91; and figures, 41, 42–43, 92–93, 264–65nn. 21–22; and imitation, 32, 37, 81–83; in nineteenth-century rhetoric, 14–16, 61–62, 66, 75–94, 228; and style, 40–43, 78–79, 91–93, 146–48, 191–93, 195–97. *See also* Composition; Criticism; Epistemological rationale, the

Berlin, James A., 10–11, 257n.1, 279n.1, 280n.9

Biography, 207

Bitzer, Lloyd F., 261–62n.3, 262n.4

Blair, Hugh, 31–46, 75, 79, 209, 264n.20; on argumentation, 48, 56, 99; on arrangement, 128, 130, 131, 134–36; and classical rhetoric, 94–95, 107, 134–35, 264nn. 17–19, 264–65n.22; on delivery, 49–50, 265n.23; on the divisions, 47, 264n.18; and the doctrine of taste, 81, 85, 91, 264n.15; influence of, 45–46, 263n.12, 270n.16; influences on, 263–64n.14, 264nn. 17–18; on style, 91, 195, 264n.15, 264–65nn. 21–22. *See also* Belletristic rationale, the

Broadus, John A., 98, 122, 137, 271nn. 23–24; on pedagogy, 114, 243–44

Bryan, William Jennings, 247

Campbell, George: and the belletristic rationale, 32, 33; and classical rhetoric, 20, 25–31, 94–95; on conviction, 5–6, 98–99; and the epistemological rationale, 20–31, 46, 262nn. 4–5; influences on, 4–5, 261–62n.3, 262n.4; on invention, 23–25, 47–49; on style, 28–31, 262n.8, 263n.10. *See also* Epistemological rationale, the

Canby, Henry Siedel, and John Baker Opdycke, 281–82n.13

Canons of rhetoric, the, 37–38, 91, 101–3, 223–24; in the New Rhetoric, 6, 27, 28, 32, 102–3. *See also* Arrangement; Delivery; Invention; Style

Channing, Edward T., 70, 107–8, 158–59, 218–19, 268n.8; on the divisions, 88–89, 103; on style, 139, 140

Index

Cicero, 95, 155, 264n.17, 264–65n.22

Classical rhetoric, 11–12, 23, 126, 195, 259–60nn. 13–14; and arrangement, 39, 127–28, 131, 134–35; and the belletristic rationale, 32, 38–39, 41, 42–43, 44–46, 94–95; and composition, 174, 183, 279n.1; and the New Rhetoric, 20, 25–31, 41–43, 50, 264nn. 17–19, 264–65n.22; and nineteenth-century rhetoric, 14–16, 62, 66, 94–110, 228; and oratory, 155, 166, 265n.23; and pedagogy, 103–6, 218

Classicist stance, the, 11–12, 259–60nn. 13–14

Common sense, 23–25, 48, 77

Composition, 10–11, 13, 173–225; argumentative, 180, 184, 187–89, 200–202, 280n.6, 281–82n.13; arrangement in, 181–91, 279nn. 4–5; and classical rhetoric, 174, 183, 279n.1; descriptive, 177–78, 184–85, 202–5, 282n.14; and the epistemological rationale, 174–80, 199–200; epistolary, 211–12, 283n.17; expository, 179–80, 185, 187–88, 208–11, 282–83n.16; and fundamental rhetorical principles, 173–74, 201–2; invention in, 174–80, 279nn. 2, 4; and literature, 204–5, 218–19, 221–25, 285n.26; modes of, 177–80, 185–91, 199–216, 281n.12; narrative, 178–79, 185, 189–91, 205–8, 282n.15;

and pedagogy, 212–25, 232–33, 265n.25, 286n.2; species of, 177–80, 185–91, 199–216, 281n.12; style in, 191–99. *See also* Criticism

Connors, Robert J., 281n.12, 282n.16

Connors, Robert J., Lisa S. Ede, and Andrea A. Lunsford, 10

Conviction, 5–6, 52–58, 70–72, 74–75, 98–99. *See also* Argumentation; Persuasion

Criticism, 212–25; and the belletristic rationale, 31–46, 79–87, 216, 218–19, 283–84n.20; and the critical essay, 214–15, 283n.18; and the doctrine of taste, 34–35, 76–77, 79–87, 215–16, 264n.15; and pedagogy, 81–83, 215, 216–18, 221–25, 283n.19, 285n.25. *See also* Belletristic rationale, the; Composition; Poetics; Taste, doctrine of

Day, Henry N., 106, 134, 164, 167, 175–76; on the divisions, 88, 270n.19, 271n.24; and the doctrine of taste, 78, 85–86; *Elements of the Art of Rhetoric,* 15, 268n.10; and the epistemological rationale, 71, 120–21, 275n.19; and the principle of adaptation, 97–98, 99; on style, 92, 139, 147–48

De copia, 6

Delaware College, 237

Delivery, 6, 40, 43–45, 148–56, 265n.23; and elocution, 9, 149–

307

Index

55, 275–77nn. 20–25, 284–
85n.24, 285n.26; and the epistemological rationale, 49–50,
75, 150–51, 155–56, 275n.19
De Mille, James, 80, 109, 139,
269–70n.15; on arrangement,
131–32, 186; on the canons and
divisions, 102–3, 270n.19; on
oratory, 159–60, 169–70
De Quincey, Thomas, 274n.18
Description, 177–78, 184–85, 202–
5, 282n.14
Dickens, Charles, 207–8
Dispositio. See Arrangement
Division, the. *See* Arrangement
Divisions of rhetoric, the, 223, 224;
and the belletristic rationale,
32–34, 37–39, 87–91, 270n.19;
and the epistemological rationale, 27–28, 38–39, 47, 68–72,
90; in the New Rhetoric, 5–6,
27–28, 32–34, 46–47, 102–3,
264n.18; in nineteenth-century
rhetoric, 87–91, 93, 101–3,
229–30, 271n.24, 277–78n.26.
See also Composition; Oratory
Doxa, 4

Education, higher, 240–47; and rhetoric, 240, 243–45, 287n.7; social and cultural benefits of,
241–43, 245–47, 286n.3,
288n.9. *See also* Pedagogy,
rhetorical
Eighteenth-century rhetoric. *See
names of individual rhetoricians;* New Rhetoric, the
Eliot, Charles W., 286n.6

Elocution, 9, 149–55, 275–77nn.
20–25, 284–85n.24, 285n.26.
See also Delivery
Emerson, Ralph Waldo, 163–64
Epistemological rationale, the, 19,
20–31, 50–63; and argumentation, 51–59, 72–74, 116–22,
265n.28; and arrangement, 22–
25, 39–40, 75, 127–28, 135–39,
181–91; and the associative principle, 22–23, 24, 262n.4; and
composition, 174–80, 184–85,
189–91, 199–200, 205, 208–9;
and delivery, 49–50, 75, 150–
51, 155–56, 275n.19; and the divisions, 27–28, 38–39, 47, 68–
72, 90; and the doctrine of taste,
31–32, 34–37, 77; and ethos,
26–27, 49, 124, 125–26; and
faculty theory, 5, 21–23, 24; and
figures, 30–31, 73–74, 92–93,
197–99; and invention, 23–25,
47–49, 74, 262n.5; and the
modes, 28, 68–69, 185–87; in
nineteenth-century rhetoric, 60–
61, 66–75, 227–30; and oratory,
115–27, 144–46, 164–65, 229–
30; and pathos, 26, 27, 49, 124–
25, 126; and persuasion, 25–26,
52, 58–59, 116, 118, 122–27;
and the principle of adaptation,
98–101, 228–30; and style, 28–
31, 40–43, 59–60, 91–93, 144–
46, 191–93, 195; and vivacity,
22, 29, 30. *See also* Belletristic
rationale, the
Epistolary form, the, 211–12,
283n.17

308

Index

Index

Imagination, the, 35, 36–37, 41. *See also* Epistemological rationale, the

Imitatio. See Imitation

Imitation, 105–6, 147–48, 218, 237–40, 285–86n.1; and the belletristic rationale, 32, 37, 81–83

Introductions, 57–58, 130, 131, 137, 273n.10. *See also* Arrangement

Inventio. See Invention

Invention: and argumentation, 119, 121–22; and arrangement, 57, 175–76, 181, 185–88, 280nn. 7–8; in composition, 174–80, 279nn. 2, 4; and the epistemological rationale, 23–25, 47–49, 74, 262n.5, 264n.20. *See also* Argumentation; Arrangement

Jamieson, Alexander, 15, 76–77, 104, 269n.19

Kames, Henry Home, Lord, 31

Kellog, Brainerd, 214

Kidder, Daniel P., 149, 272n.4, 275–76n.21

Kitzhaber, Albert Raymond, 259n.11, 260n.15, 280n.9

Letter writing, 211–12, 283n.17

Lewis, E. H., 284n.23

Logic, 23–25, 48, 262n.5, 264n.20. *See also* Argumentation; Epistemological rationale, the; Invention

Macaulay, Thomas, 193–94

McElroy, John G. R., 283n.17

Mann, Horace, 241–42, 286–87n.4

Medieval rhetoric, 5, 12, 258n.5, 259–60n.13

Modes of discourse: in composition, 177–80, 185–91, 199–216, 281n.12, 282n.15; and the epistemological rationale, 28, 68–69, 185–87; in nineteenth-century rhetoric, 224, 229, 230. *See also* Argumentation; Description; Exposition; Narration

Murphy, James J., 9–10, 258n.5

Murray, Lindley, 284–85n.24

Narration, 178–79, 185, 189–91, 205–8, 282n.15. *See also* Arrangement

Neoclassical rhetoric. *See* Classical rhetoric; New Rhetoric, the

Newman, Samuel, 15, 68–69, 88, 129, 267n.6, 270n.19; on composition, 183, 187, 189, 211; and the doctrine of taste, 77, 85; literary examples in, 83, 270n.16, 285n.25; on pedagogy, 104, 231–32, 233–34, 261n.17; on style, 146, 194–95, 197–98, 274n.18

New Rhetoric, the, 12, 19–63, 174, 261n.1, 271n.23; and argumentation, 47–49, 51–59; and the canons, 6, 27, 28, 102–3; and classical rhetoric, 20, 25–31, 32, 41–43, 50, 94–95, 264nn. 17–19, 264–65n.22; and the divisions, 5–6, 27–28, 32–34, 46–47, 70–72, 102–3, 264n.18;

310

Index

fundamental assumptions of, 46–50, 51; influence of, on nineteenth-century rhetoric, 14, 19–20, 60–63, 65–67, 106–10, 113–14, 227–30, 266–67nn. 1–2; and the principle of adaptation, 27–28, 144; and style, 6, 28–31, 33–34, 49, 59–60, 140–41. *See also* Belletristic rationale, the; Blair, Hugh; Campbell, George; Epistemological rationale, the; Whately, Richard

Nineteenth-century rhetoric, 7–17, 267n.3; and argumentation, 72–75, 116–22; and arrangement, 75, 121–22, 127–39; and the belletristic rationale, 14–16, 45–46, 61–62, 66, 75–94, 228, 266n.1; and the canons, 74, 75, 101–3; and classical rhetoric, 14–16, 62, 66, 94–110, 228; and the divisions, 68–69, 70–72, 87–91, 93, 101–3, 229–30, 271n.24; and the doctrine of taste, 32, 61–62, 76–87, 93; and elocution, 9, 149–55, 275–77nn. 20–25, 284–85n.24, 285n.26; and the epistemological rationale, 60–61, 66–75, 227–30; and imitation, 32, 105–6; influence of Blair on, 45–46, 263n.12, 270n.16; influence of Campbell on, 20–21; influence of Whately on, 58–60, 265n.24, 266nn. 30–32; and liberal ideals, 16–17, 86–87, 230–31, 245–47; and the modes, 224, 229, 230; and the New Rhetoric, 19–20, 60–63, 65–67, 106–10, 113–14, 227–30; and persuasion, 75, 94, 122–27; and poetics, 218–19, 225; and the principle of adaptation, 96–101, 227–30; reliance of, on fundamental principles, 114–15, 138–40, 227–29, 239–40; and style, 73–74, 75, 91–93, 139–48; synthetic nature of, 14–17, 75, 94, 95–96, 114–15, 227, 259n.11. *See also* Composition; Criticism; *names of individual rhetoricians;* Oratory; Pedagogy, rhetorical

Oratory, 9–10, 13, 113–70; argumentation in, 98–99, 116–22, 158–61, 278n.28; arrangement in, 127–39; and classical rhetoric, 155, 166; deliberative, 145, 162–63, 169–70; and democratic idealism, 167–70, 274n.16; and the epistemological rationale, 115–27, 144–46, 164–65, 229–30; and ethos, 124, 125–26; judicial, 145, 158–59; moral and social benefits of, 166–70, 278–79n.30; and pathos, 124, 125–26; persuasion in, 116, 118, 122–27, 161–64; popular, 145, 156–57, 163–65, 229–30, 278n.27, 278–79n.30; and the principle of adaptation, 144–46, 164–65, 272n.7; reliance of, on fundamental principles, 114–15, 138–39, 144; religious, 145, 160–62, 229, 277–78n.26; and the speaker's qualifications,

Index

Index

Sheridan, Thomas, 6, 44, 155, 277n.24

Smith, Adam, 33

Specialization bias, 12–14, 260nn. 14–15

Speech communication departments, 7–10, 277n.25

Style, 191–99, 270n.21, 280–81n.9; and the belletristic rationale, 40–43, 78–79, 91–93, 146–48, 191–93, 195–97; and elegance, 195–97, 220; and eloquence, 33–34, 146–48, 274n.18; and the epistemological rationale, 22, 28–31, 59–60, 144–46, 194–95; as governed by fundamental principles, 139–44, 274n.15; models of, 193–94, 197, 264n.16, 281n.10; in the New Rhetoric, 6, 28–31, 33–34, 49, 59–60, 140–41; in oratory, 139–48, 274n.18; and perspicuity, 29–30, 40, 192–93, 194; and vivacity, 22, 29, 30, 194–95. *See also* Figures

Swinton, William, 283–84n.20

Taste, doctrine of: and the belletristic rationale, 34–37, 45–46, 79–87, 91; and criticism, 34–35, 76–77, 79–87, 215–16, 264n.15; and the epistemological rationale, 31–32, 34–37, 77; moral and social benefits of, 35–36, 45–46, 84–87; in nineteenth-century rhetoric, 32, 61–62, 76–86, 93; and style, 146,

274n.18. *See also* Belletristic rationale, the

Theremin, Franz, 146–47, 167, 273n.10

Topoi. *See* Arrangement; Invention; Modes of discourse

Trollope, Anthony, 193

Twentieth-century rhetoric, 15, 267–68n.7, 270n.21, 282n.15; and literary study, 219, 222, 284nn. 22–23

Vickers, Brian, 260n.15

Walker, John, 6, 155, 277n.24

Wallace, Karl R., 8

Ward, J. O., 259–60n.13

Webster, Daniel, 270n.18

Welsh, Alfred H., 161–62, 211, 213–14, 270–71n.22; on composition, 177, 178, 183, 201, 203; on the divisions, 87–88, 109–10, 271n.24; on pedagogy, 105, 219–20; on style, 91–92, 141–42, 281n.10

Whately, Richard, 50–60, 94–95, 265n.15; on argumentation, 51–59, 118–19, 265–66nn. 28–29; on arrangement, 128, 130–31, 273n.9, 280n.8; on conviction, 5–6, 52–58; influence of, 58–60, 265n.24, 266nn. 30–32; on persuasion, 58–59, 99, 123, 125; on style, 59–60, 195. *See also* Epistemological rationale, the

Wilson, Thomas, 13

Wordsworth, William, 220

Wyoming, University of, 238–39

Nan Johnson received her doctorate from the University of Southern California in 1981. She taught rhetoric in the Department of English at the University of British Columbia until 1990, when she joined the faculty of the rhetoric and composition program in the English Department at Ohio State University. She specializes in the history of rhetoric, critical theory, and composition studies. Her plans for future research include a study of the rhetorical education of nineteenth-century women orators and writers and an analysis of the movement of nineteenth-century academic rhetoric into popular culture.